First World War

and Army of Occupation

War Diary

France, Belgium and Germany

48 DIVISION
144 Infantry Brigade
Gloucestershire Regiment
1/4th (City of Bristol) Battalion (T.F.)
30 March 1915 - 31 October 1917

WO95/2758/1

The Naval & Military Press Ltd
www.nmarchive.com
Published in association with The National Archives

Published by

The Naval & Military Press Ltd

Unit 10 Ridgewood Industrial Park,

Uckfield, East Sussex,

TN22 5QE England

Tel: +44 (0) 1825 749494

www.naval-military-press.com

www.nmarchive.com

This diary has been reprinted in facsimile from the original. Any imperfections are inevitably reproduced and the quality may fall short of modern type and cartographic standards.

Contents

Document type	Place/Title	Date From	Date To
Heading	WO95/2758/1 1/4 Battalion Gloucestershire Regiment		
Heading	48th Division 144th Infy Bde 1-4th Bn Glos Regt Apr 1915 1917 Oct		
Heading	144th Inf. Bde. 48th Div War Diary 1/4th Battn. The Gloucestershire Regiment April (30.3.15 To 30.4.15) 1915		
Heading	War Diary Of 1/4th Battn Gloucestershire Regt From 30th March 1915 To 30th April 1915 (Volume I)		
War Diary	Maldon Essex	30/03/1915	30/03/1915
War Diary	Danbury	31/03/1915	31/03/1915
War Diary	Boulogne	01/04/1915	01/04/1915
War Diary	Winnezeele	02/04/1915	05/04/1915
War Diary	Le Petit Mortier	06/04/1915	10/04/1915
War Diary	Armentieres	11/04/1915	30/04/1915
Heading	144th Inf. Bde. 48th Div. War Diary 1/4th Battn. The Gloucestershire Regiment May (1.5.15 To 30.5.15) 1915		
War Diary	Pont De Nieppe	01/05/1915	06/05/1915
War Diary	Roegsteert	06/05/1915	19/05/1915
War Diary	Pont De Nieppe	20/05/1915	23/05/1915
War Diary	Roegsteert	24/05/1915	30/05/1915
Heading	144th Inf. Bde. 48th Div. War Diary 1/4th Battn. The Gloucestershire Regiment June (31.5.15 To 30.6.15) 1915		
War Diary	Roegsteert	31/05/1915	04/06/1915
War Diary	Pont De Nieppe	05/06/1915	07/06/1915
War Diary	Roegsteert	08/06/1915	26/06/1915
War Diary	Bailleul	27/06/1915	27/06/1915
War Diary	Vieux Berquin	28/06/1915	28/06/1915
War Diary	Robecq	29/06/1915	29/06/1915
War Diary	Hurionville	30/06/1915	30/06/1915
Heading	144th Inf. Bde. 48th Div. War Diary 1/4th Battn. The Gloucestershire Regiment July (1.7.15 To 30.7.15) 1915		
War Diary	Hurionville	01/07/1915	12/07/1915
War Diary	Hesdigneul	13/07/1915	13/07/1915
War Diary	Brebis	14/07/1915	16/07/1915
War Diary	Hurionville	17/07/1915	18/07/1915
War Diary	Lillers	19/07/1915	19/07/1915
War Diary	Louvincourt	20/07/1915	20/07/1915
War Diary	Bois Du Warnimont	21/07/1915	30/07/1915
Heading	144th Inf. Bde. 48th Div. War Diary 1/4th Battn. The Gloucestershire Regiment August (31.7.15 To 30.8.15) 1915		
War Diary	Colincamps	31/07/1915	09/08/1915
War Diary	Courcelles Au Bois	10/08/1915	15/08/1915
War Diary	Colincamps	16/08/1915	23/08/1915
War Diary	Courcelles Au Bois	24/08/1915	30/08/1915
Heading	144th Inf. Bde 48th Div. War Diary 1/4th Battn. The Gloucestershire Regiment September (31.8.15 To 30.9.15) 1915		

War Diary	Courcelles Au Bois	31/08/1915	04/09/1915
War Diary	Hebuterne	05/09/1915	17/09/1915
War Diary	Authie	18/09/1915	28/09/1915
War Diary	Hebuterne	29/09/1915	30/09/1915
Heading	144th Inf. Bde. 48th Div. War Diary 1/4th Battn. The Gloucestershire Regiment October 1915		
War Diary	Hebuterne	01/10/1915	11/10/1915
War Diary	Authie	12/10/1915	18/10/1915
War Diary	Hebuterne	19/10/1915	26/10/1915
War Diary	Authie	27/10/1915	31/10/1915
Heading	144th Inf. Bde. 48th Div. War Diary 1/4th Battn. The Gloucestershire Regiment November 1915		
War Diary	Authie	31/10/1915	03/11/1915
War Diary	Hebuterne	04/11/1915	12/11/1915
War Diary	Authie	13/11/1915	19/11/1915
War Diary	Hebuterne	20/11/1915	28/11/1915
War Diary	Authie	29/11/1915	30/11/1915
Map	Map		
Heading	144th Inf. Bde 48th Div. War Diary 1/4th Battn. The Gloucestershire Regiment December 1915		
War Diary	Authie	01/12/1915	05/12/1915
War Diary	Hebuterne	06/12/1915	14/12/1915
War Diary	Authie	15/12/1915	21/12/1915
War Diary	Hebuterne	22/12/1915	28/12/1915
War Diary	Authie	29/12/1915	30/12/1915
Map	Map		
Heading	144th Brigade 48th Division 1/4th Battalion Gloucestershire Regiment January 1916		
War Diary	Authie	31/12/1915	02/01/1916
War Diary	Hebuterne	03/01/1916	09/01/1916
War Diary	Authie	10/01/1916	14/01/1916
War Diary	Hebuterne	15/01/1916	21/01/1916
War Diary	Authie	22/01/1916	26/01/1916
War Diary	Hebuterne	27/01/1916	30/01/1916
Heading	144th Brigade 48th Division 1/4th Battalion Gloucestershire Regiment February 1916		
War Diary	Hebuterne	31/01/1916	02/02/1916
War Diary	Authie	03/02/1916	10/02/1916
War Diary	Souastre	11/02/1916	17/02/1916
War Diary	Hannescamps Trenches	17/02/1916	21/02/1916
War Diary	Bienvillers	22/02/1916	24/02/1916
War Diary	Hannescamps Trenches	25/02/1916	28/02/1916
Heading	144th Brigade 48th Division 1/4th Battalion Gloucestershire Regiment March 1916		
War Diary	Hannescamps	29/02/1916	29/02/1916
War Diary	Souastre	01/03/1916	03/03/1916
War Diary	Courcelles	04/03/1916	05/03/1916
War Diary	Serre Trenches	06/03/1916	07/03/1916
War Diary	Courcelles	08/03/1916	11/03/1916
War Diary	Serre Trenches	12/03/1916	30/03/1916
Heading	144th Brigade 48th Division 1/4th Battalion Gloucestershire Regiment April 1916		
Heading	War Diary Of 1/4th Battn Gloucestershire Regiment From 31.3.16 To 30.4.16 Volume 13		
War Diary	Serre Trenches	31/03/1916	02/04/1916
War Diary	Couin	03/04/1916	07/04/1916

War Diary	Hebuterne Trenches	08/04/1916	14/04/1916
War Diary	Sailly Au Bois	15/04/1916	19/04/1916
War Diary	Coigneux	20/04/1916	24/04/1916
War Diary	J Sector Hebuterne Trenches	25/04/1916	30/04/1916
Heading	144th Brigade 48th Division 1/4th Battalion Gloucestershire Regiment May 1916		
Heading	War Diary Of 1/4th Battalion Gloucestershire Regiment From 1/5/16 To 30/5/16 Volume 14		
War Diary	Hebuterne Trenches	01/05/1916	02/05/1916
War Diary	Authie	03/05/1916	03/05/1916
War Diary	Beauval	04/05/1916	14/05/1916
War Diary	Couin	15/05/1916	23/05/1916
War Diary	Couin and Trenches Hebuterne	24/05/1916	24/05/1916
War Diary	Trenches Hebuterne	25/05/1916	30/05/1916
Heading	144th Brigade 48th Division 1/4th Battalion Gloucestershire Regiment June 1916		
Heading	War Diary Of 1/4th Bn Gloucestershire Regt From 31.5.16 To 30.6.16 Volume 15		
War Diary	Trenches	31/05/1916	31/05/1916
War Diary	Couin	01/06/1916	01/06/1916
War Diary	Gezaincourt	02/06/1916	03/06/1916
War Diary	Maison Rolland	04/06/1916	11/06/1916
War Diary	Yvrench	12/06/1916	13/06/1916
War Diary	Yvrench and Occoches	14/06/1916	14/06/1916
War Diary	Occoches and Couin	15/06/1916	15/06/1916
War Diary	Covin	16/06/1916	21/06/1916
War Diary	Covin and Sailly	22/06/1916	22/06/1916
War Diary	Sailly Bivouacs (pt 126)	23/06/1916	30/06/1916
Heading	144th Inf. Bde 48th Div. War Diary 4th Battn. The Gloucestershire Regiment July 1916		
War Diary	Pt 126 (S. of Sailly)	01/07/1916	01/07/1916
War Diary	P 18e (Mailly Maillet)	02/07/1916	02/07/1916
War Diary	Withington Avenue Trench	03/07/1916	03/07/1916
War Diary	P.10.e	03/07/1916	03/07/1916
War Diary	J 16.a (S Of Sailly)	03/07/1916	04/07/1916
War Diary	Courcelles	05/07/1916	07/07/1916
War Diary	Courcelles & Trenches	08/07/1916	08/07/1916
War Diary	Trenches Front Of Serre	09/07/1916	12/07/1916
War Diary	Courcelles	12/07/1916	13/07/1916
War Diary	Courcelles and Bouzincourt	14/07/1916	14/07/1916
War Diary	Bouzincourt and Trenches W. Of Ovillers	15/07/1916	15/07/1916
War Diary	Trenches Neighbourhood Of Ovillers	16/07/1916	16/07/1916
War Diary	Trenches Near Ovillers	16/07/1916	16/07/1916
War Diary	Trenches Ovillers	17/07/1916	19/07/1916
War Diary	Trenches Ovillers and Donnet Post Ribble Street	20/07/1916	20/07/1916
War Diary	Donnett Post and Ovillers Trenches	21/07/1916	21/07/1916
War Diary	Ovillers Trenches	22/07/1916	23/07/1916
War Diary	Ovillers Trenches and Crucifix Corner	24/07/1916	26/07/1916
War Diary	Ovillers Trenches and Crucifix Corner and Hedauville	27/07/1916	27/07/1916
War Diary	Hedauville and Arqueves	28/07/1916	28/07/1916
War Diary	Arqueves and Beauval	29/07/1916	29/07/1916
War Diary	Beauval and Franqueville (In Domart)	30/07/1916	30/07/1916
War Diary	Franqueville	31/07/1916	31/07/1916
Map	Map		
Heading	144th Brigade 48th Division 1/4th Battalion Gloucestershire Regiment August 1916		

War Diary	Franqueville	01/08/1916	07/08/1916
War Diary	Autheux	08/08/1916	08/08/1916
War Diary	Franqueville	09/08/1916	09/08/1916
War Diary	Puchevillers	10/08/1916	11/08/1916
War Diary	Hedauville	12/08/1916	12/08/1916
War Diary	Hedauville and Support to Ovillers Sector in Ribble Street	13/08/1916	13/08/1916
War Diary	Ovillers Trenches To Ribble Street	14/08/1916	14/08/1916
War Diary	Ovillers Trenches	15/08/1916	15/08/1916
Diagram etc	Diagram		
War Diary	Ovillers Trenches	16/08/1916	16/08/1916
War Diary	Bouzincourt	16/08/1916	18/08/1916
War Diary	Ribble Street	19/08/1916	21/08/1916
War Diary	Trenches Leipsie Redoubt	21/08/1916	21/08/1916
War Diary	Leipsic Redoubt	21/08/1916	22/08/1916
War Diary	Leipsic Redoubt And Bouzincourt	23/08/1916	23/08/1916
War Diary	Bouzincourt	24/08/1916	25/08/1916
War Diary	Forceville	26/08/1916	26/08/1916
War Diary	Trenches S Of Auchonvillers	27/08/1916	31/08/1916
Heading	144th Brigade 48th Division 1/4th Battalion Gloucestershire Regiment September 1916		
Heading	War Diary Of 1/4th Battn. Gloucestershire Regiment From 1.9.16 To 30.9.16 Volume 18		
War Diary	Trenches Q.17.A.5.3 To Q10.D.5.2	01/09/1916	05/09/1916
War Diary	Trenches Q.17.A.5.3 To Q10.D.5.2 and Bois de Warnimont	06/09/1916	08/09/1916
War Diary	Bois De Warnimont	09/09/1916	10/09/1916
War Diary	Bois de Warnimont	11/09/1916	12/09/1916
War Diary	Bus & Orville	13/09/1916	14/09/1916
War Diary	Orville	15/09/1916	18/09/1916
War Diary	Autheux	18/09/1916	29/09/1916
War Diary	Autheux and Sus-St-Leger	30/09/1916	30/09/1916
Heading	144th Brigade 48th Division 1/4th Battalion Gloucestershire Regiment October 1916		
Heading	War Diary Of 1/4th Battalion Gloucestershire Regiment From 1-10-16 To 31-10-16 Volume 19		
War Diary	Sus-St-Leger and Halloy	01/10/1916	01/10/1916
War Diary	Halloy	02/10/1916	02/10/1916
War Diary	Halloy And Souastre	03/10/1916	03/10/1916
War Diary	Souastre	04/10/1916	06/10/1916
War Diary	Souastre and Trenches	07/10/1916	07/10/1916
War Diary	Trenches Opposite Gommecourt	08/10/1916	11/10/1916
War Diary	Trenches Opposite Gommecourt and Souastre	12/10/1916	12/10/1916
War Diary	Souastre and Warlincourt	13/10/1916	13/10/1916
War Diary	La Haie and Warlincourt	14/10/1916	14/10/1916
War Diary	Warlincourt and La Haie	15/10/1916	17/10/1916
War Diary	Warlincourt La Haie and Trenches	18/10/1916	18/10/1916
War Diary	Trenches Yankee St to Warrior St or K.10.B.1.5 to K.16.B.9.5.8	18/10/1916	19/10/1916
War Diary	Warlincourt & Grincourt	20/10/1916	20/10/1916
War Diary	Sus-St-Leger	21/10/1916	24/10/1916
War Diary	Transport Sus-St-Leger and Talmas	24/10/1916	24/10/1916
War Diary	Sus-St-Leger & Bresle	25/10/1916	25/10/1916
War Diary	Bresle & Albert	31/10/1916	31/10/1916
War Diary	Albert	31/10/1916	31/10/1916

Heading	144th Brigade 48th Division 1/4th Battalion Gloucestershire Regiment November 1916		
Heading	War Diary Of 1/4th Battalion Gloucestershire Regiment From 1/11/16 To 30/11/16 Volume 20		
War Diary	Albert	01/11/1916	01/11/1916
War Diary	Bazentin Le Petit & Trenches	02/11/1916	04/11/1916
War Diary	Bazentin Le Petit and Martinpuich	05/11/1916	05/11/1916
War Diary	Martinpuich Support Trenches	06/11/1916	06/11/1916
War Diary	Le Sars and Martinpuich	07/11/1916	07/11/1916
War Diary	Le Sars	08/11/1916	09/11/1916
War Diary	Contalmaison	10/11/1916	19/11/1916
War Diary	Contalmaison & Martinpuich	20/11/1916	20/11/1916
War Diary	Martinpuich	21/11/1916	22/11/1916
War Diary	Le Sars	23/11/1916	23/11/1916
War Diary	Le Sars Contalmaison	24/11/1916	24/11/1916
War Diary	Contalmaison	25/11/1916	30/11/1916
Heading	144th Brigade 48th Division 1/4th Battalion Gloucestershire Regiment December 1916		
Heading	War Diary Of 1/4th Gloucestershire Regiment From 1st December 1916 To 31st December 1916 Volume 21		
War Diary	Contalmaison	01/12/1916	01/12/1916
War Diary	Contalmaison & Martinpuich	02/12/1916	02/12/1916
War Diary	Martinpuich	03/12/1916	04/12/1916
War Diary	Martinpuich & Contalmaison	05/12/1916	05/12/1916
War Diary	Contalmaison	06/12/1916	09/12/1916
War Diary	Contalmaison & Le Sars	10/12/1916	10/12/1916
War Diary	Le Sars	11/12/1916	13/12/1916
War Diary	Le Sars & Martinpuich	14/12/1916	14/12/1916
War Diary	Martinpuich & Scots Redoubt South	15/12/1916	15/12/1916
War Diary	Scots Redoubt South	16/12/1916	16/12/1916
War Diary	Scots Redoubt South & Mametz Wood	17/12/1916	21/12/1916
War Diary	Mametz Wood	22/12/1916	22/12/1916
War Diary	Mametz Wood & Fricourt Camp	23/12/1916	23/12/1916
War Diary	Fricourt Camp	24/12/1916	28/12/1916
War Diary	Fricourt Camp & Becourt Camp	29/12/1916	29/12/1916
War Diary	Becourt Camp & Contay	30/12/1916	30/12/1916
War Diary	Contay	31/12/1916	31/12/1916
Heading	War Diary Of 1/4th Bn. Gloucestershire Regiment From 1.1.17 To 31.1.17 Volume 22		
War Diary	Contay	01/01/1917	07/01/1917
War Diary	Contay & Huchennville	08/01/1917	08/01/1917
War Diary	Huchennville & Caumont	09/01/1917	28/01/1917
War Diary	Cerisy	29/01/1917	31/01/1917
Heading	War Diary Of 1/4th Battalion Gloucestershire Regt From 1/2/17 To 28/2/17 Volume 23		
War Diary	Cerisy & Cappy	01/02/1917	01/02/1917
War Diary	Cappy	02/02/1917	07/02/1917
War Diary	Marly Camp	08/02/1917	15/02/1917
War Diary	Cappy	16/02/1917	21/02/1917
War Diary	Sophie Trench	22/02/1917	24/02/1917
War Diary	Marly	25/02/1917	28/02/1917
Heading	1/4th Bn Gloucestershire Regiment War Diary For March 1917 Volume 24		
War Diary	Cappy	01/03/1917	12/03/1917
War Diary	Cappy & Sophie	13/03/1917	14/03/1917
War Diary	Sophie	15/03/1917	24/03/1917

War Diary	Sophie & Cartigny	25/03/1917	25/03/1917
War Diary	Cartigny	26/03/1917	28/03/1917
War Diary	Cartigny & Villers Faucon	29/03/1917	29/03/1917
War Diary	Villers Faucon	30/03/1917	31/03/1917
Heading	War Diary Of 1/4th Bn The Gloucestershire Regt T.F From 1/4/17 To 30/4/17 (Vol. XXIV)		
War Diary		01/04/1917	30/04/1917
Heading	War Diary Of 1/4th Bn The Gloucestershire Regt 1st May To 31st May 1917 (Vol XXVI)		
War Diary		01/05/1917	29/05/1917
Heading	War Diary Of 1/4th Bn The Gloucestershire Regt (T.F) From 1st June To 30th June 1917 (Vol XXVII)		
War Diary	Lebucquiere	01/06/1917	06/06/1917
War Diary	Louverval	06/06/1917	15/06/1917
War Diary	Le Bucquiere	15/06/1917	22/06/1917
War Diary	Louverval	23/06/1917	30/06/1917
Miscellaneous	1/4th Battalion Gloucestershire Regiment	12/06/1917	12/06/1917
Miscellaneous	1/4th Battalion Gloucestershire Regiment	14/06/1917	14/06/1917
Miscellaneous	1/4th Battalion Gloucestershire Regiment	25/06/1917	25/06/1917
Heading	War Diary Of 1/4th Batt Gloucestershire Regt From 1 July 1917 To 31 July 1917 Volume28		
War Diary	Louverval	01/07/1917	01/07/1917
War Diary	Fremicourt	02/07/1917	02/07/1917
War Diary	Achiet Le Petit	03/07/1917	03/07/1917
War Diary	Blaireville	04/07/1917	21/07/1917
War Diary	Berles-Au-Bois	22/07/1917	22/07/1917
War Diary	Poperinghe	23/07/1917	25/07/1917
War Diary	St Janter Biezen	25/07/1917	31/07/1917
Heading	War Diary Of 1/4th Batt. Gloucestershire Regt From 1.8.17 To 31.8.17 Volume 29		
War Diary	Camp At A29c	01/08/1917	05/08/1917
War Diary	Dambre Camp	06/08/1917	06/08/1917
War Diary	Front Line	08/08/1917	09/08/1917
War Diary	Support	09/08/1917	11/08/1917
War Diary	Front Line	13/08/1917	16/08/1917
War Diary	Reigersburg Camp	16/08/1917	20/08/1917
War Diary	Canal Bank	21/08/1917	21/08/1917
War Diary	Front Line	22/08/1917	25/08/1917
War Diary	Canal Bank	25/08/1917	25/08/1917
War Diary	Reigersburg Camp	26/08/1917	26/08/1917
War Diary	Brown Camp	27/08/1917	27/08/1917
War Diary	School Camp	29/08/1917	31/08/1917
Heading	1/4th Battalion Gloucestershire Regt. War Diary Period No.30 Sept 1st 1917 To Sept 30th 1917 Vol 30		
War Diary	School Camp	01/09/1917	17/09/1917
War Diary	Nielles (les Ardres P de C)	18/09/1917	30/09/1917
Heading	1/4th Gloucestershire Regiment War Diary 1st October-31st October 1917 Volume XXXI		
War Diary	Nielles Les Ardres (P.de.C)	01/10/1917	01/10/1917
War Diary	Brake Camp	02/10/1917	05/10/1917
War Diary	Reigersberg Camp	06/10/1917	07/10/1917
War Diary	Dambre Camp	08/10/1917	10/10/1917
War Diary	Siege Camp	11/10/1917	11/10/1917
War Diary	School Camp	12/10/1917	13/10/1917
War Diary	Savy	14/10/1917	15/10/1917
War Diary	Villers-Au-Bois	16/10/1917	17/10/1917

War Diary	Front Line	18/10/1917	23/10/1917
War Diary	Ottawa Camp	24/10/1917	31/10/1917
Miscellaneous	1/4th Battalion Gloucestershire Regiment		
Miscellaneous	1/4th Battalion Gloucestershire Regiment	14/10/1917	14/10/1917
Operation(al) Order(s)	Operation Orders No.38 By Lt. Col. H. St. G. Schomberg, Comdg. 1/6th Bn. Gloucestershire Regt.	11/10/1917	11/10/1917
Operation(al) Order(s)	Operation Orders No.39 By Lt. Col. H. St. G. Schomberg, Comdg. 1/6th Bn. Gloucestershire Regt	12/10/1917	12/10/1917
Operation(al) Order(s)	Operation Orders No.40 By Lt. Col. H. St. G. Schomberg, Comdg. 1/6th Bn Gloucestershire Regt	14/10/1917	14/10/1917
Operation(al) Order(s)	Operation Orders No.37a By Lt. Col. H. St. G. Schomberg, Comdg. 1/6th Bn Gloucestershire Regt.	10/10/1917	10/10/1917
Operation(al) Order(s)	Operation Orders No.41 By Lt. Col. H. St. G. Schomberg, Comdg. 1/6th Bn Gloucestershire Regt	17/10/1917	17/10/1917
Operation(al) Order(s)	Operation Orders No.41a By Lt. Col. H. St G. Schomberg, Comdg. 1/6th Bn Gloucestershire Regt	21/10/1917	21/10/1917

WO/95/2758/1

1/4 Battalion Gloucestershire Regiment

48TH DIVISION
144TH INFY BDE

1-4TH BN GLOS REGT.

APR 1915-~~MAR 1919~~.

1917 OCT

TO ITALY

144th Inf.Bde.
48th Div.

Battn. disembarked
Boulogne from
England 31.3.15.

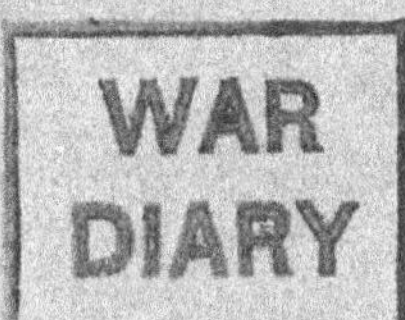

1/4th BATTN. THE GLOUCESTERSHIRE REGIMENT.

A P R I L

(30.3.15 to 30.4.15)

1 9 1 5

1

Mar '19

Confidential

WAR DIARY

of

1/4th Batt^n GLOUCESTERSHIRE REG^T

from 30th March 1915 to 30th APRIL 1915

(Volume I).

Instructions regarding War Diaries and Intelligence Summaries are contained in F. S. Regs., Part II. and the Staff Manual respectively. Title pages will be prepared in manuscript.

WAR DIARY
or
INTELLIGENCE SUMMARY
(Erase heading not required.)

Army Form C. 2118

Hour, Date, Place	Summary of Events and Information	Remarks and references to Appendices
10.20 P.M. 30.3.15 MALDON ESSEX	Transport left MALDON EAST at 10.20 P.M. – Strength 2 Officers, 77 horses and Mules, 23 Vehicles, 84 other Ranks.	
1.0 p.m. 31.3.15. DANBORY	Battalion left DANBORY in two train loads – left MALDON EAST at 3.20 pm and 3.50 pm – Strength 26 Officers and 999 other ranks (2 short) – Telegram from Lichfield saying Pte HOLLAND of Transport left at SOUTHAMPTON – arrived FOLKESTONE 8.0 pm – BOULOGNE 10.0 pm. – Camp 11.30 pm.	
1.4.15. BOULOGNE	Left Camp 9.0 AM. – Entrained at PONT de BRIQUES at 10.0 AM. on same train as transport which had come from HAVRE – arrived CASSEL 2.0 pm. – Left CASSEL 5.0 pm. by march route for WINNEZEELE about 9 miles away and arrived there at 8.45 pm and went into scattered billets. Sergt ROWLANDS proceeded from HAVRE to A.G.'s Office at Base – L/Cpl Cox from BOULOGNE to Base records – Total marching in state 29 Officers 997 other ranks including interpreter.	
2.4.15. WINNEZEELE	Missed Censor Stamp No 2700 and reported it to C2 Troopers and G.H.Q I(d) Issued to Companies copies of special routine order by G.O.C. 2nd Army about penalties for certain offences.	
3.4.15. " "	2 supply waggons, with 2 drivers A.S.C., 1 Cpl and 2 men of C Coy and 4 horses A.S.C. out this day to join No 3 Coy: S.M.D train at STEENVOORDE. Battalion paraded at Brigade Hd Qrs for inspection by Gen. Sir H. Smith-Dorrien G.C.B.D.S.O. at 11.0 AM. – Wire from O.C. details DANBURY to say Censor Stamp found and forwarded on 31.3.15 – Informed G.H.Q I(d) and C2 Troopers by wire.	
4.4.15 " " "	Lt CASTLE went to draw Cash for 1st payment at 8.0 AM. Lt PARRINSON to Bde Hd Qrs at 12 noon as billeting officer in advance. March orders from Bde received at 2.0 pm. for Battalion to pass St SYLVESTRE CAPPEL at 10.0 AM tomorrow en route to billets S. of BAILLEUL.	

Army Form C. 2118.

WAR DIARY
or
INTELLIGENCE SUMMARY
(Erase heading not required.)

Instructions regarding War Diaries and Intelligence Summaries are contained in F. S. Regs., Part II. and the Staff Manual respectively. Title pages will be prepared in manuscript.

Hour, Date, Place	Summary of Events and Information	Remarks and references to Appendices
5.4.15 WINNEZEELE	Battalion paraded at WINNIZEELE at 7.30 AM – C.S.M. Hss and Pte HOUSE and Lt MANSELL left behind sick with 1st S.M. Field Ambulance – Marched out 28 Officers, 995 other ranks, 78 horses. Bde Starting point – St SYLVESTRE CAPPEL, via METTEREN to NOOTE BOOME where Battalion separated to billeting areas. – Our billets in scattered farms about 1 miles W of DOULIEU – 1 NCO and 22 men fell out on march – arrived billets at 3.0 PM about 18 mile march – Light rain all day and very heavy rain after arrival – Battn marched well but were tired – Glouc: ARTILLERY passed us at FLETRE – one H.D. horse died during the night – this horse was allotted us at SOUTHAMPTON to complete establishment – Battn reported present at 8.0 p.m. except 1 L/Cpl and 7 men. – Hd Qrs at LE PETIT MORTIER.	
6.4.15. LE PETIT MORTIER	1 Cpl and 6 men reported 12 noon from Ambulance. – S.M.D. Q106 of 5.4.15 "For present no acknowledgement to be given for billets, but careful record to be kept." Pro: forma Returns of various kinds received. Ptes SHATTOCK and HACK reported at Bde Hd Qrs	
7.4.15 . . .	Battn present – 28 Officers, 995 including attached. – G.O.C. Bde inspected 23 men who fell out on the march on 5th inst. – 2 men to 1st S.M.F. Ambulance.	
8.4.15 . .	3rd Corps Routine Order No. 53 of 6.4.15 prohibits drink to be bought or sold except wine or light beer. 1 man of C Coy to 1st S.M.F. ambulance and 1 man of D Coy –	
9.4.15	1 Riding Horse broke away on night 7/8th and has not been found – Major & 2.M. WILSON to Field Ambulance and one man – Bde [illegible] Eggleton & S.M.2 [illegible] Head Quarters [illegible] 4 officers and 6.0. [illegible] Commenced a 3 day Bomb Throwing Course with 4th Divn Hd Qrs at NIEPPE	
10.4.15	[illegible] 2.[illegible] STEENWERCK at 2.16 p.m. Route via CROIX du BAC – ERMENTIERES Passed General HEATH Commanding 1/1 South MIDLAND DIVISION who sent a Complimentary Order to the Brigade. Passed Maj. Genl. Keir Commanding 6th Division at Croix du Bac. and Lt. General Pulteney at ERQUINGHEM – Battn Billetted in old HOSPICE CONVENT in RUE DE ROTOURS. ARMENTIERES and attached to 16th Brigade – A Coy: and 2 platoons B Coy. Sent to TRENCHES at 9.30 p.m. for instruction viz: 3 platoons to 1/K.S.L.I. – 1 platoon to 6th Yorks and LANCS: – 2 platoons to BUFFS.	

1247 W 3299 200,000 (E) 8/14 J.B.C. & A. Forms/C. 2118/11.

WAR DIARY
or
INTELLIGENCE SUMMARY.
(Erase heading not required.)

Army Form C. 2118.

Instructions regarding War Diaries and Intelligence Summaries are contained in F. S. Regs., Part II. and the Staff Manual respectively. Title pages will be prepared in manuscript.

Hour, Date, Place		Summary of Events and Information	Remarks and references to Appendices
9.30 AM	11.4.15. ARMENTIERES	Lectures to all Officers and N.C.O.s on Sanitation by M.O. Loyal North Lancs.	
10.30 AM.		4 platoons to R.E. Stores to see trench stores being made and for instruction in their use.	
12.0 noon.		Inspection by G.O.C. 16th Bde in Square.	
1.0 pm.		" " " " of Transport.	
2.30 pm.		Instruction in Bomb throwing to all Officers and N.C.O.s at 16th Bde Hd Qrs.	
6.0 pm.		1 Platoon B Coy. and 1 Platoon C. Coy. for trench digging – Tools from 16th Bde.	
8.0 pm.		1 " B " " " " " "	
		Three men wounded ~~[illegible]~~ in Platoon att^d^ to BUFFS & sent to Hospital. – Wounded by bomb from Trench Mortar. J.C.T.	
6.30 – 10.30 AM.	12.4.15	C.O. and Adjt were taken round trenches of 16th Infy Brigade	
9.30 "		Lecture to Officers & N.C.O.s on Trench Warfare – by an Officer, 1/K.S.L.I.	
10.30 "		D. Coy. to R.E. Stores to see types of works.	
10.45 "		Machine Gun detachment inspected by Bde M.G. Officer & taken to Bde M.G. Range for firing.	
11.0 "		Officers visited billets of 1/K.S.L.I. & saw general arrangements.	
9.0 pm.		3 platoons of D Coy. for trench digging.	
		Platoons in trenches relieved by C. Coy. and 2 Platoons B Coy. ~~Coy~~ for instruction viz. 3 platoons to 2/York & Lancs. 1 platoon to 5/N. Lancs. and 2 platoons to 1/Leicester Regt. J.C.T.	
9.30 AM.	13.4.15	1 Coy. to R.E. depot to see types of Works.	
11.0 AM.		Officers and N.C.O.s to see Bomb and Grenade throwing Experiments.	
6.0 pm.		3 platoons D Coy. to trenches of York and Lancs. Regt with M.G. Section – 1 platoon D Coy. with 5/L.N. Lancs. Regt	
6.0 pm.		C.O. and Adjt to Hd Qrs 1/Leic. Regt for tour of Trenches.	
		1. Heavy Draught horse died – from twisted intestines. J.C.T.	
	14.4.15	March orders for 15/4/15 recd from Bde – these were cancelled at 5 pm.	
		1. Man of D Coy. wounded during trench instruction & sent to Hospital.	
		D. Coy. in trenches as above. J.C.T.	

(73989) W4141—463. 400,000. 9/14. H.&J.Ltd. Forms/C. 2118/10.

Army Form C. 2118.

Instructions regarding War Diaries and Intelligence Summaries are contained in F. S. Regs., Part II. and the Staff Manual respectively. Title pages will be prepared in manuscript.

WAR DIARY
or
INTELLIGENCE SUMMARY.

(Erase heading not required.)

Hour, Date, Place	Summary of Events and Information	Remarks and references to Appendices
15.4.15	Batt. Pioneers rec. instruction at R.E. Stns.	All references to Map. BELGIUM. Sheet 28 $\frac{1}{40,000}$
7.0 pm.	A + B Coy. officers visited Trenches of R. Irish Regt. near PLOEGSTREET which the Batt. takes over on 17th April	
	D. Coy. and M.G. Section came out of Trenches 7.0 pm. [initials]	
16.4.15	Orders rec. re. taking over Trenches from R. Irish Regt. (2 Coys) ; 4/R. Berks. (2 Coys) ; at Ploegsteert ; O.C. Coys. visited Trenches and stayed during night.	
	C.O. visited H.Q. 2nd Royal Berks. Regt. at HAMPSHIRE FARM – arrangements made for Telephone Communication to all Trenches	
	Transport ordered to go to NIEPPE – March table rec. for 17th April. [initials]	
17.4.15	Batt. marched out of HOSPICE CIVIL – ARMENTIÈRES at 5.15 pm and took over Trenches as follows. Viz.	
	A + B Coys. took over from 2/R. Irish Regt. from R. in WARNAGE north to Fork Road South of AU GHEER.	
	C + D " " " 4/R. Berks Regt. " above Fork Road to LE GHEER.	
	Relief carried out by 10.55 pm.	
	Heavy Gun fire about 15 miles North from 8.0 pm. to 11. pm.	
	Hot Rifle fire at 8.0 pm to 9.0 pm. about 10 miles to North. (probably Hill 60)	
	2 M.Gs. from 1/6 Glouc. Regt. attached with C + D Coys. [initials]	
18.4.15	All quiet during night and day.	
6.30 AM.	3 men wounded by Rifle fire – Brig.-Genl. visited H.Q. 2nd at 1.0 pm.	
1.0 P.M.	Snipers reported firing from Trees or Houses opposite Hampshire Trench.	
	Work in Trenches during day improving breastworks + communications	
	Rt. Hon. A.J. Balfour visited Trenches in afternoon.	
8.0 P.M.	2 Sections B. Coy. from Lancashire Support Farm to RUTTER TRENCH at 8.0 p.m.	
	2 " " D. " Breastworks E of Keepers Lodge moved into HAMPSHIRE Trench.	
	1/Worcester Regt. took over the Breastworks at 8.0 pm.	
9.30 pm	Brig.-Genl. went round Trenches with C.O. at 9.30 p.m.	
	2 officers per Coy. of 1/6 Glouc. Regt. spent night in Trenches to learn about them. [initials]	

(73989) W4141—463. 400,000. 9/14. H.&J.Ltd. Forms/C. 2118/10.

Instructions regarding War Diaries and Intelligence Summaries are contained in F. S. Regs., Part II. and the Staff Manual respectively. Title pages will be prepared in manuscript.

WAR DIARY
or
INTELLIGENCE SUMMARY.
(Erase heading not required.)

Army Form C. 2118.

Hour, Date, Place	Summary of Events and Information	Remarks and references to Appendices
19. 4. 15	Battn front was calm up till 8.30 p.m. when Enemy fired about a dozen bombs from trench mortar into our lines. Effect slight as bombs fell mostly beyond our breastworks. C. Compy Headquarters at LE GHEER were set on fire but it burnt out by 10 p.m. – During this time there was continuous rifle fire by both sides – Communication was obtained with supporting batteries who fired about six Rounds. Saps from German trenches observed in front of D. Coy. – LE GHEER Cottage set on fire by shell. 1 Man in D Coy wounded in knee by Sniper. No 2583 Pte H. DYDE – C. Coy. Killed [initials]	
20. 4. 15	Corpl SELWOOD. C. Coy wounded at 2.30 p.m. while reconnoitring a party of 5 Germans on our wire in front of Picket House. whom he fired at single handed – His name has been forwarded to Bde for recommendation. Pte DYDE buried in LANCASHIRE COTTAGE CEMETERY at 5.45 P.M. 2 Shells from our own Battery burst near Hd Qrs but did no harm. Pte CONIBEAR – D. Coy. wounded in trenches – C. Coy. moved 1 NCO and 7 men from LE GHEER to BARRICADE HOUSE [initials]	Alteration in Disposition
21. 4. 15.	ENEMY'S M.G. fire on road. East + South of PLOEGSTREET WOOD prevented R.E. stores being delivered to D. Company. A Coy received a paper kite sent from German Line with message – "Please send this back when wind is favourable. As you have no ships left – why don't you come over here – we are tired of this". 1/6 Glouc. Regt relieved the Battn in trenches at 7.30 pm. Relief finished at 1.30 AM. The Germans shelled the Convent during relief and kept up sniping and occasional M.G. fire, wounding 1 man of 1/6 Glouc Regt. Enfilade trench had some shots in from rear and HAMPSHIRE trench some from the left. It is doubtful whether these are German shots or from our trench N of BIRDCAGE held by 1/7 Worc Regt. L/Corpl Phillips (D Coy) Pte Turner " " Do Brodrib . A. Coy } all wounded in trenches. 3 men wounded [initials]	
22. 4. 15	Battn in Billets in PLOEGSTREET in Bde Reserve – Working parties in Evening – digging in Sheet 28 – T.18 [initials]	
23. 4. 15	Do: Do: Do: 2 men slightly wounded – Do: Do: [initials]	

(73989) W4141—463. 400,000. 9/14. H.&J.Ltd. Forms/C. 2118/10.

Instructions regarding War Diaries and Intelligence Summaries are contained in F. S. Regs., Part II. and the Staff Manual respectively. Title pages will be prepared in manuscript.

WAR DIARY
or
INTELLIGENCE SUMMARY.
(Erase heading not required.)

Army Form C. 2118.

Hour, Date, Place	Summary of Events and Information	Remarks and references to Appendices
24.4.15	Batt: in Billets in PLOEGSTREET in Bde Reserve – Quiet day. J.H.T.	
25.4.15.	Batt: relieved 1/6 Glouc: Regt in trenches – beginning at 8.0pm. Relief completed by 12.15 midnight – No casualties – quiet night. J.H.T.	
26.4.15	Batt: in trenches. Day quiet. Telephone communication arranged from hut at U.27 G.3.8 to all Companies as fighting HQ 2rs – Sniping by enemy at night – Pte H. POUND. No 2657 of A Coy: killed and also No 2458 Pte A. VOISEY of C Comp'y both shot in head – J.H.T.	
27.4.15	1 Cpl. + 2 men sent for Machine Gun course at WISQUES. 1 Sergt + 7 men sent to S.M.D HQ 2rs for permanent duty.	
3.0pm.	S.M.D. G.B. 8 d/d 26.4.15 directs all wire in front of trenches to be inspected nightly. C. Coy reports 3 white rockets sent up by Germans at U.28 C.2.9 and B. Coy reports 5 white and 1 blue sent into their trench on right of C. Coy at same time.	
5.30.pm.	2 Rifle grenades fell in A. Coy. trenches and 1 grenade in B. Coy's trench – result 6 men of A. Coy. wounded 2 seriously – No 1859 Pte O.H. BADMAN died during the night –	
11.30 pm.	Cessation of all work ordered from 1.30 AM to 2.0 AM for listening throughout Brigade – Nothing doing. Orders rec'd from Brigade to take over line from GERMAN HOUSE exclusive to PLOEGSTEERT – LE GHEER Road – U 21.D.8 from 1/7 Worcester Regt before daylight – 1½ Platoons, B Co from support behind CONVENT U.27.B.2 were moved at once and 1 Machine Gun from right advanced trench U.28.C.1.7 to U 21.d.5.7. About Pte Betts. A. Coy. No 2224. – Communication trench dug towards Convent. J.H.T.	
28.4.15	Relief of 1/7 Worcester trenches completed by 3.0 AM. — Several rifle grenades were fired at A + B Coy's trenches from point U 22.C 5.5. but did no damage. In return this point was shelled by 126th Battery. Snipers located by D. Coy: at U.22 C.6.7 and Machine Gun located there too. Quiet day and night – One man wounded (slight) – Communication trench continued – J.H.T.	
29.4.15	Pte E.H. NIEHOS – C. Coy given Commission to Special Reserve – L/Cpl T.A.H. NASH given Commission to 16th (1st City) Batt: Manchester Regt	

(73989) W4141—463. 400,000. 9/14. H.&J.Ltd. Forms/C. 2118/10.

Instructions regarding War Diaries and Intelligence Summaries are contained in F. S. Regs., Part II. and the Staff Manual respectively. Title pages will be prepared in manuscript.

WAR DIARY
or
INTELLIGENCE SUMMARY.
(Erase heading not required.)

Army Form C. 2118.

Hour, Date, Place	Summary of Events and Information	Remarks and references to Appendices
29.4.15	S.M.D. 191. A.X. recd with instructions regarding rendering of Casualty Estimate in Action and (3) daily Casualty returns showing names of Officers and Numbers of Other Ranks, Killed, wounded or missing –	
	Sap from Enfilade to Rotten trenches got through – Sap started from BURNT OUT FARM towards HEDGE TRENCH. Communication trench from Support farm to CONVENT. Continued –	
6.0pm.	12 Shrapnel burst over B. Coy. breastworks in Wood.	
9.30pm.	A Rifle Grenade fell in A. Coy's advanced trench wounding 2 men –	
10.50pm.	Several Grenades were fired at CONVENT and ROTTER trenches.	
	4 Shrapnel burst over CONVENT trenches – No damage done – H.T.	
30.4.15. 7.30 AM. 11.0 AM. 2.0 PM.	Morning foggy – No 2920 Pte H. E. STENNER wounded seriously in head – and No 25. Sergt W. T. BRADLEY – C Coy. Seriously wounded at 7.30 AM. both by rifle fire – C.O in Conference with Brigadier at 11.0 AM. Our trenches visited by General YARMALOFF (Russian) at 2.0pm. –	
	Hedge at U.28.c.4.8. (A. Coy. trenches) reconnoitred by Sergt GRIMSHAW and L/Cpl MURPHY but no signs of enemy occupation found.	
	About 50 German Shells fell near RIFLE HOUSE in PLOEGSTEERT WOOD during afternoon.	
	Battn was relieved at 8.0pm. by 1/6 Glosc. Regt. – Relief completed without casualty at 11.0pm – Battn arrived at billets at PONT de NIEPPE at 12.0 midnight. – H.T.	

144th Inf.Bde.
48th Div.

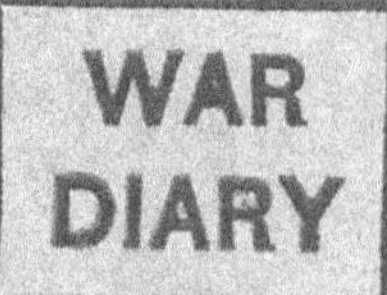

1/4th BATTN. THE GLOUCESTERSHIRE REGIMENT.

M A Y

(1.5.15 to 30.5.15)

1 9 1 5

Instructions regarding War Diaries and Intelligence Summaries are contained in F. S. Regs., Part II. and the Staff Manual respectively. Title pages will be prepared in manuscript.

WAR DIARY
or
INTELLIGENCE SUMMARY.
(Erase heading not required.)

Army Form C. 2118.

Hour, Date, Place	Summary of Events and Information	Remarks and references to Appendices
1.5.15 PONT de NIEPPE	Battalion in Billets at PONT de NIEPPE in Divisional Reserve. No 2920 Pte H.E. STENNER of D. Coy died of wounds received 30-4-15. Strength - 27 Officers - 926 other ranks.	Reference to MAP BELGIUM. sheet 28 Scale - 1:40,000
2.5.15 " "	Battalion in Divisional Reserve - Divine Service held in the Baths, address delivered by Bishop of PRETORIA Strength - 27 officers - 919 other Ranks.	
3.5.15 " "	Battalion in Divisional Reserve - 2 men tried by F.G.C.M. for sleeping on Post - Sentenced to 5 years Penal Servitude - Sentence confirmed but committal suspended until further orders. Joined - 2/Lieut. POLACK and 2/Lieut. THOMAS from 2/4 Glouc: Regt. Strength - 29 officers - 911 other Ranks.	
4.5.15 " "	Battn in Divisional Reserve - Headquarters and Companies inspected by the Brigadier General at their billets during the morning. 5 men sent to Hospital and 1 returned. Strength - 29 Officers - 910 other Ranks.	
5.5.15 " "	Battalion in Divl Reserve during daytime. 27 men reported sick, mostly diarrhoea - 8 men sent to Hospital and 6 returned from Hospital - 2 of these men quite unfit for duty, still very sick. Strength 29 officers - 905 other ranks. Battalion relieved 1/6 Glouc: Regt in trenches U.21.22.27.28 Relief delayed by bursts of rifle fire and some shelling - No Casualties during relief - 1 man in D. Company wounded in side later.	
6.5.15	Battn in Trenches - A and C companies working on new trench to connect BURNT OUT FARM (A Coy) and HEDGE TRENCH (C. Coy) both U 28. a. - Wounded - 4 men. (1 since died) 4 men returned from Hospital - about 5 severe cases of diarrhoea are occurring daily - Instructions issued to all Ranks about use of respirators and goggles against asphyxiating Gas (S.N.D. order No 4 of 4.5.15 and III Corps Memo d/d 2nd May 1915 [illegible]) - Respirators, Goggles, and bottles of Bi-carbonate Soda solution issued. A trench mortar is now in the possession of the Battn and one telescopic sighted Rifle was recd today - Periscopes have nearly all been broken by shots and we cannot get them replaced - Eight shells fell near LE GHEER CONVENT - U 27.3. during afternoon - Capt LEWIS and 24 Battn Grenadiers were instructed by a Sergt of 2 A&S. Highlanders in attack with bombs - 4 men wounded (1 since died) 4 men returned from Hospital -	

(73989) W4141—463. 400,000. 9/14. H.&J.Ltd. Forms/C. 2118/10.

Instructions regarding War Diaries and Intelligence Summaries are contained in F. S. Regs., Part II. and the Staff Manual respectively. Title pages will be prepared in manuscript.

WAR DIARY
or
INTELLIGENCE SUMMARY.
(Erase heading not required.)

Army Form C. 2118.

Hour, Date, Place	Summary of Events and Information	Remarks and references to Appendices
6.5.15 PLOEGSTEERT	One Machine Gun moved out of T Trench. U21.D Strength. 29. Officers, 905 O.R. J.C.T.	
7.5.15 " "	Batt in the Trenches – Quiet night – Silence observed from 1.30 AM – 2.0 AM. for listening – nothing heard. Lieut: J.H. KNIGHT-ADKIN and L/C HOLLAND (D. Coy) approached to 15 yards of German trench in U22.C. and threw 2 bombs – both of which exploded in Enemy's trench, getting away safely under rifle fire. 6 Shells (German) fell near KEEPER'S COTTAGE (U27.B.5) in PLOEGSTEERT WOOD. 2 Trench Mortars, with 1 officer and detachment from 1/7 Worcester Regt were sent to C. Coy 220 Boxes. S.A.A. and 400 Grenades and 150 Mortar bombs were carried up to trenches during night 7/8 4 men returned from Hospital and 4 men sent there. 8 men of D. Coy wounded and 1 not reported to Dr and duty. Strength 29 Officers – 899. O.R. J.C.T.	
8.5.15. " "	Batt in the Trenches – Ammunition Carrying Completed 3.0 AM. Work on new trench (U28.a) delayed owing to Bursts of rapid fire on our working parties – C. Coy reconnoitred old sap head from German lines – coming to centre of our new trench – and found unused and full of water. Very quiet day but Enemy's snipers were busy and several men were hit, two of them in the wood by overs. – Orders issued for tomorrow in accordance with Bde programme Lieut. NEWTH and 1 platoon of B. Coy. moved from Lancashire Support Farm (U.27.B) to dug-outs in HUNTERS AVENUE (U21.C) after midnight. 4 men sent to Hospital – 3 men returned from Hospital + 2 wounded men sent during the day. 2 men wounded in A. Coy. 3 men in B Coy and 3 men in C. Coy. Strength. 29 Officers and 892. O.R. J.C.T.	
9.5.15 " "	Batt in the Trenches – During the night 8/9 May. A. Coy. sent out 5 patrols to German wire under Lieut: MANSELL – They cut the wire and put boards on and marked. All patrols were fired on, and returned by 2.30 AM. with 2 Casualties (1 died before 7.0 AM.) Major BAKER – O.C. A. Coy. reports, in connection with the above that PTE BEES, who was slightly	

(73989) W4141—463. 400,000. 9/14. H.&J.Ltd. Forms/C. 2118/10.

Instructions regarding War Diaries and Intelligence Summaries are contained in F. S. Regs., Part II. and the Staff Manual respectively. Title pages will be prepared in manuscript.

WAR DIARY
or
INTELLIGENCE SUMMARY.
(Erase heading not required.)

Army Form C. 2118.

Hour, Date, Place	Summary of Events and Information	Remarks and references to Appendices
9.5.15. PLOEGSTEERT	Slightly wounded in the leg, reported at 2.15 A.M. that L/c PEARCE was wounded and that he had been sent back to get help – Meanwhile Pte STEPHENS had carried L/c PEARCE in from a point 15 yards from the German trenches, under a heavy fire (rifle) he was assisted by Pte BROWN, while Pte SANTER carried all the rifles – At 3.0 A.M. our Snipers were active and throughout the day heavy rifle fire was kept up on the German trenches in U21 b, U22 a.c. & U28 a and Mortars and rifle grenades were also used successfully, and our Machine Guns active all day, supported by 3 Guns 1/6 Glouc. Regt. dug in during night 8/9 in U.27 b.3.5 employing overhead fire on U29.a.1.6, U22.d.5.5. in accordance with programme recd from Glouc. & Worc. Brigade with object of holding enemy to their trenches and thus assisting attacks being made Elsewhere. Howitzers, Mountain Battery and Field Batteries also shelled German trenches and lines in rear. Our trenches, especially those of A. Coy in U27b.+d and B. Coy in U21.d. heavily shelled by German Artillery as well as LE GHEER Convent. U27.b. The German wire entanglements much damaged by our Artillery and their parapets breached in several places in front of A and C. Coys in U.28 a and U.22. Capt SLADE – O.C. C Coy. specially complimented by our Artillery observing Officer who stated that 90% of his trench Mortar bombs had landed either on the German parapets or in their trenches, while Capt LEWIS. A Coy. made several breaches in German parapet with a trench mortar. 5 Men returned from Hospital 2 Men Killed in A. Coy. – 8 men wounded including 1 detained at Dressing Station & 1 at duty. Strength 29. officers – 890. O.R. [initials]	This incident and those concerned in it have been reported to the Brigade
10.5.15. "	Battn in the trenches. during night 9/10 May. our Machine Guns sent bursts of fire on roads and road junctions in rear of German trenches on points previously arranged on map. and bursts of rapid fire from our trenches produced showers of Star Shells from the Germans who seem the very suspicious of our intentions, though comparatively little firing was done by them except	

Instructions regarding War Diaries and Intelligence Summaries are contained in F. S. Regs., Part II. and the Staff Manual respectively. Title pages will be prepared in manuscript.

WAR DIARY
or
INTELLIGENCE SUMMARY.
(Erase heading not required.)

Army Form C. 2118.

Hour, Date, Place	Summary of Events and Information	Remarks and references to Appendices
10.5.15 PLOEGSTEERT	Except on our Machine Guns - A Coy's support trench enfiladed by German M.G. and traverse built to protect same. Several trench mortar bombs fell in C. Coy's trenches, only one man injured. L/C STIDSTON proceeded to ENGLAND to take up Commission. 3 men wounded (1 at duty) - 2 men returned from Hospital & 4 men sent to Hospital. Strength - 29 Officers - 886. O.R.	
11.5.15	During night 10/11 May - Sergt STRICKLAND and Pte HOLLAND (D Coy) went over to the German wire and threw 2 Hand Grenades into the German trench, both of which exploded. Afterwards the Battn was relieved in the trenches by the [illegible] Regt. LIEUT. MANSELL's platoon (of A Coy) was caught on the way back by M.G. fire & had to lie down. No casualties but one man grazed and a bullet in LIEUT. MANSELL's pack. 3 Coys took up Support trenches from 8.0 pm to 2.0 AM. 2 Limber wagons [illegible] to Ordnance. 6 men returned from Hospital - 4 men sent to Hospital including [illegible] Corpl BETTS (A Coy) Strength - 29 Officers - 888. O.R.	
12.5.15	Battn in Brigade Reserve at PLOEGSTEERT - Quiet day - strong N.E. wind. LIEUT. J. KNIGHT-ADKIN and 6 men sent to Hospital. A Coy to Baths at Pont de Nieppe. Strength 28 Officers - 882. O.R.	
13.5.15	Battalion in Bde Reserve. Hot & Misty morning - wind changed to S.W. Cpl REX and 6 men to Hospital, and 3 men returned from Machine Gun Course. Strength - 28 Officers - 878. O.R.	
14.5.15	Battn in Bde Reserve. Quiet day. B Coy to Baths at PONT de NIEPPE - Lecture delivered at LONDON SUPPORT FARM to Officers and N.C.Os by O.C. 1st S.M. FIELD AMBULANCE on Asphyxiating Gas as used by the Germans, and the precautions to be taken in consequence. Very heavy rain early. 2 Men sent to Hospital. Strength - 28 Officers - 876. O.R.	

(73989) W4141—463. 400,000. 9/14. H.&J.Ltd. Forms/C. 2118/10.

Instructions regarding War Diaries and Intelligence Summaries are contained in F. S. Regs., Part II. and the Staff Manual respectively. Title pages will be prepared in manuscript.

or

INTELLIGENCE SUMMARY

(Erase heading not required.)

Hour, Date, Place	Summary of Events and Information	Remarks and references to Appendices
15.5.15. PLOEGSTEERT	Battalion in Brigade Reserve. Quiet day. Issue of new respirators completed and men instructed in their use. Instructions re: use of Sodium Thiosulphite (Hypo) etc. 3rd Corps. Q 2839/15 received & acted on. After dark the Battn. relieved 1/6 Glouc. Regt. in trenches – relief completed by 10.50 p.m. 4 men sent to Hospital and 4 men returned from Hospital. Strength – 28 Officers – 876 O.R. J.C.T.	
16.5.15 . . .	Battalion in trenches – weather very hot. Message received at 9.0 A.M. from Bde. to harass enemy during day with long-range Machine Gun fire, Rifle fire and Motars. – this was carried out and enemy replied with Mortar. 3 men sent to Divisional Signal Co. for Course. 1 man wounded and 1 Drummer sent to Hospital. Strength 28 Officers – 871 O.R. J.C.T.	
17.5.15 . . .	Battalion in trenches. Brig. Genl. went round trenches with C.O. in the morning. Wet day and very quiet. German Airship sighted to North moving East at 4.20 A.M. 2 men sent to Hospital – and 2 men returned to duty from Hospital. Strength 28. Officers – 871 O.R. J.C.T.	
18.5.15 . . .	Battalion in trenches – Very quiet day and very wet all day. Letter from Mil. Secretary to Lord Kitchener, stating that Officers' revolvers had been issued when demanded, sent on to Bde. as although constantly demanded none were issued to this Battalion. Original letter to Lord Kitchener was written by an Officer's wife. Revolvers required by fifteen Officers. Cpl. Rice – RAMC. attd. and 3 men returned to duty from Hospital and 2 men sent to Hospital. Strength 28. Officers – 873 O.R. J.C.T.	
19.5.15 . . .	Battalion in trenches – Wet day and very quiet, though a few shells were dropped all along Battalion trenches, wounding one man in PLOEGSTEERT WOOD. Another periscope has been hit & broken and man cut about the face by same. It seems impossible to get periscopes replaced and Battn. will soon be left without any. 1 man sent to S. Mid. Divn. for duty. 1 man wounded by Shrapnel – Captain TILLY and 1 man sent to Hospital. 1 man returned from Hospital. 1/6 Glouc. Regt. relieved us at night, without casualty. Last Company reached its billets in NIEPPE at 1.30 A.M. Strength 27. Officers – 871. O.R. J.C.T.	

1247 W 3299 200,000 (E) 8/14 J.B.C. & A. Forms/C. 2118/11.

Instructions regarding War Diaries and Intelligence Summaries are contained in F. S. Regs., Part II. and the Staff Manual respectively. Title pages will be prepared in manuscript.

or

INTELLIGENCE SUMMARY

(Erase heading not required.)

Hour, Date, Place	Summary of Events and Information	Remarks and references to Appendices
20.5.15. PONT de NIEPPE	Battalion in Billets in PONT de NIEPPE in DIVISIONAL RESERVE. – Sergt SAUNDERS (B. Coy) wounded in face by broken periscope – 4 men sent to Hospital sick and 1 man returned from Hospital. C. Coy. Bathed. Strength – 27 Officers – 867. O.R. J.C.T.	
21.5.15 " "	Battn in Billets in Divnl Reserve. C.S.M. BROWNING and 5 men to Hospital – Sergt STRICKLAND and 4 men returned to duty from Hospital. Strength 27 Officers and 866. O.R. J.C.T.	
22.5.15 " "	Battn in Billets in Divnl Reserve. Brigr General inspected Battn by Companies at their Billets 10.0 AM to 1.0 PM. 5 men sent to Hospital sick and Sergt SAUNDERS (B Coy) and 2 men returned to duty. Strength. 27 Officers. 864 O.R. J.C.T.	
23.5.15 " "	Battn in Divnl Reserve – Brigd Chaplain held voluntary Communion Service at 8.30 AM. Battn attended Divine Service at the Baths at 12 Noon. – Battn relieved 1/6 Glouc. Regt in trenches by 10.20 pm. – Officers patrols from all Companies inspected wire. German Working party reported in T in front of No 17 trench. O.28 a.2.7. At 11.0 pm. cheering and rapid fire for 10 minutes from Brigade on left of our line. One red flare reported 500x distant opposite BURNT OUT FARM (O28. a) at 11.52 p.m. – New Advanced trench proceeded with from both flanks and Centre. Latrine trench begun in it, wire knife-rests put out in front of new work. Extension of No 11 trench improved. Communication trench to No 23 trench continued, and Comm trench to No 17 trench begun. Wire improved in front of No 19 trench – O.22.B. Lieut. SAVILE and 6 men to Hospital – 1 man returned to duty from Hospital. Strength. 26 Officers – 858 O.R. J.C.T.	
24.5.15 Ploegsteert	Battn in Trenches – Quiet morning – day fine & hot. Germans shelled PLOEGSTEERT from O27. b.9.4 at 12. Noon. – Artillery informed of point observed. More shells into PLOEGSTEERT at 3.15 pm. and twelve shells into LE GHEER Convent. New trenches continued and flooring, draining done to old trenches and new latrines made. New trench now manned though about 120 yards still remain to be made – ITALY declared war on AUSTRIA. Major T. WILSON and Lieut. J.H. KNIGHT-ADKIN and 6 O.R. returned from Hospital. Wounded. 1 man. To Hospital 1 man. Strength – 28 Officers and 862. O.R. J.C.T.	

Instructions regarding War Diaries and Intelligence Summaries are contained in F. S. Regs., Part II. and the Staff Manual respectively. Title pages will be prepared in manuscript.

or

INTELLIGENCE SUMMARY

(Erase heading not required.)

Hour, Date, Place	Summary of Events and Information	Remarks and references to Appendices
29.5.15 ROEGSTEERT	Battalion in Brigade Reserve at ROEGSTEERT .. "B" Company to Baths at PONT de NIEPPE 6 men to Hospital – 2 men returned from Hospital – Strength 27 Officers – 857 O.R. J.C.T.	
30.5.15 " " "	Battalion in Brigade Reserve at ROEGSTEERT.– Voluntary service of Holy Communion at Headquarters Billet at 9.0 AM and Divine Service held at Company Billets. 10 men to Hospital – 6 men returned from Hospital – Strength 27 Officers – 853 O.R. J.C.T.	

1247 W 3299 200,000 (E) 8/14 J.B.C. & A. Forms/C. 2118/11.

144th Inf.Bde.
48th Div.

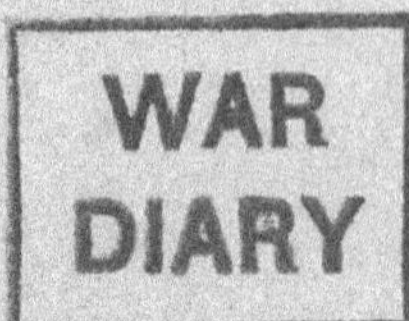

1/4th BATTN. THE GLOUCESTERSHIRE REGIMENT.

J U N E

(31.5.15 to 30.6.15)

1 9 1 5

Instructions regarding War Diaries and Intelligence Summaries are contained in F. S. Regs., Part II. and the Staff Manual respectively. Title pages will be prepared in manuscript.

or

INTELLIGENCE SUMMARY

(Erase heading not required.)

Hour, Date, Place	Summary of Events and Information	Remarks and references to Appendices
31.5.15. PLOEGSTEERT	Battalion in Brigade Reserve at PLOEGSTEERT C.I.D.3.3. At 1.30pm Enemy shelled PLOEGSTEERT BRASSERIE in which A Co is billetted and set the ESTAMINET there on fire. The Company was taken away quickly and at 2.0pm. Eight high explosive shells were put into the billet. The Enemy then shelled PLOEGSTEERT X Roads U.25.C.8.5. with Shrapnel causing 1 Casualty. 1 Vermorel Sprayer was broken by a shell. Battalion relieved 6th Glouc Regt in the trenches. 2 Companies of Seaforth Highlanders attached for instruction and 2 platoons went into the trenches with each of our Companies. Had to withdraw one platoon per Coy. to HUNTER'S AVENUE from B. C. & D Coys. and from A Coy to LANCS. SUPPORT FARM in order to make room in the trenches – Relief completed by 10.5pm without casualty. Much sniping by enemy all night. Work on BRISTOL trench & wire continued. One German hit in front of Trench No 22. In front of Trench No 19 a German Patrol, with flag, was fired on by C Co listening post and one man reported hit. Later the flag – PRUSSIAN Colours was brought in by C Co. 3 men to Hospital – 1 man returned from Hospital. Strength 27 Officers – 851 O.R.	Map: Belgium. Sheet 36. B. Series. 1:40,000 Sheet 28 – 1:40,000
1.6.15	Battalion in the Trenches – Major General Fanshawe Comdg 48th Division went round trenches at 7.30 AM. – Wind N.E. – Orders received from Brigadier General to alter disposition and watch whole front of our trenches by day with 2 platoons only and by night with 2 Companies. By day front line Companies to have 3 platoons in Support Trenches. Remaining Companies to occupy supporting points in rear. Much work done on new Bristol trench. U.28.a. – PALK Villa Communication trench now very good and new Communication trench started from point just South of PALK Villa U.21.D.6.6. to Trench 23. Covering party of C. Company sent out at night 2/3rds way to German line to prevent Snipers or patrols interfering with work on trench – result very satisfactory. – It is thought that the Germans send out listening posts with string communication and turn fixed rifles on working parties when string is pulled. – 2 men to 3rd Corps Workshops – 5 men wounded. Strength – 27 Officers – 844 O.R.	

1247 W 3299 200,000 (E) 8/14 J.B.C. & A. Forms/C. 2118/11.

Instructions regarding War Diaries and Intelligence Summaries are contained in F. S. Regs., Part II. and the Staff Manual respectively. Title pages will be prepared in manuscript.

or

INTELLIGENCE SUMMARY

(Erase heading not required.)

Hour, Date, Place	Summary of Events and Information	Remarks and references to Appendices
2.6.15. PLOEGSTEERT	The Battalion in Trenches. The 2 Companies of Seaforth Highlanders, under Major LUMSDEN, vacated the trenches at 1.30 A.M. without casualty. New dispositions as directed by Brigadier General taken up mid-day. LANCASHIRE SUPPORT FARM U.27.d. and RED FARM U.27.C. was being fortified, also LAWRENCE FARM U.27.C. Sergt C.H. WAKLEY. A.Cy was killed by rifle bullet on 1.6.15 at 3.30pm - 1 man slightly wounded - still at duty - 2 men to Hospital and 2/Lieut. TRAPNELL - Capt W.S. CLARKE and 5 men returned from Hospital. Strength 27 Officers - 846. O.R. JGT	Map. BELGIUM. Sheet 28. - 1/40,000
3.6.15. . . .	Battalion in Trenches - Left end of BRISTOL Trench was joined up to Centre T piece U.2 & A.25. leaving about 70 yards on right to complete - Our Snipers compelled Germans to lower all their permanent periscopes, several being hit by our shots, and one German killed. Sniper shooting being directed by Capt GUETERBOCK. One mountain gun was moved to Trench 20 at LE GHEER U.22.a.0.3. and at 2.54 AM. fired 4 rounds lyddite and 6 shrapnel into German barricade across WARNETON Road where there appears to be a gun emplacement U.16.D. making a big breach into which one of our Machine Guns fired 1000 rounds. - Germans shelled PLOEGSTEERT Village, and put several high explosive shells over ESSEX Farm U.26.A and into wood and field just North of Bde H.Q. at HANTS FARM U.26.B.6.8. - Brigadier General went round Trenches in afternoon and approved of distribution of posts &c. - LOG BOOKS started for each Company in trenches with Maps for same. - 1 man wounded, 1 man to Hospital sick - 5 men returned from Hospital - Strength 27 Officers - 849. O.R. JGT	
4.6.15 . . .	Battalion in the Trenches - Enemy kept up bursts of Machine Gun fire from 9.0pm to 11.0pm. and long range Artillery fire on our Communications. G.O.C. Division proposes to make a new Roster of Battalions in the trenches which will necessitate each Battn occupying part of the whole Divisional line in turn. Battn was relieved by 6/Glouc: Regt at 8.0p.m. - Last platoon arrived at Billets at PONT de NIEPPE at 12 midnight. Wounded - LIEUT. MANSELL (slight and at duty) 2 men (one at duty). Strength 27 Officers - 848. O.R. JGT	
5.6.15 PONT de NIEPPE	Battalion in billets at PONT de NIEPPE - C Coy to Baths at 9.0 AM. - 1 man sick to Hospital - 2/Lieut. TRAPNELL and 6 men returned from Hospital - 1 man to Hospital - Strength 28 Officers - 853 O.R. JGT Wind W. day fine and hot.	
6.6.15 . . .	Battalion in billets in Divisional Reserve. Orders recd at 11.0pm. to move to Bde Reserve tomorrow at HUNTERS TOWN PLOEGSTEERT WOOD U.19.D. with one Company in trenches 31 - S.24 U.21.D. and HUNTERS AVENUE. Transport to move to Sheet 36 B.8.b. - D Coy to Baths at 9.0 AM. - Battalion attended Divine Service at 11.30 AM at Baths and Lecture at same place at 2.30pm on Asphyxiating Gas - G.O.C. 4th Division attended same - The Mine under Birdcage U.21.b. in front of trench 31 was exploded at 10.0 AM. destroying German counter mine and 30 yards of Enemy's parapet. - LIEUT. SAVILE and 1 man returned from Hospital. Strength 29 Officers and 854. O.R. JGT	

1247 W 3299 200,000 (E) 8/14 J.B.C. & A. Forms/C. 2118/11.

Instructions regarding War Diaries and Intelligence Summaries are contained in F. S. Regs., Part II. and the Staff Manual respectively. Title pages will be prepared in manuscript.

or

INTELLIGENCE SUMMARY

(Erase heading not required.)

Hour, Date, Place	Summary of Events and Information	Remarks and references to Appendices
7-6-15. PONT de NIEPPE	Battalion in Divisional Reserve at PONT de NIEPPE, but moved at 2.0 p.m. to HUNTERSTON – South and North and relieved 1/4 Oxford and Bucks: L.I. and 1 Coy of the 1/4 Berks: Battalion in PLOEGSTEERT WOOD. 1 Company to hold trench 31. U.21. B.3.1-6 and supporting breastworks – 3 Coys in Brigade Reserve (viz 2 Coys. in huts and 1 Coy. in tents) Wind N. – Very hot day – Relief completed by 6.0 p.m. No Casualties. – 12 men returned from Hospital – 2 men sent to Hospital – Strength – 29 Officers – 865 O.R. [initials]	
8-6-15. PLOEGSTEERT	Dispositions as yesterday afternoon – and at 6.0 pm D Coy relieved C. Coy in Trench 31 and supporting breastworks. – G.O.C. 48th Division visited trenches and Batt: Head Quarters at 9.0 A.M. – Brigadier General also visited trenches during the morning – Wind N.W. Very hot morning – Thunderstorm with some rain at 5.0 pm – Four shells burst close to Hd. Qrs at 3.0 pm but did no damage. – Orders received for Batt. to continue to hold trench 31. and to give up trenches 11.12.13. which will be taken over by Batt. on our right. Our Right will now be from Burnt Out Farm – U.28.a.3.3 and our left Communication trench leading to Trench 32., U21. B. 3. 6. both exclusive – Sergt. GREGORY. D.Coy joined III Corps: Workshops – 1 man returned from Divisional Guard – 4 men returned from Hospital – 1 man sick to Hospital – Strength 29. Officers – 868. O.R. [initials]	
9-6-15 . . .	Disposition in morning as yesterday – Batt. Hd. Qrs. and 3 Companies relieved 1/6 Glouc: Regt. in Trenches 14 to 24. – Dispositions. 1 Company trenches 14-18 inclusive with supporting points in rear – 1 Company trenches 19 to 24 inclusive and Breastwork 23, and supporting points in rear in the Wood, and 1 company in KEEPERS COTTAGE breastworks and HUNTERS AVENUE all in PLOEGSTEERT WOOD – and 1 Company remains in trench 31. etc as yesterday. Relief completed at 6-30 p.m. – Wind N.W. – ~~Returned from Hospital~~ Joined the Batt: from [illegible] 1 man. Sick to Hospital – 1 man. – Strength – 29. Officers and 868. O.R. [initials]	[initials]
10-6-15. . . .	Dispositions as yesterday – At 6.55. A.M. the Germans exploded a mine 20 yards N of the HAMPSHIRE T in trench 24 – U.21.d.8.9 making a crater 30 yards long E & W, 20 feet deep and 20 yards wide – no damage done to our trenches – Immediately afterwards they shelled Trench 22 and Trenches 31 & S.24 and Area U.21. part of a & b and all of d. – chiefly with "Little Willies". Parapet of Trench 23 was damaged and 1 Officer (LIEUT: H.G. PHIPPEN) and 3 men wounded in trench S.24 – and 3 men wounded in trenches S.22 and S.23 – LIEUT: J.A. KNIGHT-ADKIN was hit in stomach by a spent bullet – his belt saving him. – A man had a large splinter of shell through cigarette case in breast pocket – – Continued on next folio –	

Instructions regarding War Diaries and Intelligence Summaries are contained in F. S. Regs., Part II. and the Staff Manual respectively. Title pages will be prepared in manuscript.

INTELLIGENCE SUMMARY

(Erase heading not required.)

Hour, Date, Place	Summary of Events and Information	Remarks and references to Appendices
10. 6. 15 PLOEGSTEERT	Continued The Brigadier General was in the trenches at the time – Arrangements have been made for occupying Crater and joining it to HAMPSHIRE T trench. 5000 Sandbags and many [illegible] etc. [illegible] got up [illegible] for [illegible] night. A party of 1 N.C.O (Sergt. SAUNDERS) occupied Crater at 8.30 pm. and dug themselves in on our side – A shallow communication trench was made by daylight on the 11th June – The Enemy shelled the whole area intermittently during day – wounding 1 man – and fired Rifle Grenades at night into HAMPSHIRE T. wounding 3 men – Rest of front quiet – 1 wounded – LIEUT. H. G. TRIPPEN + 3 men to Hospital + 5 men sick to Hospital + 2 men slightly wounded but at duty – 2 men returned from Div.l SIGNAL Course, 1 man from DIV.L REST STATION, 21 men [illegible] No. 3 Coy [illegible] for Shoeing Course – Strength – 28. Officers – 862 O.R.	
11. 6. 15 . . .	Battalion in trenches – Dispositions as previously – Wind N.E. Day quiet. At 9 pm. B. Coy occupied Crater [illegible] with 8 men. – Germans fired Grenades into HANTS trench 21.d.8.8. We replied with rifle grenades into BIRDCAGE 21.b.7.2 – Two [illegible] were spotted by their flashes in German line opposite trench 31. at close range. U.21.d.9.5. R.E. working party with [illegible] from C. Coy on Communication trench from Hants trench T to Crater. – Crater was found to be nearly circular 30 yds × 25 yds × 25 feet deep – walls not perpendicular enough to get [illegible] dug in. – A German working party was on this side of Crater at 11.55 pm. and withdrew about 1.15 A.M. – Our party withdrew at 1.45 A.M. except 2 men [illegible] dug in. Wire was put out in front of HANTS trench. Parapet along trench 31 improved U.21.3.4. – A platoon of C. Coy worked at completing BRISTOL trench U.28.a.3.4. and 2/Lt. H. MERRICK was shot in jaw and seriously wounded. Trench 31. was shelled by German from 10.45 pm to 11.30 pm. and at 3.45 A.M. about 40 German shells fell all round AU GAFER 27.B.8.8 but several did not explode – 1 man transferred to No. Cas.ty Clearing Station – 1 man went to Hospital sick – LIEUT. CASTLE and 6 men wounded and 4 men returned from Hospital. 1 man to Hospital as servant to LIEUT TRIPPEN – LIEUT. L. TARKINSON attached to 81st Bde for instruction & [illegible] with him. Strength 26. Officers – 859. O.R.	
12. 6. 15 . . .	Dispositions as previously. Very quiet day – A few shells fell in PLOEGSTEERT Wood U.30.D. and U.26.b. in afternoon. Brigadier visited trenches early in morning with C.O. and arranged plan to try & catch German party at Crater. Smoke helmets issued to all ranks. – Notice rec.d that if quite necessary leave can be given to 8 men per Battalion for 6 days. 1 man died of wounds. Returned to duty 2. O.R. – wounded to Hospital 2/Lt. H. MERRICK and 2. O.R. and Servant for 2/Lt. MERRICK. Sick to Hospital 2. Returned to duty from Courses 2 + 2 to Course – Strength 25 Officers and 855. O.R.	

1247 W 3299 200,000 (E) 8/14 J.B.C. & A. Forms/C. 2118/11.

Instructions regarding War Diaries and Intelligence Summaries are contained in F. S. Regs., Part II. and the Staff Manual respectively. Title pages will be prepared in manuscript.

INTELLIGENCE SUMMARY

(Erase heading not required.)

Hour, Date, Place	Summary of Events and Information	Remarks and references to Appendices
13.6.15. PLOEGSTEERT.	Battalion in trenches. Dispositions as before. Night quiet. Enemy's transport reported on move earlier than usual last night & many working parties busy. - A patrol from B. Coy reconnoitred all round Crater and up to Enemy Sapad in front where they were bombed by Germans and replied with hand grenades and returned without casualty. Digging party on trench at Crater and communication with same now established. Wire now strong all along front of HAMPSHIRE T and Crater - Crater visited by Brigade Major and full report rendered with sketch. Decided not to hold Crater by day as Germans could not reach it. - A periscope about 12 feet high has been put up in the BIRDCAGE. U.21.b. for past 3 mornings but has always been shot down at once by Sergt. BIZLEY. - Work continued on BRISTOL TRENCH. U.25.a. and now only 2 bays remain to be revetted up. - Brigade working party on LANCASHIRE SUPPORT FARM U.27.D. - A mine was exploded near LE TOUQUET, on our right, opposite of WORCESTER Regt. about 7.0 AM. 6/Glouc. Regt. relieved this Battn. in trenches 14 to 31 and we relieved 8/WORCESTER Regt. in BRIGADE RESERVE at HUNTERSTON, in PLOEGSTEERT WOOD. U.19.d. - 15 Officers &c. of WARWICK Regt. visited our trenches 14 - 31 to learn them. - 1 Man killed in action. - 1 Man wounded. Sick to Hospital 4. Wounded to Hospl. 1. Returned from Hospital 3. Strength 25 Officers - 852. O.R. [initials]	
14.6.15 . . .	Battalion in Brigade Reserve at HUNTERSTON. - PLOEGSTEERT WOODS. - Wind E.N.E. - About 2.0 AM a mine was exploded by the Enemy opposite trench 32 - evidently a counter mine. 2 Engineers reported killed and 9 buried (who were extricated safely 22 hours later.) Much rapid fire, machine guns & shelling ensued for half an hour after the explosion - Battalion stood to arms - Quiet day followed. - 2 working parties of 50 men each at 9.0 AM and 1.0 pm getting sandbags out of mine in trench 32 & using them to build parapet to connect breastworks of trench 31 - 1 man killed, 1 man wounded (at duty) 1 man sick to Hospital and 1 man returned from Hospital. Strength 25 Officers and 857. O.R. [initials]	
15.6.15 . . .	Battalion in Brigade Reserve as before. Memo. re: regarding temporary promotion of Officers supernumerary to Establishment and temporary rank to officers performing duties of higher rank - Two working parties of 50 men each supplied at 9.0 am and 1.0 pm getting sandbags out of mine. 2 men slightly wounded. - Disposition of Division in trenches again readjusted - Two Brigades now to hold trenches with one Brigade in Reserve. - 144th Brigade to become Divisional Reserve - 6/Glouc: relieved by late at night by 7/Warwicks - all Battalion Machine Guns brought back to Battn. Hd. Qrs. - We become Divisional Reserve - 2 Companies to remain at HUNTERSTON South and 2 Companies to the PIGGERIES U.19.c.5.9. Sheet 28 - Move completed by 6.0 pm. except Machine Guns which were back at 11.30 pm (1 man wounded). Sick to Hospital 2.O.R. Returned from Hospital 7.O.R. - Strength. 25 Officers 851. O.R. [initials]	
16.6.15 . . .	Battalion in Divisional Reserve at HUNTERSTON and PIGGERIES - Situation - Wind N.E. - 2 men sick to Hospital returned from Hospital LIEUT. CASTLE and three men. Wounded 1 man. Strength 851 O.R. and 25 Officers. [initials] Lieut. CASTLE promoted Captain 1.5.1915. 2/Lieut. WOOKEY . . . Lieut. 23.4.1915. 2/Lieut. WARD . . . Lieut. 1.5.1915.	

1247 W 3299 200,000 (E) 8/14 J.B.C. & A. Forms/C. 2118/11.

Instructions regarding War Diaries and Intelligence Summaries are contained in F. S. Regs., Part II. and the Staff Manual respectively. Title pages will be prepared in manuscript.

or

INTELLIGENCE SUMMARY

(Erase heading not required.)

Hour, Date, Place	Summary of Events and Information	Remarks and references to Appendices
17. 6. 15. PLOEGSTEERT	Battalion in Divisional reserve in the Piggeries and [illegible] as previously. Wind N.E. Major General FANSHAWE Commanding 48th (S.M.) Division inspected the Battalion in field adjoining the Piggeries at 8.0 AM. Present on parade 24 Officers and 734 O.R. – The C.O. and Adjutant visited trenches 64 to 73 U.1.a.6c. U.2.b. U.8.a. which this Battalion takes over on 19.6.15. – No 2750 Pte W. Brickwell (A.C.) to Div. Hd 2rs as clerk to Camp Comdt. 2 men severely wounded by shell fire whilst passing PLOEGSTEERT Church on pass. 3 men sick to Hospital. 1 man returned to duty from [illegible]. 2 men returned from Hospital. Strength 26 Officers and 850 O.R. J.C.T.	
18. 6. 15 . . .	Battalion in Divisional Reserve in The PIGGERIES. Company Commanders visited trenches 64 to 73. The "Stand By" was ordered at 6.0 p.m. and dismissed at 8.10 p.m. – 3 men to Hospital wounded – 3 men sick to Hospital 4 men returned from Hospital. Strength 26 Officers – 848 O.R. J.C.T.	
19. 6. 15 . . .	Battalion in Reserve, as above. Relieved 1/4 BUCKS. Battn in trenches 64–73 opposite MESSINES at 9.0 p.m. – Relief completed, without casualty by 10.30 p.m. – Captain W. LEWIS and 6 O.R. granted leave to proceed to England – LIEUT: J KNIGHT-ADKIN and 5 O.R. sick to Hospital and 1 Officers Servant. Strength 24 Officers and 836 O.R. J.C.T.	
20. 6. 15 . . .	Battalion in trenches 64–73 – Wind N.E. 2/LIEUT. G.K. SAVILE was killed by a bullet at 6.25 AM. while walking down the trench – Brigadier-General visited trenches with C.O. at 10.0 AM. – Lt Colonel RAYMER 5/S. Staffords visited Head Quarters from 46th Division on our left. – LIEUT F. WARD and L/Cpl HOLLAND reconnoitred German trenches in front of trench 72 from 3.0 p.m to 7 p.m. in daylight and got within 30 yards of German wire discovering German listening posts and tracks taken by enemy patrols [illegible] discovered. A flight of 20 Aeroplanes passed over from British lines at 3.45 AM – Enemy's aeroplane active dropping smoke signals and lights over trench 72 on NEUVE EGLISE – MESSINES road – A coys trenches were shelled during the day and also enfiladed by rifle fire from PETIT DOUVE Farm. From 10.0 pm to 1.0 am officers patrols went out to front and crossed ground all along our trenches to within 100 yards of enemy's trenches in front of MESSINES and 50 yards from PETIT DOUVE FARM. Enemy's [illegible] appear to be brought in transport down to trenches along [illegible] roads. 2/LIEUT. POLACK patrolled from trench 71 to house at U.1.b.6.6 where he encountered enemy's patrols – Hand grenades were thrown by both sides and Enemy fled. Enemy quiet on our front. Ground in rear of trenches reconnoitred by Hd 2rs and communications studied. 2/LIEUT. G.K. SAVILE killed in Action. 3 O.R. wounded. 1 O.R. underage and unfit transferred to Base (off strength). 3 men returned from Hospital. – Strength – 23 Officers + 835 O.R. – 2/Lieut SAVILE buried in Cemetery on W. side of road leading LA PLUS DOUVE Farm. J.C.T.	
21. 6. 15 . . .	Battalion in trenches. Wind N.E. Enemy put 6 "Little Willies" into Hd 2rs farm at LA PLUS DOUVE at 10.0 AM. buildings still further damaged but no one was hurt.	

Instructions regarding War Diaries and Intelligence Summaries are contained in F. S. Regs., Part II. and the Staff Manual respectively. Title pages will be prepared in manuscript.

INTELLIGENCE SUMMARY

(Erase heading not required.)

Hour, Date, Place	Summary of Events and Information	Remarks and references to Appendices
21.6.15. PLOEGSTEERT	Brigadier-General visited Battalion area at 10.15.AM. – Quiet day – work done improving Communication trenches in rear of fire trenches and extending them – and digging wells in trenches 67 and 70. – Officers patrols again went well to front all along line and report Enemy only working inside their own line and no patrols met. Our Snipers think they accounted for 3 or 4 Germans including an Artillery Observation Officer in trench N. of DOLLS HOUSE at MESSINES. – LIEUT. TARKINSON returned from attachment to 2/Glouc: Regt and his Servant and 7 men from Hospital. 1 man sick to Hospital. Strength 24 Officers and 836. O.R. J.C.T.	
22.6.15 . . .	At 1.15.AM. Enemy opened rapid rifle fire opposite trenches 64 to 69 and kept same up at intervals for an hour. Wind N.E. At 10.30.AM. Enemy put 12 high Explosive Shells into trench 68 and made 2 small holes in parapet. – 1st S.M. F.A. Brigade replied and put 3 Shots into same trench – one in Capt GUETERBOCK'S dug-out. Intermittent shelling during day – no harm done – LIEUT. WARD and L/Cpl HOLLAND made another daylight patrol north of MESSINES – WOLVERGHEM Road and got close to German trenches observing their wire and Sentry-posts. – Our Snipers disabled a Machine-Gun at PETIT DEUVE Farm by knocking away Embrasure – LIEUT: WARD and patrol of 7 men lay out for Enemy patrol opposite 73 trench but none came. LIEUT: and 6 men 9/NORFOLKS attached to D. Co having volunteered to catch a prisoner – work done same as yesterday and much grass cut in front of wire. – Trial message to 1st S.M. F.A. Brigade for Artillery Support on 65. trench – took 4½ minutes to open fire and got the Battery covering 71 trench. Appreciation of Situation by G.O.C. 48th Division read to Co Commanders showing why Enemy is likely to attack our trenches within next few days. 1 man to Hospital wounded – LIEUT. BEAVEN and 2 men sick to Hospital and 3 men returned from Hospital. – Strength 23. Officers and 836. O.R. Light rain at night. J.C.T.	
23.6.15 . . .	Battalion in trenches as before – Wind N.E. Cloudy + Cool. – Major BARKER reports sounds of mining under No 65 Trench – and message sent to Brigade for R.E. expert to listen. Work continued on communication trenches. Day and night quiet. – Message received from Brigade at 9.0.AM. warning relief of the Division by 12th DIVISION – 6/Glouc: Regt relieved Battalion in trenches at 9.30 P.M. Relief Completed by 12.30 midnight with 2 Casualties. – 1 man sick to Hospital and 2 men returned from Hospital. Strength. 23 Officers and 837. O.R. – J.C.T.	

1247 W 3299 200,000 (E) 8/14 J.B.C. & A. Forms/C. 2118/11.

Instructions regarding War Diaries and Intelligence Summaries are contained in F. S. Regs., Part II. and the Staff Manual respectively. Title pages will be prepared in manuscript.

WAR DIARY
or
INTELLIGENCE SUMMARY.
(*Erase heading not required.*)

Army Form C. 2118.

Hour, Date, Place	Summary of Events and Information	Remarks and references to Appendices
24.6.15. PLOEGSTEERT	Battalion in Brigade Reserve at COURT DREVE Farm N. of PLOEGSTEERT. Quiet day. The Germans patrol attacked 8/WORCS: Regt about trench 62 at 12 midnight (night 24-25) with bombs - much firing took place and one German Officer was killed on parapet. 2 men to Hospital wounded. 5 men to Hospital sick - 2 men returned from Hospital. Capt. W. LEWIS and six men taken on strength from leave. Strength 24 Officers - 838. O.R. J.T.	
25.6.15.	Battalion in Billets at COURT DREVE Farm in Brigade Reserve. Very quiet day - 1 man sick to Hospital, 3 men returned from Hospital. Armr. staff Sergt. Small and 3 O.R. returned to duty and taken on strength. Strength 24 Officers - and 844 O.R. J.T.	
26.6.15.	Battalion in Brigade Reserve as above, - Division relieved by 12th Division and Canadians. Battalion relieved in Bde. Reserve by 8th Canadians at 9.30 p.m. and marched at 10.0 p.m. arriving BAILLEUL at 2.0 A.M. on 27.6.15. No one fell out. - Major H.L. BAKER to Hospital sick - No. 3066. Pte C. MOSS returned to duty from cold shoeing course. Strength 23. Officers and 845. O.R. J.T.	
27.6.15. BAILLEUL	Battalion in Billets at BAILLEUL. Major Genl. PULTENEY, Commanding 3rd Army Corps, inspected the Battalion in fatigue dress at 11.45. A.M. and expressed his satisfaction. Marched at 9.0 p.m. to VIEUX BERGUIN, 5 miles and took 4 hours to do it being delayed by other troops on road. No one fell out. 1 man sick to Hospital. Strength 23 Officers - 844. O.R. J.T.	
28.6.15 VIEUX BERGUIN	Battalion in Billets at VIEUX BERGUIN - Marched at 6.15 p.m. through MERVILLE and arrived at ROBECQ at 11.0 p.m. - The 48th DIVISION now in 4th Corps with 1st and 47th DIVISIONS. 3 men sick to Hospital. Strength 23. Officers and 841. O.R. J.T.	
29.6.15. ROBECQ	Battalion in Billets at ROBECQ - Marched at 6.0 p.m. through LILLERS and arrived at HURIONVILLE at 8.30 p.m. Bad billets in Mining Village. 2 men sick to Hospital. Strength. 23. Officers and 829. O.R. J.T.	
30.6.15 HURIONVILLE	Battalion in Billets at HURIONVILLE Strength 23. Officers and 839. O.R. J.T.	

(73989) W4141—463. 400,000. 9/14. H.&J.Ltd. / Forms/C. 2118/10.

144th Inf.Bde.
48th Div.

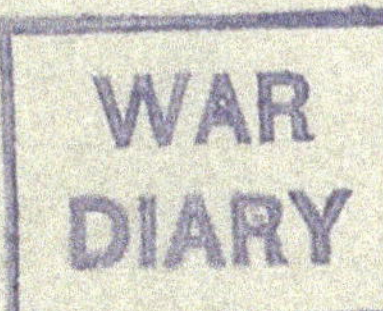

1/4th BATTN. THE GLOUCESTERSHIRE REGIMENT.

J U L Y

(1.7.15 to 30.7.15)

1 9 1 5

Instructions regarding War Diaries and Intelligence Summaries are contained in F. S. Regs., Part II. and the Staff Manual respectively. Title pages will be prepared in manuscript.

WAR DIARY
or
INTELLIGENCE SUMMARY
(Erase heading not required.)

Hour, Date, Place	Summary of Events and Information	Remarks and references to Appendices
1-7-15. HORIONVILLE	Battalion in Corps Reserve at HORIONVILLE. Company training. Grenadiers and Machine Gun training. Ground East of BURBURE reconnoitred for Brigade training. J.G.T.	
2-7-15 . . .	Lieut. PARKINSON gazetted Captain from 2-6-15. – Captain VEALE, 2/Lieut. TRIPPEN, and 2/Lieut MERRICK to ENGLAND and off Strength – 1 Man sick to Hospital. 2 men returned from Hospital. Strength 26 Officers & 849. O.R.	
	Battalion in Corps Reserve at HORIONVILLE – General Sir D. HAIG. Comdg 1st Army rode round Brigade area in afternoon. Company training as above – 1 Man sick to Hospital. Strength 26. Officers and 849 O.R. J.G.T.	
3-7-15 . . .	Battalion in Corps Reserve – Company training. B and C. Company to Baths at CALONNE-RICOUART. C.O. and Adjutant to Brigade Conference at 2.0 p.m. at BURBURE. 1 Man returned to duty from C.C.S. and 2 men sick to FIELD AMBULANCE. Strength. 26 Officers and 850. O.R. J.G.T.	
4-7-15 . . .	Battalion in Corps Reserve. ~~Company training~~ J.G.T. Very hot day. Divine Service in field at 6.30 p.m. 2/Lieut. MASTER to be Temp. Lieut. dtd 2.6.15. – 2 men sick to Field Ambulance, 1 man returned from 7 Coy. R.E. Strength 26. Officers and 851. O.R. J.G.T.	
5-7-15 . . .	Battalion in Corps. Reserve. Company training proceeding. Lt. Col. DAVENPORT and Capt. Mc. CARRE to ENGLAND on 7 days leave. 1 Man off strength to C.C.S. 4 men sick to Field Ambulance, 1 Man returned from Field Ambulance and [illegible] men from C.C.S. – Strength 26. Officers and 853 O.R. J.G.T.	
6-7-15 . . .	Battalion in Corps Reserve. Company training 5.30 to 8.0 A.M. – Battalion paraded at 5.0 p.m. and carried out a Brigade Exercise at LE MARQUET Wood in area D. 14 and 15 & 13. – Battalion was in Brigade reserve and was pushed forward at 3.0 A.M. through imaginary German Trenches, which had been already carried by 7th and 8th WORC: Regts to Eastern edge of Wood – arrived back to billets at 6.30 A.M. on 7/7/15. LIEUT. J. H. KNIGHT-ADKIN, to England sick, 2 men returned from Field Ambulance. Strength 25 Officers and 852 O.R. J.G.T.	
7-7-15 . . .	Battalion in Corps Reserve. Company training 6 p.m. to 8.0 p.m. High Wind and rain. 2 men returned from Field Ambulance and 1 from C.C.S. – Strength 25. Officers and 854. O.R. J.G.T.	
8-7-15 . . .	Battalion in Corps Reserve – Battalion paraded 8.30 A.M. and Marched to LILLERS to line road along with other Units for LORD KITCHENER – back in Billets at 11.30 A.M. – Company training 6–8 p.m. Strength. 25. Officers and 854. O.R. J.G.T.	

1247 W 3299 200,000 (E) 8/14 J.B.C. & A. Forms/C. 2118/11.

Instructions regarding War Diaries and Intelligence Summaries are contained in F. S. Regs., Part II. and the Staff Manual respectively. Title pages will be prepared in manuscript.

WAR DIARY
or
INTELLIGENCE SUMMARY.
(Erase heading not required.)

Army Form C. 2118.

Hour, Date, Place	Summary of Events and Information	Remarks and references to Appendices
9-7-15 HORIONVILLE	Battalion in Corps Reserve. Started Musketry in old Chalk Quarry. Firing in Quarry by Snipers and Platoon firing, Company training. Adjutant visited 1st Glouc: Regt at LABEUVIERE. – 1 man to Field Ambulance and 3 men returned from F.A. – Strength. 25 Officers and 854. O.R. H.T.	
10-7-15. " "	Battalion in Corps Reserve. Musketry and Company training continued. Firing at 50yds Range not very satisfactory. Men have got into bad habits from snapping over parapets in the trenches. – Light portable tripods for Machine Guns received. 2 men to Field Ambulance. Strength 25 Officers – 855 O.R. H.T.	
11-7-15 " " "	Battalion in Corps Reserve. Attended Divine Service at 11.0AM. in Field. Lt Col. G.F. GARDINER, Comdg 1st Glouc: Regt visited us. Major THOMPSON and 3.O.R. went on 7 days leave to ENGLAND – D. Company Completed musketry practice. 1. man to Field Ambulance. Strength 25. Officers and 855. O.R. H.T.	
12-7-15 " " "	Battalion paraded at 8.0pm. and marched to HESDIGNEUL with the Brigade, about 9 miles, and Bivouacked on the Village Green. 2 men sent to a Trench Mortar Course at ST VENANT. Lieut MANSELL and 2/Lieut THOMAS and 2. O.R. to Field Ambulance. Strength 25 Officers and 854 O.R. H.T.	
13-7-15. HESDIGNEUL	Lt Col. DAVENPORT and Capt W.S. CLARKE returned from leave 5.0AM. and 1 N.C.O. of A Coy went on leave to ENGLAND. Battalion paraded 9.0pm. and marched with the Brigade to BREBIS – a model mining village near and 2nd line trenches to Billets, which were overcrowded. Another march with 200yds interval between Companies and 50 yds between platoons. Arrived at 1.0AM. but owing to late billeting did not settle in till 2.30 AM. Transport except Cookers, returned to HESDIGNEUL. 4 men to Field Ambulance. – LIEUT. BEAVEN returned from Field Ambulance. Strength 25. Officers and 854. O.R. H.T.	
14.7.15 BREBIS	300 men of A + B Companies paraded at 7.15 AM. for digging at 8.0AM. in reserve trenches – 300 men. C + D " " " " 12.30 Noon " " – they were several times shelled by German and Quit home at 4.0pm. with 2 Casualties. 2 men to Field Ambulance Strength 25. Officers 854. O.R. H.T.	
15-7-15 " " "	Two Reliefs of 300 men each, as yesterday from 8-12 P.M. and 12 midnight to 4 A.M. on the 16th inst. digging. No casualties – 1 man to C.C.S. off strength. 2 men to Field Ambulance. 2 men returned from F.A. – Strength 25 Officers & 853. O.R. H.T.	
16.7.15 " " "	LIEUT. NEWTH returned from duty at HAVRE – Very hot day – Battalion marched at 9.0pm. via NOEUX les MINES and MARLES MINES back to old billets at HORIONVILLE. 15 Miles and roads very muddy after LOSINGHEM. 12 men fell out but rejoined on arrival at billets which were reached at 4.0AM. – Joined us from 2/4th Battalion 2/LIEUTS: ANDERSON and SYMES – 8 men to Field Ambulance. Strength 27. Officers and 853. O.R. H.T.	

(73989) W4141—463. 400,000. 9/14. H.&J.Ltd. Forms/C. 2118/10.

Instructions regarding War Diaries and Intelligence Summaries are contained in F. S. Regs., Part II. and the Staff Manual respectively. Title pages will be prepared in manuscript.

WAR DIARY
or
INTELLIGENCE SUMMARY.
(*Erase heading not required.*)

Hour, Date, Place	Summary of Events and Information	Remarks and references to Appendices
~~16.7.15. BREBIS~~	~~Lieut. NENTH returned from day at HAVRE. Very hot day.~~ See preceding day. J.C.T.	
17.7.15 HURIONVILLE	Battalion arrived at HURIONVILLE at 4.10. A.M. – 2 Blanket Wagons (complete turnouts) returned to No 3. Coy. TRAIN at 12 noon. – Orders received no superstructures allowed on Cookers. Battalion will now be very short of Transport and it is a problem how rations will be carried if delivered late before a March. Extra Equipment now in possession to that laid down for 2 baggage Wagons does not appear to be taken into consideration – Brigade Operation Order No 12 Copy No 4 received at 8. 0 p.m. with orders for move by train on morning of 19th inst. 1 Man returned from C.C.S. and 5 Men from Field Ambulance and 2 Men sent to Field Ambulance. Strength 27 Officers and 853. O.R. J.C.T.	
18.7.15. . . .	A. Company and Transport marched to LILLERS at 10.30 p.M. to entrain – remainder of Battalion marched at 12.45 Midnight 2 Men returned from Field Ambulance and 2 sent sick to Field Ambulance, and 2 Men to No 3 Train and 3 Men returned from No 3 Train. Strength 27 Officers and 853. O.R. J.C.T.	
19.7.15 LILLERS	Battalion left LILLERS by train at 3.1. AM and arrived MONDICOURT at 9.30. A.M. detrained and whole clear of Station at 10.20 AM. Marched to LOUVINCOURT, about 8 miles – day very hot – and road hilly – 5 Men fell out and 2 of these fainted – Found billets, which had been vacated by the FRENCH the day before, very clean –	
20.7.15. LOUVINCOURT	2 Men returned from Mortar Course, 3 Men to Brigade as grooms and orderly – Strength 27 Officers and 853. O.R. J.C.T. Recd orders in morning to be ready to move – Actual order to move recd at 3.0 p.M. [illegible] Battalion was parading. Moved into bivouac in BOIS du WARNIMONT – S.E. of AUTHIE. about 2 miles – No water nearer than AUTHIE 2 miles off. Had to double space transport up steep lane into woods – 5 Men to Field Ambulance – Strength 27 Officers and 853. O.R. J.C.T.	
21.7.15. Bois du WARNIMONT	Battalion in bivouac in WARNIMONT wood. Company training being carried on by all Companies – 5 Men sick to Field Ambulance – 3 Men returned from F.A. Strength 27 Officers and 853. O.R. J.C.T.	
22.7.15. . . .	Battalion in bivouac as above – Company training and the whole Battalion fired 5 rounds standing and 15 rounds lying with ball cartridge. Very heavy rain all night. 1 Man transferred to No 6. C.C.S. and 1 Sergt. to ADMS [illegible] Div. and 1 Man to Brigade H.Q. 4 Men to Field Ambulance. Strength 27 Officers and 852. O.R. J.C.T.	
23.7.15 . . .	Battalion in Bivouac as above – Company training continued – Roads reconnoitred through BUS, BERTRANDCOURT, SAILLY, COURCELLES and BAYENCOURT. – 1 Man returned from Command and 1 from Field Ambulance – 2 Men sick to Field Ambulance. Strength 27 Officers and 852. O.R. J.C.T.	

(73989) W4141—463. 400,000. 9/14. H.&J.Ltd. Forms/C. 2118/10.

Instructions regarding War Diaries and Intelligence Summaries are contained in F. S. Regs., Part II. and the Staff Manual respectively. Title pages will be prepared in manuscript.

WAR DIARY
or
INTELLIGENCE SUMMARY.
(Erase heading not required.)

Army Form C. 2118.

Hour, Date, Place	Summary of Events and Information	Remarks and references to Appendices
24.7.15. Bois du WARNIMONT	Battalion in Bivouac in WARNIMONT Wood. Company training continued. Inspected at 2.55 pm. after only 1 hours notice by General MONRO Commanding 3rd ARMY – found guard of 1 N.C.O and 3 men over sources of AUTHIE river. 1 man to No 2 C.C.S and 3 men to No 4. C.C.S. (off strength) 2 men sick to Field Ambulance and 2 men returned from same. Strength 27 officers and 848. O.R. J.C.T.	
25.7.15 . . .	Battalion in Bivouac as before – C.O. Adjutant and Coy Commanders went round trenches at HEBOTERNE – Company training continued. Names of Miners called for, for new Mining Companies. 48th Divn letter, No S. 69a d/d 21.7.15. All smoke helmets in future to have date of issue entered on them. 48 Divn 394 A.X. 18.7.15. – 1 man to Command to Divl H.Q. 1 man to C.C.S. No 4. – 3 men sick to Field Ambulance and 3 men returned from same. Strength 27. officers. and 847. O.R. J.C.T.	
26.7.15 . . .	Battalion in Bivouac as before – Company training continued – Battalion inspected in bivouac lines at 4 pm. by Maj-General SNOW, Commanding VII Corps – Brigade Orders received for occupying trenches on 28th inst. 2/Lieut CRUMP went on special leave to ENGLAND. 1 man returned from Field Ambulance – 2 men sick to Field Ambulance – Strength 27 officers and 847. O.R. J.C.T.	
27.7.15 . . .	Battalion in Bivouac as before – Company training continued – Major, Adjutant and Company Commanders, M.G. officer, and Medical Officer visited trenches occupied by 5th WARWICKS at HEBUTERNE to arrange about relief tomorrow – Working party of 2 officers and 100 men found for R.E. Store. Heavy rain last night and from 3.0 pm to 5.0 pm today. 4 officers joined without notice, at 7.30 pm. viz: – 2/Lieuts: W.E. FISHER, A.H. CLARK, R.I. HAWKINS, F.D. ANDREWS. advised of 1 man sent to England sick (off strength) Capt W. LEWIS and 5 men sick to Field Ambulance, 2 men to Base and 2 men returned from F.A. Strength 31. officers and 844. O.R. J.C.T.	
28.7.15 . . .	Battalion in Bivouac as before. Preparation made for vacating same, but message recd at 12.10 pm. Cancelling move to trenches – Transport was ready packed & shelters pulled down. Applied for LIEUT: W.E. FISHER to revert to 2/LIEUT: in proper sequence junior to 2/LIEUT: IRVING – Authority recd (A.G.s branch of Staff No B/2055 and 48th Divl 1003 A.X. d/d 22.7.15) for N.C.O.s and men re-engaging for duration of war to receive 1 months furlough to ENGLAND. – Sergt 7. HARRIS to Base (off strength) 3 men sick to Field Ambulance and 3 men returned from Field Ambulance. Strength 31. officers & 843. O.R. J.C.T.	

(73989) W4141—463. 400,000. 9/14. H.&J.Ltd. Forms/C. 2118/10.

Instructions regarding War Diaries and Intelligence Summaries are contained in F. S. Regs., Part II. and the Staff Manual respectively. Title pages will be prepared in manuscript.

WAR DIARY
or
INTELLIGENCE SUMMARY.
(*Erase heading not required.*)

Army Form C. 2118.

Hour, Date, Place	Summary of Events and Information	Remarks and references to Appendices
29.7.15 Bois de WARNIMONT	Battalion in Bivouacs in WARNIMONT woods as before. Fatigue party of 400 men on H.Q. line at COIGNEUX from 8.30 A.M. to 12.30 p.m. 48th Divn Order No 21 received detailing new disposition for taking over trenches at 9.30 pm. This Battalion to hold Section E for 8 days alternately with a Battn of 143rd Bde. 144th Bde Operation order No 15 recd at 9.30 p.m. This Battalion to take over from TROIS ARBRES HEATTRES (right of DUBLIN Fus(?)) to Copse NNE of TOUVENT FARM (Exclusive). C.O. reconnoitred new trenches with the Brigadier 2 men sick to F.A. (including L/Cpl BEES of B.C. who was accidentally injured by pick when digging – 2 men returned from F. Ambulance and also Captain LEWIS. Strength 31 officers and 843 O.R. [initials]	
30.7.15 . . .	Battalion in Bivouacs, as above. Major, Adjutant, M.G. officer, & Company Commanders reconnoitred new trenches in the morning and returned to camp. Battalion marched at 6.0 pm. via: COURCELLES. Relief commenced at 9.0 pm. and was completed, without casualty at 11.20 pm. – Men's water from SUCRERIE about two miles. 3 men sick to Field Ambulance. 4 men returned from Field Ambulance. Strength 31 officers & 843 O.R. [initials]	

(73989) W4141—463. 400,000. 9/14. H.&J.Ltd. Forms/C. 2118/10.

144th Inf.Bde.
48th Div.

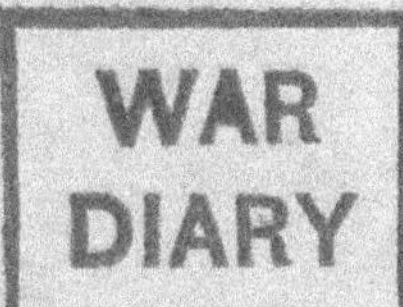

1/4th BATTN. THE GLOUCESTERSHIRE REGIMENT.

A U G U S T

(31.7.15 to 30.8.15)

1 9 1 5

Instructions regarding War Diaries and Intelligence Summaries are contained in F. S. Regs., Part II. and the Staff Manual respectively. Title pages will be prepared in manuscript.

WAR DIARY
or
INTELLIGENCE SUMMARY.
(Erase heading not required.)

Army Form C. 2118.

Hour, Date, Place	Summary of Events and Information	Remarks and references to Appendices
31.7.15. COLINCAMPS	Battalion in the trenches - Day fine and bright - G.O.C. Division and Brigadier inspected trenches 9.0 AM. Day quiet. Great difficulty with water as pump is situated in IV Divisional Area at SUCRERIE and all water has to be carried from there 1½ miles. There is so much carrying to be done that few men are available for anything else - though there is a great deal of work that needs putting in hand. The trench had 2 men to every 1 in this portion of the line and the Dublin Fusiliers had 4 Coys: to our 3. - Two nights ago the Germans started a sap head opposite to the left of our line and are continuing it - This is the only place opposite our line where we can see them. A German was shot at 5.0 AM. by B. Coy: Sentry while standing on their parapet. Captain LEWIS returned from Field Ambulance. 3 Men to F.A. 4 Men to Composite C. 7th Corps H.Q. Strength 31 Officers and 839 O.R. J.C.	
1.8.15 . . .	Battalion in the trenches - Night cold and fine - German saphead prolonged about 10 yards in night. Enemy shoulder remarks over to us. They include an American German believed to be 170th Regt. The Battalion front is now covered by 1 trench 2 gun battery, the 125th Battery and 2nd Gloucester Battery. 5 Enemy shells burst over B Coys fire trench 8.30 AM. Enemy shelled all along fire trenches & LAVANT and MORRISON Communication trenches 4.15 - 4.30 PM. Cor: Sergt: Major Gabb of C. Coy: wounded. He will be a great loss to the Battalion - Originally in 2/Glosters he came out as a National Reserve on mobilization. Thunderstorm at 5.30 pm. Hours for drawing water restricted to 2-4 AM. 12-2 pm. and 6-8 pm. Men will get no wash of any kind while in trenches although the pipe line to barrels in Bois des OBSERVATEUR close to H.Q. could be fixed in a day - appears to be a difficulty between Divisions - 125th Battery shelled German Sap at 7.0 pm. - 1 Man returned from F.A. 3 Men sent to F.A. Strength 31 Officers and 839 O.R. J.C.	
2.8.15 . . .	Battalion in the trenches - South wind - Dull cold morning and night wet - trenches in awful state of mud and water - No wood available for making trench flooring - Heavy thunderstorm at 4.0 pm. with hail - Enemy working on their sap head all during night and large working party to south. Opened machine gun fire on them and drove them in - Again had sap shelled during the morning - MOINE trench evidently rebuilt after a heavy shelling and it dips down in places requiring much repair.	

(73989) W4141—463. 400,000. 9/14. H.&J.Ltd. Forms/C. 2118/10.

Instructions regarding War Diaries and Intelligence Summaries are contained in F. S. Regs., Part II. and the Staff Manual respectively. Title pages will be prepared in manuscript.

WAR DIARY
or
INTELLIGENCE SUMMARY.
(Erase heading not required.)

Army Form C. 2118.

Hour, Date, Place	Summary of Events and Information	Remarks and references to Appendices
2-8-15 COLINCAMPS	Promiscuous shelling by the Enemy during day but no harm done – Enemy had working parties out in front during night, our Machine Guns drove them in about 12 midnight. – Bomb traps placed by LIEUT: IRVING along line where their covering parties had been the night before but they did not approach. Wet night – trenches awful – great difficulty in getting up Rations and Stores. – 1 man returned from C.C.S. 2 men returned from F.A. Coy. Sergt. Major Gabb (C Coy) wounded to Hospital (Rejoins?) LIEUT: F. WARD and 1 man sick to Hospital. Strength 31 Officers and 840. O.R. J.G.T.	
3.8.15 " "	Battalion in the trenches. Very wet morning – trenches 2 feet under water in places – Quiet day and situation normal – German sap fired on by Trench Guns and 125th Battery. 3 men returned from F.A. and 3 men sent sick to F.A. Strength 31. Officers and 838. O.R. (2 men to C.C.S. off strength) J.G.T.	
4-8-15 " "	Battalion in the trenches – weather still wet. Day quiet & situation normal. Work done on trench repair & fix our Communication trenches. R.E. Stores in Bois being daily sorted into order. Captain & Adjt. R. I. RAWSON and 5 N.C.Os + men went on 8 days leave to ENGLAND to 11th inst. Armr. Sergt. SMALL to Div! Amm: Shop – 1 Corpl 2 men + 2 A.S.C. drivers to No 3 Coy. Train – 5 men sick to F.A. and 2 men returned from F.A. Strength 31 Officers and 838. O.R. J.G.T.	
5-8-15 " "	Battalion in trenches – weather finer but trenches still in shocking state – Day quiet and situation normal – Usual shelling by Enemy but no harm done – Our Artillery fired on German sap head in afternoon and 3 Rounds H.E. on same spot (pt. 311) where working party was located at 11.20 p.m. – C.O. and H.Q. Officers of 5th Warwick Regt. reconnoitred our line of trenches – 2 water barrels secured and fixed at foot of Communication trench to be filled by our water carts at night – so that pure drinking water may be secured. 2 men returned from F.A. – 1 man injured, accidentally, by bomb, to F.A. and 2 men sick to F.A. Strength 31 Officers and 838. O.R. – 3 N.C.Os + men on 8 days leave to ENGLAND to 12th inst. J.G.T.	

Instructions regarding War Diaries and Intelligence Summaries are contained in F. S. Regs., Part II. and the Staff Manual respectively. Title pages will be prepared in manuscript.

WAR DIARY
or
INTELLIGENCE SUMMARY.
(Erase heading not required.)

Army Form C. 2118.

Hour, Date, Place	Summary of Events and Information	Remarks and references to Appendices
6.8.15 COLINCAMPS	Battalion in the trenches – Morning very wet and trenches in a bad state. Day quiet and situation normal. Several shells sent over by Germans but no harm done. Our front is now covered by 2nd Glose Battery the 125th Battery having taken over a zone to our right in IV Div^n area. The Brigadier and Brigade Major inspected our trenches. and the Company officers of 5/Warwicks reconnoitred them, also their M.O. – 1 man returned from Div^n C Coy and 2 men from F.A. – 2 men sick to F.A. Strength 31 officers & 839 O.R. J.G.	
7.8.15 . . .	Battalion in the trenches – Morning wet but rain stopped midday – A few rounds High Explosive were fired by the Enemy on our trenches MOINE near its junction with tranchée LAVANT. No damage done – Battalion was relieved by 5/Warwicks – Relief commenced at 10.30 p.m. but owing to the water & mud in the trenches was not completed until very late. A and D Companies marched to Billets in COLINCAMPS and B and C Companies to COURCELLES au BOIS by Sections – the last arriving at 3.0 AM – 1 man returned from C.C.S. and 1 man from F.A. Strength 31 officers and 839 O.R. J.G.	
8.8.15 . . .	Battalion in Reserve at COLINCAMPS and COURCELLES. D Company supplied a working party of 120 men and C Company one of 120 men at Pt 127 – 3/4 mile N.W. of COURCELLES at noon – B Company at Baths at SAILLY-au-BOIS 10.0 AM – 12 noon – 3 men sick to F.A. and 3 men returned from F.A. Strength 31 officers and 839 O.R. J.G.	
9.8.15 . . .	Battalion in Reserve as above – Day fine and warm until 7.0 p.m. when terrific thunderstorm and torrents of rain fell – Working parties of 50 men each found by A Coy 8.0 AM – 2.0 pm and 8.0 pm – 2.0 A.M. at LA SIGNY Farm – D Coy: 125 men and B Coy. 125 men at COIGNEUX. B Coy. 25 men making Corduroy paths at R.E. Stores. C Company at Baths at SAILLY 10.0 AM – 12 noon – Police post of 1 NCO and 3 O.R. found by us at BERTRANCOURT. 1 man returned from C.C.S. and 2 men from F.A. – 10 men sick to F.A. – Captain R.C. CLARKE. R.A.M.C. (attached) sick to F.A. and Capt SHERRARD from 2/1st Amb. arrived to take his place. – LIEUT. MANSELL and 2/LIEUT. THOMAS reported as having been transferred to ENGLAND sick on 28/7/15 and 2 O.R. (off strength) Strength 29 officers and 838 O.R. J.G.	

WAR DIARY
or
INTELLIGENCE SUMMARY.
(*Erase heading not required.*)

Instructions regarding War Diaries and Intelligence Summaries are contained in F. S. Regs., Part II. and the Staff Manual respectively. Title pages will be prepared in manuscript.

Army Form C. 2118.

Hour, Date, Place	Summary of Events and Information	Remarks and references to Appendices
10.8.15 COURCELLES-au-BOIS	Battalion in reserve at COURCELLES and COLINCAMPS. Day fine and warm. Working parties found as follows, viz: A.Coy. LA SIGNY defences two parties 50 men each. – B. Coy. 150 men Corps work, C. Coy. 150 men Corps work. D Coy. 100 men COLINCAMPS defences and 25 men R.E. Stores on Corduroy paths. F.G. Court Martial on No 2547 Pte WESTON – C. Coy. "Sleeping on his post." – 1 man (under age) to Base, 8 men sick to F.A. 2 men returned from F.A. Strength 29 Officers and 837 O.R. – C.O. and Company Commanders visited HEBUTERNE and [illegible] defences. H.T.	
11.8.15 . . .	Battalion in reserve as above – Rain early morning, fine & [illegible] remainder of day. B and C Companies, Machine Gun Sections and H.Q. details inspected by Brig. General 10.0 AM. Sentence on Pte WESTON promulgated. Capt. SLADE and LIEUT. NEWTH and 6 O.R. left on short leave to ENGLAND and C.Q.M. Sergt TAYLOR (A Coy) left on 1 Month's leave to ENGLAND after signing on again till end of war. – 2 men discharged (time expired) and 3 men sick to F.A. and 7 men returned from F.A. Strength 29 Officers 835 H.T.	
12.8.15 . . .	Battalion in reserve as above. Day fine. Working parties of 50 men each in reliefs on LA SIGNY defences. 5 N.C.O.s and men left on 8 days leave to ENGLAND – 4th Machine Gun received – 4 O.R. transferred to C.C.S. 2 O.R. on Command to Divl. Salvage Coy. 3 O.R. sick to Field Ambulance. & 2 men returned from F.A. Strength 29 Officers and 831. O.R. H.T.	
13.8.15 . . .	Battalion in Reserve as above – day fine with heavy showers – Working parties as usual – B Coy: had baths at SAILLY – F.G.C.M. on Pte Guest, transport, for striking an N.C.O. – Major H.L. BAKER transferred to Base (permanent) 2 O.R. transferred to C.C.S. (No 4) 1 man on Command attached to Divl. Signal Coy – 6 O.R. sick to F.A. – Off Strength Sergt EVES to Base, 7 men with Corps Comp Coy and 2 A.S.C. ~~strength~~ 3 O.R. returned from Field Ambulance. Strength 28 Officers and 819 O.R. H.T.	
14.8.15 . . .	Battalion in Reserve as above – Day fine – Working parties as usual – 2 platoons of C Coy had Baths at SAILLY. 1 Case of suspected German Measles reported from COLINCAMPS. – German Aeroplane passed over Village flying N. at 5.0 pm and returned about 6.0 pm. flying very high – 3 O.R. transferred to No 4. C.C.S (off strength) 8 men sick to F.A. & 4 men returned from F.A. Strength 28 Officers + 816. O.R. H.T.	

(73989) W4141—463. 400,000. 9/14. H.&J.Ltd. Forms/C. 2118/10.

Instructions regarding War Diaries and Intelligence Summaries are contained in F. S. Regs., Part II. and the Staff Manual respectively. Title pages will be prepared in manuscript.

WAR DIARY
or
INTELLIGENCE SUMMARY.
(Erase heading not required.)

Army Form C. 2118.

Hour, Date, Place	Summary of Events and Information	Remarks and references to Appendices
15.8.15 COURCELLES au BOIS.	Battalion in Reserve. Very wet morning – but fine after mid-day – Relieved of WARWICKS in the trenches without Casualties – Relief completed by 5.30 p.m. – M.G.s left billets at 8.45 A.M. – all Bde. C. Grenadiers to be in trenches – Trenches very muddy and Communication trenches over boots in mud & water in valleys – New dump for rations and stores, 800 yards forward used. Rations stored in dugouts adjoining dump and taken up after "Stand-down" in morning – LIEUT. F. WARD sick to ENGLAND on 8.8.15. (off strength) LIEUT. CLARK and 5 O.R. sick to F.A. – 1 man to No. 4 C.C.S. – 5 men returned from F.A. and 3 O.R. returned from Div. Salvage C. Strength 27 officers and 815 O.R. J.C.T.	
16.8.15. COLINCAMPS	Battalion in Trenches – Intermittent shelling 9 a.m. – 11 a.m. and 2 p.m. to 3.50 p.m. No harm done – Arrangements made for fixing 4 water barrels at new dump to be filled by water carts at night. Party of 12 men on pumping out well at LA SIGNY. – Draining Communication trenches and work started on new H.Q.rs – Germans busy digging on saps opposite our line – Sniped them all day. Orders rec'd. from Division to sap across our front to straighten line, thus advancing about 40 yards, began sapping to the front at night in three places – 1 man slightly wounded (at duty). Sick in Billet 2/LIEUT. IRVING 1 man sick to Highland C.C.S. and 1 man to No. 4 C.C.S. (off strength) 2 men returned from F.A. Strength 27 officers and 813 O.R. J.C.T.	
17.8.15 . . .	Battalion in Trenches – Morning fine – wet afternoon – Trenches very bad. Parties at work on parapets to prevent them falling in – R.E. stores very scarce and no revetting material available. Captains CASTLE and WADE & 6 O.R. proceeded on leave to ENGLAND at 5 p.m. – 2/LIEUT. IRVING and 7 men sick to F.A. – 1 man to Highland C.C.S. and 1 man to No. 4 C.C.S. (off strength) 1 man returned from F.A. Strength 27 officers & 811 O.R. J.C.T.	
18.8.15 . . .	Battalion in Trenches – Very wet day – Trenches very bad, very muddy and slippery – working on drainage, cutting drains and sump holes through clay into the chalk & clearing out those silted up with mud – improving parapets which are only about 2 ft. thick in places – thickening to 5 feet – sapping new fire trench; laying trench flooring. Orders rec'd. to return all boxes of S.A.A. marked. B. & all French bombs to be returned. – LIEUT. BEAVEN and 3 O.R. proceeded on 6 days leave to ENGLAND. – 9 men (on Command) to 178 Tunnelling C. 1 man transferred to No. 4 C.C.S. and 1 man returned from No. 4 C.C.S. (on strength) 4 men sick to F.A. and 5 men returned from F.A. Strength 27 Officers and 811 O.R. J.C.T.	
19.8.15 . .	Battalion in Trenches. Fine day but mud very bad – 3rd Army Gas Expert visited Batt. Trenches. Boxes of S.A.A. marked B total 12 returned. Establishment of bombs in future to be	

(73989) W4141—463. 400,000. 9/14. H.&J.Ltd. Forms/C. 2118/10.

Instructions regarding War Diaries and Intelligence Summaries are contained in F. S. Regs., Part II. and the Staff Manual respectively. Title pages will be prepared in manuscript.

WAR DIARY
or
INTELLIGENCE SUMMARY.
(Erase heading not required.)

Army Form C. 2118.

Hour, Date, Place	Summary of Events and Information	Remarks and references to Appendices
19.8.15. COLINCAMPS.	to be 25 per platoon in front line (150) 100 per Coy Support line (400) 100 Bn Reserve. Total 650. Bde letter T/898 of 18/8/15. Shelling of our fire trenches 3–3.15 pm. – No 18 Bay hit – no casualties. – Some activity on both sides with shells and more rifle and M.G. fire than usual during the day. Our heavy Battery shelled points 311–312 at 3.0 pm. 3 Explosions, like Aerial Torpedoes, at 9.10 pm. just South of junction DELAUNDY and LAVAND trenches – Water from LA SIGNY reported fit to drink and being laid into barrels in Bois des OBSERVATEURS through canvas pipe line 400 yds. from Bn Hd Qrs – 2 men to ENGLAND sick, and 1 man returned from No 4. C.C.S. & 2 men returned from F.A. Strength 27 Officers & 810. O.R. J.T.	
20.8.15 . . .	Battalion in trenches – Night quiet. Day fine but dull. Intermittent shelling and a 5.9 Howitzer shell landed in junction of trenches MOINE and LAVAND but only damaged parapet. – 3 cases of German Measles confirmed by F. Amb. and 4th case today – all in No 1 Platoon of A Coy. Amounts to an epidemic and contracted in COLINCAMPS. 1 man wounded to Field Ambulance (slight) 4 men sick to F.A. 1 man to Highland C.C.S. + 1 man to No 4. C.C.S. (Comp. ? already off strength) 3 men returned from F.A. Strength 27 Officers and 809. O.R. J.T.	
21.8.15 . . .	Battalion in trenches – day fine with showers – New Machine Gun emplacement in RABAUD finished and one in fire trench partly rebuilt, work on new Hd 2nd trench flooring in TESSIER and EXUPERY, sumps in TESSIER and LAVAND; Rebuilding parapet in RABAUD, continuing saps to fire trench. Our heavy battery shelled SERRE at 3.0 pm. – New arrangements in case of Alarm while in reserve billets recd from Bde D/69 dtd 21.8.15. To No 4. C.C.S. 1 man – To Divl. Rest Station 1 man (on strength from C.C.S.) 1 man wounded to F.A. 3 men sick to F.A. – 2/LIEUTS IRVING and CLARK returned from F. Ambulance. Strength 27 Officers and 809. O.R. J.T.	
22.8.15 . . .	Battalion in trenches. Work on parapets and trenches as before. Day fine and cold. Trenches drying up; Sandbags recd last night from R.E. & used on parapets. A draft of 20 O.R. arrived from HAVRE, these are all men who have been sick at the Base except 3 – Artillery shelling by both sides intermittently. Bde No T/942 dtd 22.8.15 concerning training while in Divl. Reserve received. – 4 men transferred to No 4. C.C.S. and 1 man to Highland C.C.S. – 1 man sick to F.A. Strength 27 Officers and 804. O.R. J.T.	
23.8.15 . . .	Battalion in trenches – day fine, bright & warm. Relief by 5/WARWICKS began at 10.30. AM. for 2 Coys and M.Gs remaining 2 Coys. at 3.0 pm. Whole four Battn. now billetted at COURCELLES and Grenadiers at COIGNEUX. 2/LIEUT. SELLMAN joined from No 1. Prov: Entrenching Battn. at POPERINGHE with which our draft now is. News of German naval defeat in Gulf of RIGA recd. 1 man to No 4. C.C.S. and 1 to Highland C.C.S. 4 men returned from F.A. Strength 28. Officers and 822. O.R. J.T.	

Instructions regarding War Diaries and Intelligence Summaries are contained in F. S. Regs., Part II. and the Staff Manual respectively. Title pages will be prepared in manuscript.

WAR DIARY
or
INTELLIGENCE SUMMARY.
(*Erase heading not required.*)

Army Form C. 2118.

Hour, Date, Place	Summary of Events and Information	Remarks and references to Appendices
24. 8. 15. COURCELLES au BOIS	Battalion in Reserve at Courcelles au Bois. Very fine + warm day. Instructions received defining new boundaries to Divisional Area, as 4th Division takes over line now occupied by 4th + 6th Gloucester Regts and over an to [illegible] North of HEBUTERNE – C.S.M. GABB and 1 O.R. to England, two men to Field Ambulance 1 man returned from C.C.S. (on strength) 4 men returned from F.A. Strength 28 Officers + 821 O.R. J.G.	
25. 8. 15 . . .	Battalion in Reserve. – C + D Companies on digging fatigues, 50 men of A Coy. on Corps fatigue and 25 men on R.E. fatigue at R.E. Stores. 2 platoons of A + B. Coy. had baths at SAILLY – 4 men to Field Ambulance 1 man to Div^l H.Q. (on command) 2 O.R. to Bd^e H.Q. for Course of Bugler Augt 25 – Augt 30th. Strength 28 Officers + 821. O.R. 2/Lieut. BRIGGS on leave to England to 1st Sept + 6 N.C.Os + men.	
26. 8. 15 . . .	Battalion in Reserve – A + B. Companies on digging fatigues. 1 platoon of C. Coy on R.E. fatigues – C and D Companies had Baths at SAILLY – Capt^s CASTLE + WADE and 6 O.R. returned from leave. Capt PARKINSON and 3 O.R. on leave to England till 2^d Sept. – Sentence of 5 years P.S. on No 2543 P^te WESTON commuted to 3 months F.P. No 1. by order of G.O.C. in C. 3rd Army – Strength 28. Officers and 821 O.R. J.G.	
27. 8. 15 . . .	Battalion in Reserve. Lt Col. Davenport, Capt Ransom + Captn Clarke went for Bd^e tour round 3rd Army area by Motor Bus via ACHEUX and CORBY and back via QUERRIEUX – C. Coy at Company training – A + B Companies on digging fatigues. 1 Platoon D Coy on R.E. fatigues. 2 men to Field Ambulance. 1 man to C.C.S. No 4. (off strength) 2 men returned from Field Ambulance. Strength 28 Officers + 820. O.R. J.G.	
28. 8. 15 . . .	Battalion in Reserve. C and D. Companies on digging fatigue from 9.0 AM – 3.0 pm. 1 Platoon of B. Coy instruction in Grenades at COIGNEUX at 3.0 pm. – A + B. Companies marching order inspection at 4.0 pm. B Coy. had baths at SAILLY also 50 men on R.E. fatigue – A. Coy – 2 platoons had baths – 1 man to C.C.S. No 4 (off strength) 3 men to F.A. and 3 men returned from Field Ambulance. Strength 28 Officers + 819. O.R. J.G.	
29. 8. 15 . . .	Battalion in Reserve. A + B. Coys digging fatigues 9.0 AM to 3.0 pm. C. Coy. 50 men on R.E. fatigue making Stores 8 AM – 4. pm. – Divine Service conducted by the Rev. Canon W. WELCHMAN, the Batt^n Chaplain, who has lately joined the Division from BRISTOL. O.C. and mounted officers reconnoitred ground for practice attack	

Instructions regarding War Diaries and Intelligence Summaries are contained in F. S. Regs., Part II. and the Staff Manual respectively. Title pages will be prepared in manuscript.

WAR DIARY
or
INTELLIGENCE SUMMARY.
(Erase heading not required.)

Army Form C. 2118.

Hour, Date, Place	Summary of Events and Information	Remarks and references to Appendices
29.8.15. Cont. COURCELLES	attack from trenches – 2/LIEUT. IRVING, seconded for service with 178th Tunnelling Coy, proceeded to 10th Corps Hd Qrs this morning and 9 men (off strength) – 1 man to No 4. C.C.S. (off strength) 2 men to Field Ambulance and 1 man returned from F.A. and 1 man on Command. Strength 27 Officers + 808. O.R. day hot but night very wet. J.C.T.	
30.8.15. " "	Battalion in Reserve. day fine and cool, night wet. C and D Companies practice attack on imaginary trenches with all necessary tools, stores, bombs &c at 9.0 A.M. between Road BERTRANCOURT – COIGNEUX and BOIS du WARNIMONT and A and B. Companies practice same on same ground at 5.0 p.m. O.C. attended conference held by G.O.C. Division with C.Os at 2.0 pm. 2 men to Field Ambulance and 2 men returned from Field Ambulance. Strength 27 Officers and 808. O.R. J.C.T.	

(73989) W4141—463. 400,000. 9/14. H.&J.Ltd. Forms/C. 2118/10.

144th Inf.Bde.
48th Div.

WAR
DIARY

1/4th BATTN. THE GLOUCESTERSHIRE REGIMENT.

S E P T E M B E R

(31.8.15 to 30.9.15)

1 9 1 5

Instructions regarding War Diaries and Intelligence Summaries are contained in F. S. Regs., Part II. and the Staff Manual respectively. Title pages will be prepared in manuscript.

WAR DIARY
or
INTELLIGENCE SUMMARY.
(Erase heading not required.)

Army Form C. 2118.

Hour, Date, Place	Summary of Events and Information	Remarks and references to Appendices
31.8.15. COURCELLES au BOIS.	Battalion in Reserve. day cold and Cloudy. B. Company 2 Officers and 120 men on Corps fatigues – C and D Coys. and 50 men of A. Coy on R.E. fatigues. 2 men returned from Field Ambulance. Captain F.G.J. GOETERBOCK and 2 O.R. to Field Ambulance. Strength 27 Officers and 808 O.R. J.G.T.	
1.9.15. . . .	Battalion in Reserve. day cool + Cloudy with West wind. A+B Coys. inspected by C.O. in Marching Order. Corps and R.E. fatigues found by B.C.D. Coys. A+C Coys. rifles inspected by Armourer at 5.30pm. Evening wet – 1 man returned from Field Ambulance. Strength 27 Officers and 808 O.R. J.G.T.	
2.9.15 . . .	Battalion in Reserve. Wet last night – day cold and Cloudy with West wind. D Coy inspected by C.O. in Marching Order. Corps and R.E. fatigues found by A.B+C. Coys. – B and D Coys. rifles inspected by Armourer. 2/Lieut. BRIGGS and 6 men returned from LEAVE. Lecture to Officers by Brig. Genl NICHOLSON at 6.0pm. Strength 27 Officers and 808 O.R. J.G.T.	
1.9.15. . .	Lieut. WOOKEY and 2/Lieut. TRAPNELL and 9 men went on leave to ENGLAND. Sergt Lock (M.G. Section) having been ... [illegible] ... to ENGLAND.	
3.9.15 . . .	Battalion in Reserve. day cold + wet with West wind. Corps and R.E. fatigues found D and C. Coys. A.B and ½ C. Coys. and 50 men of D. Coy. had Baths at SAILLY – Capt. PARKINSON and 8 men returned from leave. – C.O. adjutant and Coy. Commanders visited trenches 11 to 18 in front of HEBOTERNE to be taken over on Sunday (5.9.15) from 145th Brigade. Major THOMPSON detailed to Command HEBOTERNE KEEP. 2/Lieut. CLARK and 1 man to Field Ambulance – 2 men returned from Field Ambulance. Strength 27 Officers and 808 O.R. J.G.T.	
4.9.15. . .	Battalion in Reserve. Day fine. C. Coy. inspected by C.O. in Marching Order. Corps and R.E. fatigues found by A+B. Coys. – D Coy. had Baths at SAILLY. 2 men to Field Ambulance. Captain GOETERBOCK and 1 man returned from Field Ambulance. Strength 27 Officers and 808 O.R. J.G.T.	
5.9.15 HEBUTERNE	Battalion relieved part of BUCKS: Batt. and 3 Coys. of 4/R. Berks: Batt. in HEBOTERNE trenches before 1.0pm. Relief completed without Casualty. A+D. Coy. in fire trenches. C Coy in Bn. Reserve in billets. B. Coy in Bde Reserve in KEEP. Bn. H.Q. in Red House. HEBOTERNE. Trenches are too shallow but otherwise good and everyone made more comfortable than the last place near COLINCAMPS. 1 man to Field Ambulance and 1 man returned from Field Ambulance. Strength 27 Officers and 808 O.R. – Captain R.C. Parke R.A.M.C. (T.) rejoined the Battalion from Hospital at Base – J.G.T.	

(73989) W4141—463. 400,000. 9/14. H.&J.Ltd. Forms/C. 2118/10.

Instructions regarding War Diaries and Intelligence Summaries are contained in F. S. Regs., Part II. and the Staff Manual respectively. Title pages will be prepared in manuscript.

WAR DIARY
or
INTELLIGENCE SUMMARY

(Erase heading not required.)

Hour, Date, Place	Summary of Events and Information	Remarks and references to Appendices
6.9.15. HEBUTERNE.	Battalion in Trenches – day fine. C.O. attended conference at Bde H.Q. All Sentries are now ordered to be doubled which takes more men. Work done on Communication trenches and traversing fire and Service trenches. A Party working under R.E. on dugouts E end of BIRON Com: trench. Very quiet day on our front. A German Aeroplane came over at 6.0pm but was at once turned back by fire and a British plane. A Patrol of 1/8th WORCESTERS met GERMAN patrol on TOISIEUX Rd in front of right of A. Coy. and killed one, bringing the body in – a man of 61st Regt (Prussn). – Capt & Adjt R. I. RAWSON promoted Major w.e.f. 1.9.15. 10 men to C.C.S. and 2 men to Field Ambulance, and 2 men returned from Field Ambulance. Strength 27. Officers and 806. O.R. J.T.	
7.9.15	Battalion in Trenches – day fine – quiet on our front with some shelling – Enemy shelled D. Coy. No 14 Trench hitting parapet three times. No damage. This was in reply to our Howitzer shelling FERME SANS NOM. Three saps started from trenches Nos 13, 14 and 15. to the front. C Coy. started continuation of MONT VALIER Communication trench. Major Osler – 19th Durham L.I. attached to us for instruction for 3 days. – 4 men to Field Ambulance. 8 men returned from F.A. – 10 men taken on Strength from 1/2nd Coy. R.E. Strength 27 Officers and 816 O.R. J.T.	
8.9.15 . . .	Battalion in Trenches. Work on fire and Communication Trenches – day fine & quiet. Captain P.G.J. GUETERBOCK and LIEUT. MASTER on leave to ENGLAND and also 9 N.C.O's & men – Pte GLOVER. C. Coy having re-engaged given 1 months leave to ENGLAND. – 5 men to Field Ambulance, Strength 27. Officers and 816 O.R. J.T.	
9.9.15 . . .	Battalion in trenches – fine day – Some shelling but otherwise quiet. Parties of Enemy seen in GOMMECOURT Wood and on roads & paths fired on by Snipers & Machine Guns. Several suspected Cases of some mild form of Enteric fever discovered in C. Coy. Divl Sanitary Officer tested the Platoon and found about 40 cases altogether – Men do not appear to be sick but have headache, temperature and diarrhoea. Issue of Straw to men in trenches and on Stone floors in billets sanctioned 3rd Army S/1384 25.8.15, 7th Corps: (Q 1027) & 48th Divn C.M. No 1529 Q.X. dated 8.9.15. 1lbs per man to last a fortnight. List to be kept of Officers, N.C.O's & men who might be useful in supervising R.E. Work. 7th Corps G.S./191 & 48th Divn 1956 A.X. dated 8/9/15. 2 Officers per Battn to be trained as Adjt. for 1 Month. Ref: 48th Divn G.X. 620 of 8.9.15 – At present we have only Captain PARKINSON available. – 1 man to No 4 C.C.S. (off Strength) 6 men to Field Ambulance & 2 men returned from F.A. Strength, 27. Officers and 815. O.R. LIEUT. WOOKEY & 9 men returned from leave – LIEUT. TRAPNELL sick in ENGLAND – J.T.	

1247 W 3299 200,000 (E) 8/14 J.B.C. & A. Forms/C. 2118/11.

Instructions regarding War Diaries and Intelligence Summaries are contained in F. S. Regs., Part II. and the Staff Manual respectively. Title pages will be prepared in manuscript.

WAR DIARY
or
INTELLIGENCE SUMMARY.
(Erase heading not required.)

Army Form C. 2118.

Hour, Date, Place	Summary of Events and Information	Remarks and references to Appendices
10.9.15. HEBOTERNE	Battalion in Trenches - day fine but cold, strong S.W. wind. day very quiet on our front. Work on fire and Communication trenches continued. Some shelling - 1 Man discharged (off strength) 17.8.15. - 1 Man returned from Field Ambulance - 2 Men to No 4 C.C.S. (off strength) 10 men to F.A., all suspected enteric, and 1 man dischd to F.A. Strength 27 Officers + 812 O.R. J.C.T.	
11.9.15 " "	Battalion in Trenches - day fine - Situation quiet on our front. B & C Coys relieved A and D in 1st line in the evening. All S.A.A. of U.S. American manufacture called in. All Pitcher bombs had [illegible] undetonated and returned. Our Howitzers dropped 12 shells short in front of wire in front of No 2 trench at 6 p.m. Enemy shelled Bn. front at intervals from 7 to 10 p.m. and fired single shots at Saps up to 12 midnight every ½ hour. — Major Osler - 19 D.L. Infantry left. 1 Water Cart returned repaired from Ordnance and the other sent for repair. 1 Man (off strength) to No 4 C.C.S. - 6 Men to Field Ambulance and 1 Man returned from F.A. Strength 27 Officers and 811 O.R. J.C.T.	
12.9.15 " "	Battalion in Trenches - Quiet day on our front. Day fine - some shelling at intervals and a visit [illegible] HEBOTERNE in the evening. - 2 Coys of 13th Manchesters attached to us for instruction - 1 Coy finds 2 platoons in trenches with each of our Coys and 1 Coy billetted and finding fatigues. These change places every 48 hours - Coy Qr Mr Sergt TAYLOR - A Co returned from 1 month's leave to ENGLAND - 4 Men to Field Ambulance and 7 Men returned from F. Ambulance. Strength 27 Officers + 811 O.R. J.C.T.	
13.9.15 " "	Battalion in Trenches - Day fine & hot - The 2 Coys of 13th Manchesters changed over. Front quiet - Arrangements made for storage of materials, tools and stores in present No 2 [illegible] in case of a forward move. vide 48th Divl Ar. Memo. 1969 QX. Extracts from Orders & Instructions re Courts-Martial Etc to be studied by all Presidents of C.M.s (3rd Army) LIEUT WOOREY patrolled beyond Poplars on PUISIEUX Road and B Coy sent a patrol towards Ferme SANS NOM but found the ground too rough to proceed without noise. 2/LIEUT CLARK C Co returned from Hospital. 3 Men returned from F.A. 2 Men to No 4 C.C.S. off strength. 5 Men to Field Ambulance. 1 Man retd from No 4 C.C.S. (on strength) Strength 27 Officers and 810 O.R. J.C.T.	

(73989) W4141—463. 400,000. 9/14. H.&J.Ltd. Forms/C. 2118/10.

Instructions regarding War Diaries and Intelligence Summaries are contained in F. S. Regs., Part II. and the Staff Manual respectively. Title pages will be prepared in manuscript.

or INTELLIGENCE SUMMARY

(Erase heading not required.)

Hour, Date, Place	Summary of Events and Information	Remarks and references to Appendices
14.9.15. HEBOTERNE	Battalion in Trenches – Rain fell during night, but fine in day. Quiet on our front. Patrols sent out during night from B & C. Coys to try and ascertain what saps the Germans have and what gaps there are in their wire. C. Coy patrol, under LIEUT. WOOKEY from trench 8 parallel to PUISIEUX Road to 100 yards from German wire near pt. 869 (Plan Direction 10000) (Sheet 24) – Grass too dry to get closer – Returned by Scout Section at junction of PUISIEUX and BUCQUOY Roads where rifle pits and dugouts exist but no barricade – Germans working on their wire. B Coy patrol got out 200 yards but found grass too dry to get closer. Pathologist came & took blood specimens from men with fever. LIEUT. TRAPNELL granted extension of leave to 29.9.15 on Medical Certificate (A.G.'s office A/77 + 48th Divn. 1003 A.X. of 13.9.15) – 9 men returned from Field Ambulance. Strength 27 Officers & 810 O.R. [initials]	
15.9.15. " "	Battalion in Trenches – Slight rain in morning. Wind N.E. – Capt. L.G. PARKINSON appointed Adjutant vice Major R.I. RAWSON – promoted. 1st Sept. 1915. Auth. "H.Q. 3rd Army 395/p dtd. 11.9.15. Usual patrols out from our front trenches last night – work as usual on trenches and dug-outs – 3 saps completed through wire. Enemy put 5 shells into HEBOTERNE at 1.0 pm. 3 of which fell in KEEP and 2 of which struck Batt. Hd. Qrs. breaking roof of shoemaker's shop & Reg[illegible] H. Qrs. details kitchen & Mess – No Casualties – Our Artillery retaliated on GOMMECOURT – Shells came from SERRE direction. 2 men on leave to ENGLAND. 4 men back from Field Ambulance, 8 men to F. Ambulance. Strength 27 Officers 810 O.R. [initials]	
16.9.15. " "	Battalion in Trenches – day cloudy and cool – Saps through our wire finished. Usual patrols out during night. Capt. GOETERBOCK and LIEUT. MASTER and 9 men returned from leave. 2 men to No. 4 C.C.S. 3 men to Field Ambulance. 1 man returned from Field Ambulance. Strength 27 Officers – 808. O.R. [initials]	
17.9.15. " "	Battalion relieved in Trenches by 1/4 R. Berks. Regt. and returned by Companies to billets in Divl. Reserve at AOTHIE – relief completed without casualty by 11.30 PM. Arrived AOTHIE by 2.0 am – Batt. Hd. Qrs. in Chateau. Capt. HOLLAND gazetted 3/LIEUT. in Regt. to date 2.9.15 – 1 man on leave to ENGLAND – 3 men return from leave – 1 man to No. 4 C.C.S. 2 men from Field Ambulance. Strength 28 Officers and 806 O.R. [initials]	

1247 W 3299 200,000 (E) 8/14 J.B.C. & A. Forms/C. 2118/11.

Army Form C. 2118.

Instructions regarding War Diaries and Intelligence Summaries are contained in F. S. Regs., Part II. and the Staff Manual respectively. Title pages will be prepared in manuscript.

WAR DIARY
or
INTELLIGENCE SUMMARY.

(Erase heading not required.)

Hour, Date, Place	Summary of Events and Information	Remarks and references to Appendices
18.9.15. AUTHIE	Battalion in Reserve at AUTHIE. Billets inspected, and arrangements made in Cottage opposite the Mairie for the Baths just rec^d to be fixed up so that Companies can have Baths in the village. There are four iron Baths, belonging to Battalion and boiler. Indent handed to C.R.E at Bus les Artois for iron pipe to take overflow from filter tanks under road to drain. – 2/LIEUT: SELLMAN went to Machine Gun School at WISQUES for 16 days course. – 3 men to Field Ambulance. Strength 28 Officers + 806 O.R.	
19.9.15 . . .	Battalion in Reserve. Church parade at 10.0 A.M. Service taken Battalion Chaplain – Canon WELCHMAN. J.G. Corps and R.E. fatigues found by A.B.+D Coys and 45 men of C. Coy. – 1 man to F.A. and 4 men returned from Field Ambulance. Men with fever isolated on high ground N. end of the village in 5 tents. Strength – 28 Officers and 806 O.R. – 2/LIEUT: BRIGGS goes to H.Q. Royal Flying School to be attached. J.G.	
20.9.15 . . .	Battalion in Reserve. Day very fine and hot. Batt^n paraded at 9.30 A.M. for Route March via Bus and LOUVENCOURT and was inspected by Div^l General and then carried out an attack practice under a scheme set by the G.O.C. 48th Div^n on the ground, who expressed his satisfaction with the appearance and work of the Battalion. 2/LIEUT: FISHER and 2/LIEUT: BRIGGS gazetted LIEUTS: from 29.7.15 and 9.8.15 respectively. – 1 man to No. C.C.S. (off strength) + 5 men returned from Field Ambulance. Strength 28 Officers + 805 O.R. J.G.	
21.9.15 . . .	Battalion in Reserve. Day very fine + warm. A and D Companies found Corps and R.E. fatigues. B+C Companies paraded 9.0 A.M. for 1 hours arms drill and 2 hours attack practice. Arrangements made with A.P.M. 48th Div^n for room in Café NATIONALE to be used as Sergts' Mess – No drinks to be served except during the allotted hours. 4 men to Field Ambulance – 2 men returned from F.A. Strength 28 Officers + 806 O.R. C Coy had Baths.	
22.9.15 . . .	Battalion in Reserve. Sniper practice range fixed up. Thresh Disinfector allotted to the Battalion from 7.0 A.M. till noon – but arrived 1 hour and 15 minutes late. B A Coy on Corps fatigue. All Officers and B.C and D Coys attended Gas lecture and demonstration by 3rd Army Gas Expert at COUIN. At 6.30 p.m. Batt^n Concert held in Chateau Grounds. B Coy had Baths. 1 man to No. 19 C.C.S. – 3 men returned from Field Ambulance – Strength 28 Officers and 800 O.R. J.G. Note. – 4 men have been taken on Strength in error – 2/LIEUT: HOLLAND and 1 man on leave to ENGLAND.	

(73989) W4141—463. 400,000. 9/14. H.&J.Ltd. Forms/C. 2118/10.

Instructions regarding War Diaries and Intelligence Summaries are contained in F. S. Regs., Part II. and the Staff Manual respectively. Title pages will be prepared in manuscript.

WAR DIARY
or
INTELLIGENCE SUMMARY.
(Erase heading not required.)

Army Form C. 2118.

Hour, Date, Place	Summary of Events and Information	Remarks and references to Appendices
23.9.15. AOTHIE	Battalion in Reserve at AOTHIE - Day fine but my close air and heavy thunderstorm about 6 p.m. followed by rain most of the night. A.B + D Coys. on Corps and R.E fatigues and farm work for villagers. C. Coy. digging trenches for practicing attack on trenches. 2 men returned from leave - Head Quarters details and part of C. Coy. had Baths - 8 men to No. 4. C.C.S. 2 men to Field Ambulance. 6 men rejd from F.A. and 1 from tunnelling Coy. - Strength 28. Officers and 792. O.R. - Capt. W.C. CARRE to No. 4. C.C.S. [signature]	
24.9.15. . .	Battalion in Reserve at AOTHIE - Warned to be ready to move at short notice to support Brigade in trenches in front of HEBOTERNE - Company parades in morning practising attack. Battn ordered to hand over the R.E. park tools recd from 1/4 Royal Berks Regt to No. LABOUR Battn R.E. - C.O attended Conference at the Brigade Hd Qrs at COIN - A. Coy. had Baths in morning and D. Coy. in the afternoon. 6 men returned from 7th Corps Rest Coy. - 2 men sent to Field Ambulance - Strength 28 Officers & 798. O.R. A Court of Enquiry (President Capt. P.G. GOETERBACK) was held to enquire into an injury recd by No. 2. Q.M. Sgt. BEER. Shoemakers' Shops stopped to facilitate possible sudden move. Mess kit bags sent to Q.M. Stores for same reason. [signature]	
25.9.15. . .	Battalion in Reserve. C.O attended Conference at Brigade Head quarters. Control post of 6 men including N.C.O posted at St. LEGER by order of 48th Division - 6 men sent to 1/5 Sussex as being unfit to move with the Battalion - 15 men to Field Ambulance - including those with fever. C.S.M. WHITE [illegible] to ENGLAND as medically unfit. French Interpreter transferred to No. 3. Coy. Train - We now [illegible] share Interpreter with the 1/4 Berks and also share the [illegible] of the 1/6 Glouc. Regt. Strength 28 Officers and 796 O.R. - D Coy. practised attack from trenches in afternoon. M.G. Section had Baths. [signature]	
26.9.15. . .	Battalion in Reserve at AOTHIE. Church parade held at 10.0 A.M. in field W. of village on AOTHIE — MARIEUX road. Voluntary service of Holy Communion held directly afterwards in [illegible] used as Sergts MESS. - B & C. Coys practised attack from trenches in afternoon - 2 men to No. 4. C.C.S. 2 men to Field Ambulance and 1 man returned from Field Ambulance. Strength 28 Officers and 794. O.R.	

Instructions regarding War Diaries and Intelligence Summaries are contained in F. S. Regs., Part II. and the Staff Manual respectively. Title pages will be prepared in manuscript.

WAR DIARY
or
INTELLIGENCE SUMMARY.
(Erase heading not required.)

Army Form C. 2118.

Hour, Date, Place	Summary of Events and Information	Remarks and references to Appendices
27.9.15. AOTHIE	Battalion in Reserve at AOTHIE. C.O. and Major visited 1/4 Berks: Regt at HEBOTERNE and arranged for relief of that Battalion in the Trenches on Wednesday next. B and C Coys. had Baths. All Company Bombers and Brigade Bombers paraded for instruction in attack from Trenches under Major RANSON and LIEUT. FISHER. C.O. attended Conference at Brigade H.Qrs at 6.0pm. 1 man to Field Ambulance. Note The six men sent to 1/5 Sussex as unfit to move with the unit are now taken on Command. Strength 28 Officers and 794 O.R. J.G.T.	
28.9.15. "	Battalion in Reserve. Orders detailed personally by C.O. for relief of Trenches held by 1/4 Berks Regt tomorrow - day week. Sergt. Major CHAPMAN gazetted officer to 2/ Gloucester Regt. Major Thompson & [illegible] visited Louvencourt to inspect Billets there. Commission - Sergt. Major CHAPMAN. 6 men to Field Ambulance. 4 men to No. 4 C.C.S. Strength 28 Officers and 789 O.R. J.G.T.	
29.9.15. HEBOTERNE	Battalion relieved 1/4 Berks: Regt in Trenches No. XI - XVIII inclusive in front HEBOTERNE. A & D Coys in fire trenches. C Coy. in Batt: Reserve and B Coy in Brigade Reserve in Keep. Major THOMPSON in Command of KEEP. First Coy: left AOTHIE at 7.0AM. Relief completed by 12 NOON. No Casualties. 2/Lieut. R.H. DOWN joined Battalion from No. 1. ENTRENCHING Batt. 6 men rejoined Batt. from 1/5 Sussex Regt. 6 men attached to 1/5 Sussex Batt. as Control Post at St LEGER (posted 25.9.15) Strength 29 Officers and 789 O.R. J.G.T.	
30.9.15. "	Battalion in Trenches at HEBOTERNE. Night of 29th - 30th quiet and fine. Salvo of small shells fired by Enemy on trenches of the Battalion on our right at 1.0pm. No patrols sent out on Night of 29/30. Very little work has been done on trenches since we went out owing to the fact that all R.E. material has been collected into forward dumps, which may not be touched except in Case of an advance. 2/Lieut. Down posted to A Coy and 2/Lieut. Holland to D Coy. No. 1 man to No. 4 C.C.S. 9 men to No. 19 C.C.S. 3 men to Field Ambulances. Strength 29 Officers and 784 O.R. J.G.T.	

W4141—463. 400,000. 9/14. H.&J.Ltd. Forms/C. 2118/10.

144th Inf.Bde.
48th Div.

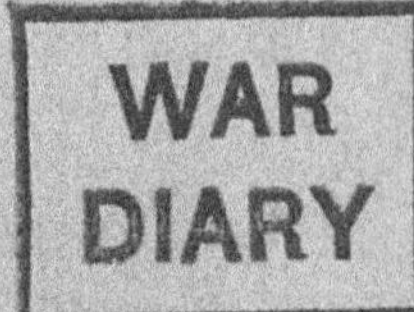

1/4th BATTN. THE GLOUCESTERSHIRE REGIMENT.

O C T O B E R

1 9 1 5

Instructions regarding War Diaries and Intelligence Summaries are contained in F. S. Regs., Part II. and the Staff Manual respectively. Title pages will be prepared in manuscript.

WAR DIARY
or
INTELLIGENCE SUMMARY.
(Erase heading not required.)

Army Form C. 2118.

Hour, Date, Place	Summary of Events and Information	Remarks and references to Appendices
1.10.15 HEBUTERNE	Battalion in Trenches at HEBUTERNE. Weather fine but much colder. Night of 30 Sept – 1st Oct quiet. Patrol from our left Coy. worked towards GOMMECOURT Wood & returned but with nothing to report. About 4.0 pm a few enemy shrapnel fell between the Glouc. Trenches and HEBUTERNE KEEP. No damage. Work begun on new dug-outs behind Battn. H^d Quarters. 2/Lieut. HOLLAND and 2 men returned from leave. 1 man to Field Amb^ce, 2 men returned from F.A. Strength 29 Officers and 784 O.R. J.C.	
2.10.15 " "	Battalion in Trenches. Weather fine but cold. Night 1-2nd quiet, day quiet. 5 Glouc. Regt. on our immediate left on patrol at 8.0 pm encountered German patrol & claim 1 German killed and 1 wounded. At 10.0 pm a great deal of bombing going on well on our right. Lieut. BRIGGS attached R.F.C. is today taken off our strength by order rec^d from Bde. – 2 men returned from F.A., 1 man from C.C.S., 3 men to F.A. and 5 men to C.C.S. – Strength 28 Officers and 780 O.R. – J.C.	
3.10.15 " "	Battalion in Trenches. Night very fine but cold + quiet except for bombing going on on right. At 9.35 AM four small shrapnel shells burst between our Reserve Coy. billets and Battal^n H.Q. – Extract from London Gazette of 29.9.15. – "Glouc. Regt. (T.F.) Capt. W. S. CLARKE to be Temp^y Major – Oct 2nd." – 1 man to F.A. and 1 man returned from F.A. Strength 28 Officers + 780 O.R. J.C.	
4.10.15 " "	Battalion in the Trenches – At 9.0 AM our 5" Howitzer shelled BUCQUOY and 1 + 2 Warwick batteries shelled German trenches. German Artillery did not reply. – Major RAWSON attached to 8/Worcester Regt. to command during Colonel PEAKE'S absence. – Lieut. TRAPNELL (sick in England) struck off strength on authority A.G. $\frac{4}{778}$ of 29.9.15. – 3 men to F.A. and 2 men returned from F.A. Strength 27 Officers and 780 O.R. J.C.	
5.10.15 " "	Battalion in the Trenches. Firing at "Stand to" both night and morning has been increasingly lively though there is no apparent reason. Patrol from our Trench BATAILLE reached German wire just to left of Trench SANS NOM, where it was challenged by German listening post. Thence it worked to the left across front of GOMMECOURT Wood & returned by right hand listening post of 6/Glouc. Regt. C Coy relieve A Coy. and B Coy relieve D Company in the Trenches. A Coy to [illegible] and D Coy to the KEEP – 1 man of A Coy. to [illegible]	

(73989) W4141—463. 400,000. 9/14. H.&J.Ltd. Forms/C. 2118/10.

Instructions regarding War Diaries and Intelligence Summaries are contained in F. S. Regs., Part II. and the Staff Manual respectively. Title pages will be prepared in manuscript.

WAR DIARY
or
INTELLIGENCE SUMMARY.
(Erase heading not required.)

Army Form C. 2118.

Hour, Date, Place	Summary of Events and Information	Remarks and references to Appendices
5.10.15. HEBOTERNE	Battalion in the Trenches – 1 man of A Coy to Control post ST LEGER vice 1 man sent to Hospital – 2 men to Corps H.Q. 5 men to Field Ambulance – Strength 27 Officers and 780 O.R.	
6.10.15 " "	Battalion in the Trenches. Night 5–6th slightly foggy. – New disposition of Companies – front line being more thinly held. We have now only four platoons in our front line – 2 platoons from each of the two Coys. in the line – Remaining two platoons of each Coy. in Battn Reserve line i.e. the outer defences of HEBOTERNE. Day quiet, but at 8.0 pm. the Germans opened rapid fire and machine guns, chiefly from the direction of GOMMECOURT, which continued for about 15 mins – There was no apparent reason for this – but the Germans were seen to first send up two green lights and the firing ended by their sending up one red light – the same procedure and firing was again opened at 8.30 pm and 9.0 pm. for 15 mins accompanied by some shelling – at 10.15 pm. our Howitzers fired several rounds on the German front line and we opened rapid fire – Total Casualties 9 men wounded – 1 man returned from F.A. and 3 men sent to Field Amb.ce + 4 men to C.C.S. Strength 27 Officers + 776 O.R. J.C.T.	
7.10.15 " "	Battalion in the Trenches – Night of 6.10.15 – 7.10.15 all quiet after 10.15 pm – Very foggy weather at Stand to and Coys. stood down about 6.0 a.m. Fine day – G.O.C. 48th Division had interview with C.O. at Battn H.Q. at 9.30 A.M. – A Coy found 67 men for R.E. fatigues for 8 hours during daytime on B. Coy. H.Q. & 24 men for carrying – Lieut. SELLMAN returned from M.G. Course. 4 men of C. Coy and 8 men of B. Coy all wounded to F.A. and 3 men sick to F.A. Strength 27 Officers + 767 O.R. J.C.T.	
8.10.15 " "	Battalion in Trenches. Night 7/8th very quiet. Day fine & quiet. but about 6.0 pm. several heavy torpedoes were fired by Germans on the Warwick trenches to our left. Several of our heavy guns replied. A Reinforcement of 2/Lieut. THIPPEN and 30 O.R. arrived at 12.15 A.M. from No 1. Entrenching Battalion. – 1 man to No 4 C.C.S. – 5 men to No 9 C.C.S. – 5 men to F.A. and 1 man returned from F.A. Strength 28 Officers + 791 O.R. J.C.T.	

Instructions regarding War Diaries and Intelligence Summaries are contained in F. S. Regs., Part II. and the Staff Manual respectively. Title pages will be prepared in manuscript.

WAR DIARY
or
INTELLIGENCE SUMMARY.
(Erase heading not required.)

Army Form C. 2118.

Hour, Date, Place	Summary of Events and Information	Remarks and references to Appendices
9.10.15. HEBOTERNE	Battalion in Trenches - Night 8/9th quiet. - day fine & normal. Col. [illegible] O.C. 4/R. [illegible] met O.C. at Trench H.Q. to discuss relief on the 11th inst. and new dispositions. 2 men to M.G. Course. 2 men to No 4. C.C.S. 3 men to F.A. - 1 man returned from F.A. 2/LIEUT. REED arrived from 1st Entrenching Battalion. Strength 29. Officers and 789. O.R. [initials]	
10.10.15. " "	Battalion in Trenches. Night 9/10th quiet. Orders for relief [illegible] detailed to Coy. Officers. - Pte. EVANS replaces Pte. HEAVEN on Control post at St. LEGER. - A patrol under LIEUT. WOOKEY and 2/LIEUT. HOLLAND left HOCHE trench at 8.15 pm and returned at 11.45 pm. They pulled up posts which the Germans had erected ready to receive wire & bombed the German wiring party when it approached. They then worked towards Gommecourt and bombed a German listening post and returned without casualty. - 1 man to No 19. C.C.S. - 2/LIEUT. ANDERSON and 2 men to F.A. & 1 man returned from F.A. & 2 O.R. from C.C.S. Strength 29. Officers & 790. O.R. [initials]	
11.10.15. " "	Battalion in Trenches. - Night of 10/11th quiet. There was rather more firing by Germans at Stand to than usual this morning. - Battn. relieved in Trenches by 4/Royal Berks. relief completed without casualty and Battn. all present in billets in AOTHIE by 5.10 pm. Coys. had dinners on way back at point 126 between SAILLY and COIGNEUX. - A Maxim gun has been [illegible] at E end of village to fire on hostile aeroplanes. 2/LIEUT. REED is posted to A. Coy. - 2 men to No 19. C.C.S. 1 man to No 4. C.C.S. - 2 men returned from F.Amb. Strength 29. Off. & 787. O.R. [initials]	
12.10.15. AOTHIE	Battalion in Reserve at AOTHIE. - O.C. inspected draft at 10.30 AM. and M.O. inspected them at same time. - draft deficient of several articles of kit. - Capt. TILLY, LIEUT. SMITH and 2/LIEUT. CORNISH joined the Battn. from ENGLAND. Capt. TILLY takes over Command & [illegible] of D. Coy. - LIEUT. SMITH posted to B. Coy and 2/LIEUT. CORNISH to C. Coy. 2 men to C.C.S. 3 men to F.Amb. and 2 men returned from F.A. Strength 32. Off. and 785 O.R. [initials]	

Instructions regarding War Diaries and Intelligence Summaries are contained in F. S. Regs., Part II. and the Staff Manual respectively. Title pages will be prepared in manuscript.

or

INTELLIGENCE SUMMARY

(Erase heading not required.)

Hour, Date, Place	Summary of Events and Information	Remarks and references to Appendices
13.10.15. AUTHIE	Battalion in Reserve at AUTHIE. Route March via AUTHIE - Road south of Bois de WARNIMONT - BUS road junction J.31.9.01 - LOUVENCOURT - Cross Road J.27 b 6.9 - AUTHIE. Head at LOUVENCOURT by 12 noon. Met the Brigadier & Staff at LOUVENCOURT and practised attack from that place towards AUTHIE with surprise incidents during same - Batt. Baths allotted to C. Coy. 1 man to No 4. C.C.S., 5 men to F. Amb. and 1 man returned from F. Amb. Strength 32 Off. + 785. O.R. J.T.	
14.10.15. " "	Battalion in Reserve. A.B & C Coys provide 100 men each for R.E. and Corps working parties. D. Coy paraded in high ground S. of AUTHIE from 9.30 AM - 12.30 PM. - Officers M.G. course (8 Battalions) under Capt. WADE and also Reserve M.G. section. Batt. Snipers firing on range and 8/Wacs. Snipers paraded with them for instruction, under Capt. GUETERBOCK. - Bombing Class under LIEUT. FISHER, with Corpl HOUGHTON and Pte LANGFORD as assistant instructors - C.O. and Capt. GUETERBOCK on F.G.C.M. at BUS at 10.0 AM - 4 special leave to ENGLAND awarded to Batt. by G.O.C. 48th Division for Sniping work and appearance of B. Coy. on March back from trenches on the 11th inst. Batt. Baths allotted to D. Coy. - 4 men to F. Amb. Strength 32. Off. and 785. O.R. J.T.	
15.10.15. " "	Battalion in Reserve. - B. C & D Coys on Corps & R.E. working parties. A. Coy paraded on high ground S. of AUTHIE 9.30 AM to 12.30 pm. - Grenadiers, M.G. Class & Reserve Section and Snipers as yesterday. Batt. Baths allotted to A. Coy & Transport Section - 8 men sent to 3rd Field Coy. R.E. as Carpenters. 25 N.C.Os + men arrived as reinforcement from 2/1 Entrenching Bn - 2 men to C.C.S. 3 men to F. Amb & 1 man returned from C.C.S and 2 from F.A. Strength 32 Off., 809. O.R. of whom 29. Off and 748 O.R. are with the Batt. - 2 Off. + 21 O.R. are in Amb. or Hospital and 1 Off. and 40. O.R. are on Command. J.T.	
16.10.15. " "	Battalion in Reserve. C. D. + A. Coys provided working parties as before. B. Coy paraded as above with dummy cartridges & sticks for bombing practice. Draft inspected by Major THOMPSON and M.O. at 9.30 AM. - Clothes in bad condition - Several deficiencies in cap badges & shoulder Titles and general physique poor, with few exceptions - Colonel DAVENPORT and LIEUT. POLACK and 9 O.R. went on leave to ENGLAND - 3 men to F. Amb. - 2/LIEUT. ANDERSON & 1 man returned from C.C.S. Strength 32. Off. and 810. O.R. J.T.	

1247 W 3299 200,000 (E) 8/14 J.B.C. & A. Forms/C. 2118/11.

Instructions regarding War Diaries and Intelligence Summaries are contained in F. S. Regs., Part II. and the Staff Manual respectively. Title pages will be prepared in manuscript.

or

INTELLIGENCE SUMMARY

(Erase heading not required.)

Hour, Date, Place	Summary of Events and Information	Remarks and references to Appendices
17.10.15. AUTHIE	Battalion in Reserve. – Voluntary Celebration of Holy Communion at 7.30 A.M. – Divine Service at [illegible] at 9.30 A.M. at which Artillery [illegible] Col. attended. D. A + B. Coys. finding Corps + R.E. fatigues. Major THOMPSON, Capt TILLY, GOETERBOCK and LEWIS visited HEBUTERNE leaving AUTHIE at 10.30 A.M. to arrange relief for the 19th inst. with the 4/Royal Berks. 4 men go on leave to ENGLAND on Special leave granted by G.O.C. Division for Sniping + Marching work. – Major R.I. RAWSON returned to Battn from Command and 2/Lieut. ANDERSON returned from C.C.S. 2 Men returned from F. Amb. 2 Men to C.C.S. and 3 men to Field Ambce. – Practice Alarm under Brigade Arrangements. Times as follows, viz: Practice Alarm message recd at 5.40 pm. – Ready to move with 1st line Transport at 6.5 pm. Moved by order from Brigade at 6.17 pm. to point 146 on St LEGER – BUS road – arrived destination at 7.0 pm. – returned to Billets at 8.0 pm. Strength 32 Off. and 808. O.R. [initials]	
18.10.15. " "	Battalion in Reserve. A.B.+C. Coys on Corps and R.E. fatigues. D. Coy paraded 9.30–12.30 as programme of B. Coy on 16.10.15. – other parades as on [illegible]. Divisional Sniping Class under Capt. HESKETH – PRICHARD – G.H.Q. – is training on Sniper Range near AUTHIE. 6 Men to F. Amb. + 1 man returned from F.A. Strength 32 Officers + 808. O.R. [initials]	
19.10.15 HEBUTERNE	Battalion relieved 4/Royal Berks. Regt in the Trenches. Coys left AUTHIE as follows – A. Coy at 7.30 A.M. D. Coy at 7.45. A.M. C. Coy at 8.0 A.M. and B. Coy at 8.15. A.M. – M.G. Section + Transport 8.30 A.M. Relief completed without casualty at 11.55 A.M. – Dispositions A Coy on right of line, B. on left. C. in Batt. Reserve and D in Brigade Reserve in KEEP. – On taking over trenches found that JENA trench required considerable repair owing to heavy shelling on it on afternoon of 18.10.15 – which trench very badly damaged. Berks had worked hard on it, but a great deal remains to be done. – at 9.0 pm. Germans fired three shells on GUDIN and JENA killing one of our Men + wounding another who were working on the repairs. – H.Q. and A. Coy. of 9/Royal Irish Fusiliers attached to us for instruction. 1 Man to No 4. C.C.S. + 1 Man to F. Amb. – 8 Carpenters returned from 3rd Field Coy. R.E. – Strength 32. Officers and 807 O.R. [initials]	
20.10.15 " "	Battalion in the Trenches. Night 19–20 quiet. – Hard at work on repairs to JENA but a lot more to be done on parapets + Shelters. – Major R.I. RAWSON left to take over Command of 1/6 A.+S. Highlanders. Major THOMPSON had interview at 10.30 A.M. with G.O.C. 48 (S.M.) DIVISION in HEBUTERNE. – 1 Man killed in action – No 2397 Pte HAMMOND and 1 man wounded – No 2296 Pte [illegible]. 2 Men to No 19. C.C.S. 1 Man to	

Instructions regarding War Diaries and Intelligence Summaries are contained in F. S. Regs., Part II. and the Staff Manual respectively. Title pages will be prepared in manuscript.

WAR DIARY
or
INTELLIGENCE SUMMARY.
(*Erase heading not required.*)

Army Form C. 2118.

Hour, Date, Place	Summary of Events and Information	Remarks and references to Appendices
20.10.15. HEBUTERNE	1 man to No 4. C.C.S. - 2 men to F. Amb. and 2 men returned from F. Amb. Strength 31 Officers and 802 O.R. [initials]	
21.10.15 " "	Battalion in the Trenches - Night 20-21 quiet and very bright. Work on TENA [illegible] proceeding and wire repaired and renewed - Most of the wooden posts were destroyed but wire itself not badly damaged. 2 platoons of 9/R.I.F. [illegible] their own line. Major THOMSON [illegible] R.E. Officer in BRICKFIELDS trench and heard their suggestions for new Right Coy. [illegible] and approved subject to certain alterations as to position. New [illegible] and plans of all trenches [illegible] started. 1 man to No 19. C.C.S. 4 men to F. Amb. & 1 man returned from F. Amb. - Head Quarters of LEFT Company in line moved down to shelter in MASSENA. Work proceeding on new Headquarters for both Companies and new shelter at Batt. H.d Quarters. Strength 31 Off. + 801 O.R. [initials]	
22.10.15. " "	Battalion in the Trenches - Night 21-22 quiet. Disposition as on previous day. Two men to C.C.S. Strength 31 offs 797	
23.10.15 "	Battalion in the Trenches. Night very bright and clear and no wind. The enemy opposite our section did not appear to do much work but were much noisier than they have been since we came to the section and were shouting and singing. In the afternoon our artillery fired heavily on enemy 1st & 2nd line trenches between PUISIEUX - HEBUTERNE and SERRE - HEBUTERNE road and also on enemy trench just S. of GOMMECOURT WOOD. Enemy artillery did not reply. Two officers and 13 men go on leave. Strength 31 offs 797. C & B Coys relieve A and D Coys in front line	
24.10.15 "	Battalion in the trenches. Night foggy at first and then clear. Our artillery fired intermittently on damaged portion of enemy's trenches and machine guns also fired. One man to C.C.S. Strength 31 offs 796	

Instructions regarding War Diaries and Intelligence Summaries are contained in F. S. Regs., Part II. and the Staff Manual respectively. Title pages will be prepared in manuscript.

WAR DIARY
or
INTELLIGENCE SUMMARY.
(Erase heading not required.)

Army Form C. 2118.

Hour, Date, Place	Summary of Events and Information	Remarks and references to Appendices
25·10·15 HEBUTERNE	Battalion in trenches. Night 24–25 very wet and work hindered. Enemy quiet. 2 officers and 13 men back from leave. Strength 31 offrs 796	
26·10·15 "	Battalion in trenches. Night 25–26 very wet and strong east wind. Work hindered by the weather. In some places the sides of the commun[n] trenches which are not revetted are begging to fall in. Enemy were very quiet. 3 men to C.C.S. Strength 31 offrs 793	
27·10·15 AUTHIE.	Battalion relieved by 4 Royal Berks regt. Relief commenced about 11 am. Companies had dinners on way back to billets. Battalion all present in billets at 5 pm and relief was carried out without casualty. Strength 31 offrs 793	
28·10·15 "	Battalion in divisional reserve. Company kit inspections. Baths for A and B coys. Men were issued with winter clothing including fur-coats, makintosh capes and lin pan gloves – all of very good quality. Strength 31 offrs. 793	
29·10·15 "	Battalion in divisional reserve. Route march AUTHIE – ST. LEGER – COIGNEUX – Road junction J 10 c.12 – BUS. Roads very bad. Bn returned to billets by 1 pm. Baths for B&C coys. Major Thompson Capt Slade and 15 men go on leave. CAPT GUETERBOCK acts as second in command during Major Thompson's absence	

Instructions regarding War Diaries and Intelligence Summaries are contained in F. S. Regs., Part II. and the Staff Manual respectively. Title pages will be prepared in manuscript.

WAR DIARY
or
INTELLIGENCE SUMMARY.
(Erase heading not required.)

Hour, Date, Place	Summary of Events and Information	Remarks and references to Appendices
30.10.15 AUTHIE	Battalion in divisional reserve. A, B, C & D Coys each find 100 men for working parties. 3 men per platoon parade for Bn Grenadier Course. Bn sappers, reserve machine gun & officers machine gun class parade 9am. 2/Lieut Andrews goes to WISQUES for machine gun course. Pte Cox with pigeon flying corps taken off strength. Pte Hampton to base time expired. Strength 31 offrs 792	
31.10.15 "	Battalion in divisional reserve. No working parties found. Parades cancelled owing to weather. Men on Bde grenade course replaced by new class. 2 offrs and 9 men return from leave. Strength 31 offrs 792.	

(73989) W4141—463. 400,000. 9/14. H.&J.Ltd. Forms/C. 2118/10.

144th Inf. Bde.
48th Div.

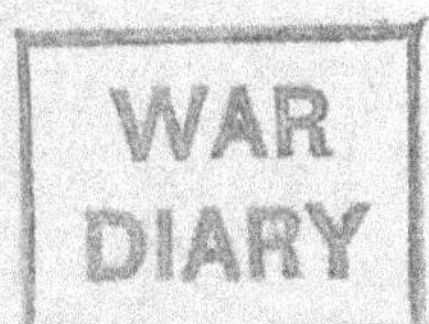

1/4th BATTN. THE GLOUCESTERSHIRE REGIMENT.

N O V E M B E R

1 9 1 5

Instructions regarding War Diaries and Intelligence Summaries are contained in F. S. Regs., Part II. and the Staff Manual respectively. Title pages will be prepared in manuscript.

WAR DIARY
or
INTELLIGENCE SUMMARY.
(Erase heading not required.)

Army Form C. 2118.

Hour, Date, Place	Summary of Events and Information	Remarks and references to Appendices
31.10.15. AOTHIE	Battalion in Divisional RESERVE – No working parties found – Parades cancelled owing to weather – Mm on Bdge. Grenade Course replaced by new class – 2 officers and 9 men return from leave – 3 men to No. 4. C.C.S and 2 men to F. amb. Strength 31. officers and 792. o.R. [initials] Battalion played Rugby Football Match against 6/Glouc. Regt. and won 6–3–	
1.11.15 ..	Battalion in Reserve – A.B.C and D Coys. provided 400 men for WORKING parties – Brigade Grenade Course paraded under Lieut. FISHER – 68 snipers per Coy. paraded under Capt. GOETERBOCK and Reserve M. Gunners under Capt. WADE and Officers M.G. Class also under Capt. WADE – FUMIGATOR allotted to the Battalion – 4. Men return from leave – 1 man to F.A. and 1 man returned from F.A. – Capt. C.C.S. TILLY to C.C.S. +1 man returned from C.C.S. – Strength 31. officers + 792. o.R. [initials]	
2.11.15 ..	Battalion in Reserve – Weather very wet – Bombers, Snipers, Reserve M.G and Officers M.G. Course parade as usual. – C.O inspected Companies in full Marching Order – Lieut. WALFORD returned from leave – 2 men to F. Amb. – Strength 31. officers and 792. o.R. [initials]	
3.11.15 ..	Battalion in Reserve – G.O.C. 48th Division called & saw C.O. – Orders for Relief tomorrow detailed to Company Commanders. A.B.C.+D Coys. provide 100 men each for Working parties – Bn. Grenadier class, Snipers, Officers M.G. Class and reserve M.G. section paraded as usual. 1 man returned from C.C.S. 2 men to C.C.S. and 3 men returned from Field Amb. – Strength 31. officers & 791. o.R. [initials]	
4.11.15 HEBUTERNE	Battalion relieved 4/Royal Berks Regt. in Trenches – Coys. left billets in following order – viz. A Coy at 8.0 A.M. D Coy. 8.15, C Coy 8.30 + B. Coy 8.45 A.M. – Transport and M.G's at 8.45 A.M. – Relief completed without Casualties at 1.0 pm. – Draft of 25 men including Sergt. WILSON arrived from Base – 5 Carpenters from R.E. at ROSSIGNOL FARM rejoined the Battalion – 1 man to C.C.S. and 7 men to F.A.s 1 man returned from F.A. – Strength 31. officers and 815. o.R. [initials]	
5.11.15 ...	Battalion in the Trenches – Night of 4th–5th fine but misty from early in morning till about 9. a.m. Enemy quiet and situation normal – Draft inspected by C.O and M.O. – two of them [illegible] to Field Ambulance. 1 man to C.C.S and 7 men returned from C.C.S 2 men to F. Amb. – Strength 31 officers and 815. o.R.	
6.11.15 ..	Battalion in the Trenches – Night 5–6th quiet and fine – Very misty during the day [initials] – consequently no observation was possible – G.O.C. 48th Division went round Trenches with the C.O.–	

(73989) W4141—463. 400,000. 9/14. H.&J.Ltd. Forms/C. 2118/10.

Instructions regarding War Diaries and Intelligence Summaries are contained in F. S. Regs., Part II. and the Staff Manual respectively. Title pages will be prepared in manuscript.

WAR DIARY
or
INTELLIGENCE SUMMARY.
(Erase heading not required.)

Army Form C. 2118.

Hour, Date, Place	Summary of Events and Information	Remarks and references to Appendices
6.11.15. HEBUTERNE	1 man to C.C.S. 1 man to No 19 C.C.S. and 1 man to No 4 C.C.S. 5 men to Field Ambulance and 3 men returned from Field Ambulance. Strength 31 Officers and 812 O.R. - 2 off. + 22 [illegible] C.T.	
7.11.15 . .	Battalion in the Trenches - Night 6-7 was quiet but much colder. Day fine. Brigadier went round the trenches with C.O. in the morning. Work as usual on trenches and new Company Headquarters; and new dugouts in Brickfield Trench - 2 men to No 4 C.C.S. 2 men to Field Ambulance 4 men returned from Field Ambulance + 1 from C.C.S. Strength 31 Officers + 811 O.R. 1 Officer and 14 O.R. returned from leave - LIEUT. NEWTH granted special leave of absence to ENGLAND in connection with award to him of MILITARY CROSS, and D.C.M. to 857 Sergt. A.L. WALFORD and 2881 Pte. H. GOULD vide Brigade Orders No 879. d/d 5/11/15 - 1 Officer and 14 men returned from leave. C.T.	
8.11.15 . . .	Battalion in the Trenches - Night 7-8 fine + quiet - day fine - work proceeding on trenches and shelters and working parties for R.E. - 1 man back from leave. 3 men to C.C.S. No 29, 5 men to Field Ambce and also 2/LIEUT. REED - 1 man returned from C.C.S and 4 men from Field Ambulance. Strength - 31 Officers and 809 O.R. C.T.	
9.11.15 . .	Battalion in the Trenches - Night 8-9 rather dull weather + quiet - at 7.5 AM. Germans fired a shell into HEBUTERNE and at 12 noon several shells - mostly shrapnel which fell between the Church + the pond - damaging one house near pond. 1 Officer returned from leave - 1 man to C.C.S. and 2 men to Field Ambulance - 1 man returned from C.C.S. Strength 31 Officers + 809 O.R. C.T.	
10.11.15 . . .	Battalion in the Trenches. Very heavy rain and high wind all night 9-10 and rain continued nearly all day - Trenches and dugouts flooded - all available men at work on drainage and repair of shelters. 2/LIEUT. BRIGGS rejoined from Flying Corps - 2/LIEUT. HANKINS attached to 2nd SEAFORTH HIGHLANDERS for training as Adjutant - No 3082 C.S.M. STONE of B Coy. to Base for 2 months duty as Instructor - 2/LIEUT. REED and 1 man to No 4 C.C.S. 4 men to Field Ambulance. 1 man returned from Field Ambulance - No 3157 Pte. BLAKE - tunnelling Coy killed in action. Strength - 32 Officers + 806 O.R.	
11.11.15 . . .	Battalion in the Trenches. Night 10-11 quiet and very wet and dark - work going on to repair damage caused by rain - but hampered sadly by lack of revetting material, Strength [illegible]	

(73989) W4141—463. 400,000. 9/14. H.&J.Ltd. Forms/C. 2118/10.

Instructions regarding War Diaries and Intelligence Summaries are contained in F. S. Regs., Part II. and the Staff Manual respectively. Title pages will be prepared in manuscript.

WAR DIARY
or
INTELLIGENCE SUMMARY.
(*Erase heading not required.*)

Army Form C. 2118.

Hour, Date, Place	Summary of Events and Information	Remarks and references to Appendices
11.11.15. HEBUTERNE	2 men to Field Ambulance – Strength 32. Officers and 806. O.R. H.T.	
12.11.15 . .	Battalion in the Trenches – Night 11–12 very dark, wet and very high wind – Trenches still in a bad state in spite of work done during past week and not possible to prevent this with men & material available. The German trenches appear to be worse than ours from the fact that enemy came out on top of parapet to bail out water – three of them were shot by us this morning while they were so employed – Battalion relieved in the Trenches by 4/Royal Berks. Regt. – Relief completed in rain, without casualty from enemy by 1.0 pm. but three men accidentally injured by falling tree in HEBUTERNE. Battalion reached billets at AUTHIE by 3.30 pm. 3 men to No. 4. C.C.S. – 4 men to Field Ambulance (including three injured by tree) – 1 man returned from Field Ambulance – Strength 32. Officers and 803. O.R. H.T.	
13.11.15. AUTHIE	Battalion in Reserve at AUTHIE – Kit inspection for all Companies and inspection of billets as usual – B and C Companies had Baths – 1 man to No. 19. C.C.S. – 2 men to Field Ambulance – 3 men returned from Field Ambulance – Strength 32. Officers and 802. O.R. H.T.	
14.11.15 . .	Battalion in Reserve – Church parade at 10.0 A.M. for those men not on fatigues – Voluntary Service of Holy Communion afterwards in Orderly Room – A.B.C.D. Companies find 100 men each for R.E. & Corps Working parties – Rugby football match at 2.30 pm against 6/Glouc. Regt. – We won by 2 pts to nil – 2/LIEUT: R.H. DOWN goes to FLIXECOURT for course – 2 men to No. 4. C.C.S. – 2 men to Field Ambulance – 1 man returned from C.C.S. & 3 men from Field Ambulance – Strength 32. Officers and 791 O.R. – H.Q. details had Baths – H.T.	
15.11.15 . .	Battalion in Reserve – Battalion paraded with first line transport for route march at 9.30 am. route – AUTHIE – VAUCHELLES – BUS – AUTHIE – reached AUTHIE at 1.0 pm – Inspected by Brigadier General at Bus – 1 man to No. 4. C.C.S. – 6 men to Field Ambulance – 5 men returned from Field Ambulance. 2 Officers and 22 O.R. return from leave – Strength 32. Officers and 790 O.R. – C and D Coys had Baths – H.T.	
16.11.15 . .	Battalion in Reserve – A.B. C and D Coys find 100 men each for Corps. and R.E. Working Parties – Heavy fall of snow during night 15–16th – Reserve M.G. section paraded at 9.0 am under Capt. WADE – Snipers paraded under Capt. GUFTERBOCK – and 2 men per platoon, as Battalion Bombing Class, under LIEUT: FISHER also at 9.0 A.M. for instruction – and Stretcher Bearers at 10.0 AM under M.O at Medical Inspection Room – a Board, composed of Capt. W. LEWIS as President and	

(73989) W4141—463. 400,000. 9/14. H.&J.Ltd. Forms/C. 2118/10.

Instructions regarding War Diaries and Intelligence Summaries are contained in F. S. Regs., Part II. and the Staff Manual respectively. Title pages will be prepared in manuscript.

WAR DIARY
or
INTELLIGENCE SUMMARY.
(Erase heading not required.)

Army Form C. 2118.

Hour, Date, Place	Summary of Events and Information	Remarks and references to Appendices
16.11.15. ~~HEBUTERNE~~ AUTHIE	and 2/LIEUT: E.J. CORNISH and 2/LIEUT. F.H. SMITH assembled at Orderly Room at 10.30 A.M. to enquire into injuries received by 3 men of C Company – owing to fall of tree tops when coming out of the trenches at HEBUTERNE on the 12th inst. – 3 men per Company paraded at 3.30 pm. for Brigade Grenade Class – 2/LIEUT: ANDREWS returns from M.G. Course. 1 Officer returns from hospital. 4 men to Field Ambulance – 1 man returned from C.C.S. Strength 32 Officers and 791 O.R.	
17.11.15 . . .	Battalion in Reserve – C.O. inspected all Companies and Hd Qrs details in full Marching Order on Coy parade grounds. Battalion Grenadier Class, Reserve M.G. Section and Snipers paraded as yesterday. Brigade Grenade Class remains at COUIN and original members return to Battalion – A and D. Companies had baths – 2 men to No 4. C.C.S. – 1 man to No 19. C.C.S. – 3 men to Field Ambulance – 3 men returned from C.C.S. and 2 men from Field Ambulance – Strength. 32. Officers and 791. O.R.	
18.11.15 . . .	Battalion in Reserve – A.B.C and D Companies provide 100 men each for Corps and R.E. working parties – Battalion Grenadier Class, Snipers and Reserve M.G. Section paraded as yesterday – Lecture to Companies by M.O. and instruction in use and adjustment of tube smoke helmets and inspection of those in possession – Baths for those men not on fatigue – 1. Officer – and 14 men proceeded on leave to ENGLAND. – Capt CASTLE takes over Command and payment of D. Coy: from this date. 1 man to No 4. C.C.S. 2 men to No 19 C.C.S. and 1 man to Field Ambulance. Strength 32. Officers and 798. O.R.	
19.11.15 . . .	Battalion in Reserve – Company Commanders instructed by C.O. as to details of relief tomorrow of 4/Royal Berks in the trenches tomorrow – Battn Grenadiers, Snipers, and Reserve M.G. Section paraded as usual – 1 Officer and 14 men returned from Brigade Grenade School. 7 Carpenters returned from R.E. Field Company at ROSSIGNAL FARM (1 to hospital out of original 8). 1. Officer and 32 men go on leave – LIEUT: NEWTH gazetted Tempy Captain from 2.10.15 – 4 men to Field Amb., + 4 men returned from Field Amb. + 1 man from C.C.S. Strength 32 Officers and 789 O.R.	
20.11.15 HEBUTERNE	Battalion relieved 4/Royal Berks Regt in the trenches – Relief of our Battn made later than usual as 4th DIVISION had arranged Bombardment of German line and 7/Worcesters, on our right, were therefore allowed to go in earlier – Companies left AUTHIE in following order – A. Coy at 11.0 A.M. D. Coy at 11.15, C. Coy at 11.30 A.M., and B. Coy at 11.45 A.M. Relief completed, without Casualty by 3.30 pm. Transport left AUTHIE at 3.0 pm. – Dispositions in Line – A Company occupy right trenches – 1 Company 13/R. Irish Rifles (attached for instruction) occupy left of line – D and C Companies in reserve, B. Coy in Keep. Major THOMPSON in Command of KEEP – 1 Company and Battn Hd Qrs 13th Royal Irish Rifles attached	

(73989) W4141—463. 400,000. 9/14. H.&J.Ltd. Forms/C. 2118/10.

Instructions regarding War Diaries and Intelligence Summaries are contained in F. S. Regs., Part II. and the Staff Manual respectively. Title pages will be prepared in manuscript.

WAR DIARY
or
INTELLIGENCE SUMMARY.
(*Erase heading not required.*)

Army Form C. 2118.

Hour, Date, Place	Summary of Events and Information	Remarks and references to Appendices
20.11.15 HEBOTERNE	attached to our Battalion for instruction – The line on our immediate Divisional Right is held by the IV DIVISION and on our Battalion right by the 8th Worcesters with 7th Worcesters on their right – our immediate Divisional left is held by the ~~6th Gloucester Regt~~ XXXVII DIVISION and our Battalion left by the 6th Glouc. Regt. – 2/LIEUT: STEGER joined the Batt. from No 1 ENTRENCHING Batt. – 2 men from M.G. course for m days to WISQUES – 2 men to C.C.S. – 3 men to Field Amb. – 2 men returned from Field Amb. – Strength 33 Officers and 786. O.R. J.G.T.	
21.11.15 . . .	Battalion in the Trenches – Night of 20/21 Quiet – C.O. went round the Trenches at 10.30 p.m. – Field Artillery and Howitzers carry out pre-arranged bombardment of German Trenches at 3.0 p.m. Patrol of 15 men of 18/R.I.R. went out under 2/LIEUT. HOLLAND, of our Batt., at 7.45 p.m. and returned about 9.0 p.m. – 2/LIEUT: CRUMP gazetted LIEUT: from 5.10.15 – 3 men to No 4. C.C.S. 4 men to Field Amb. 1 man returned from C.C.S. Strength 33. Officers and 785. O.R. Work as usual on line. J.G.T.	
22.11.15 . . .	Battalion in the Trenches. Night 21/22 fine and Quiet – heavy fog in early morning – this fog continued all day enabling men to work on parapets and on wire – Work on trenches, cutting back berms and emptying sumps & repairing covers – Building new shelter in Brickfield trench and Ramsand and new left Company Hd. Quarters in Brian and revetting sides of trenches – Observation of enemy's lines impossible on account of the fog – 4 men to Field Ambulance – 1 man returned from Field Amb. Strength 33 Officers and 784. O.R. J.G.T.	
23.11.15 . . .	Battalion in the Trenches – Night 22/23 Quiet and fine but foggy – fog continued during early morning but lifted very suddenly at 11.0 a.m. and 2 men were wounded and 1 killed by German rifle fire while being brought in from wiring party – Work on trenches as usual. Brigadier went round trenches with C.O. in the morning – 1 man killed and 2 wounded – 3 men to Field Ambulance, 2 men to C.C.S. 1 man returned from Field Amb. – Strength 33. Officers and 778 O.R. Weather very cold – J.G.T.	
24.11.15 . . .	Battalion in the Trenches – Night 23/24. Quiet and some rain – weather rather warmer – the enemy shelled IV Division front at 7.0 a.m. to which our Artillery made some reply – our artillery was active during the whole day, especially in the afternoon – work on our trenches and shelters as before – 1 man wounded in action – 4 men to C.C.S. 2 men to Field Amb. 1 man returned from C.C.S. Strength 33. Officers and 773. O.R. J.G.T.	

(73989) W4141—463. 400,000. 9/14. H.&J.Ltd. Forms/C. 2118/10.

Instructions regarding War Diaries and Intelligence Summaries are contained in F. S. Regs., Part II. and the Staff Manual respectively. Title pages will be prepared in manuscript.

WAR DIARY
or
INTELLIGENCE SUMMARY.
(*Erase heading not required.*)

Army Form C. 2118.

Hour, Date, Place	Summary of Events and Information	Remarks and references to Appendices
25.11.15. HEBUTERNE	Battalion in the Trenches – Night 24/25 very cold but quiet – foggy in early morning but the mist lifted early – Work on trenches as usual – During afternoon our Artillery bombarded S.E. Corner of GOMMECOURT WOOD and CHEMIN CREUX making very good shooting on the Wood. 1 Man to C.C.S. LIEUT. E. WOOKEY and 1 O.R. to Field Ambulance & 1 Man from Field Ambulance – Strength 33 Officers and 772 O.R. – R.I. Rifles left HEBUTERNE. J.C.T.	
26.11.15 . . .	Battalion in the Trenches – Night 25/26 fine, dry & very cold with bright moonlight at intervals – Successful enterprise carried out on our left by 6. Glouc. Regt. when 2 parties of 25 men each and an Officer, entered enemy's trench at pt. on either side of S.E. Corner of GOMMECOURT WOOD. Our Artillery formed a barrage of fire around the Corner – Several Germans were bombed and shot in the trench and shelters and one prisoner (wounded) was brought back to 6/Glouc. Lines. The parties returned covered by our Artillery – Our Machine Guns were ordered, if necessary, to support the Glosters. Work on trenches, shelters and communication trenches as usual during the day. Sergt. NICHOLLS goes on M.G. Course for instruction in use of Lewis Gun. 1 Man to Field Amb.ce, Sergt. SHIPWAY to England and off Strength – Strength 33. Officers and 771. O.R. J.C.T.	
27.11.15 . . .	Battalion in the Trenches – Night 26/27th very cold with hard frost but quiet – Work during day on trenches, shelters &c as usual – Draft of 1 Officer and 35. O.R. arrived from No. 1. Entrenching Battalion – 1 Officer and 14 men returned from leave and 2 Officers and 32 men go on leave to England – 1 Man to C.C.S. & 1 Man returned from C.C.S. 1 Man to Field Ambulance – Strength 33 Officers and 806. O.R. J.C.T.	
28.11.15 . . .	Battalion in the Trenches – Night of the 27/28th fine but very cold with hard frost. Very disturbed by enemy's fire. Very heavy Machine Gun and Rifle fire beginning at about 11.0 pm with very heavy shelling of our trenches, rear trenches and villages with small & heavy shells from 1.0 AM to 3.0 AM – No casualties except one man very slightly wounded by splinter – and very little damage done & that chiefly to wire – Battalion relieved in the trenches by 4/Royal Berks Regt. – relief began at 12.30 noon and Battalion all present in Billets at AUTHIE at 5.0 pm – without casualty. 4 Men to Divisional Band, 1 Man to C.C.S. and 1 Man to Field Ambulance. 2 men returned from C.C.S. and LIEUT. WOOKEY and 1 man returned from Fd. Amb.ce – Strength 33 Officers and 807 O.R. J.C.T.	

(73989) W4141—463. 400,000. 9/14. H.&J.Ltd. Forms/C. 2118/10.

Instructions regarding War Diaries and Intelligence Summaries are contained in F. S. Regs., Part II. and the Staff Manual respectively. Title pages will be prepared in manuscript.

WAR DIARY
or
INTELLIGENCE SUMMARY.
(*Erase heading not required.*)

Army Form C. 2118.

Hour, Date, Place	Summary of Events and Information	Remarks and references to Appendices
29.11.15. AUTHIE.	Battalion in Reserve at AUTHIE. Companies had free day for inspection of kits, billets etc by Company Commanders - Billets inspected by Major THOMPSON. 2/LIEUT. SYMES and 14 O.R. at Brigade Grenadier Course at COUIN. 1 Officer and 30 men return from leave. LIEUT. BIRD joined Battalion on 28th from 3/4 Battn on the 28th inst. He is posted to C. Coy. and reverts to 2/LIEUT on posting. 2 men to Field Ambulance and 2 men returned from Field Ambulance - very wet day - Strength 34 Officers and 807 O.R. J.C.	A map is attached showing the position of Battalion Headquarters - front line trenches, support + reserve trenches and communication trenches from HEBUTERNE and REEP. and the position of GOMMECOURT WOOD and GERMAN front line trenches -
30.11.15 " "	Battalion in Reserve at AUTHIE. - A.B.C. and D. Companies each provide 100 men for working parties on Corps Line etc and road repairing - Battn Grenade Class (2 men per platoon), Bn Runners M.G. Section, Snipers and Reserve Signallers paraded at 9.0 AM for instruction under their respective officers. - 1 Officer and 14 O.R. at Brigade Bombing Class - COUIN - 1 man returned from leave - 2 men to C.C.S. - 2 men to Field Ambulance and 2 men returned from Field Ambulance - Arrangements made for starting a Tailor's Shop so that repairs may be done quickly done whilst the Regt is in billets; and for using the School as a Church [illegible] for Recreation etc - [illegible] set aside as Sergts Mess room and arrangements progressing for fixing up Battn Recreation Room - Strength 34 Officers and 805 O.R. J.C.	

(73989) W4141—463. 400,000. 9/14. H.&J.Ltd. Forms/C. 2118/10.

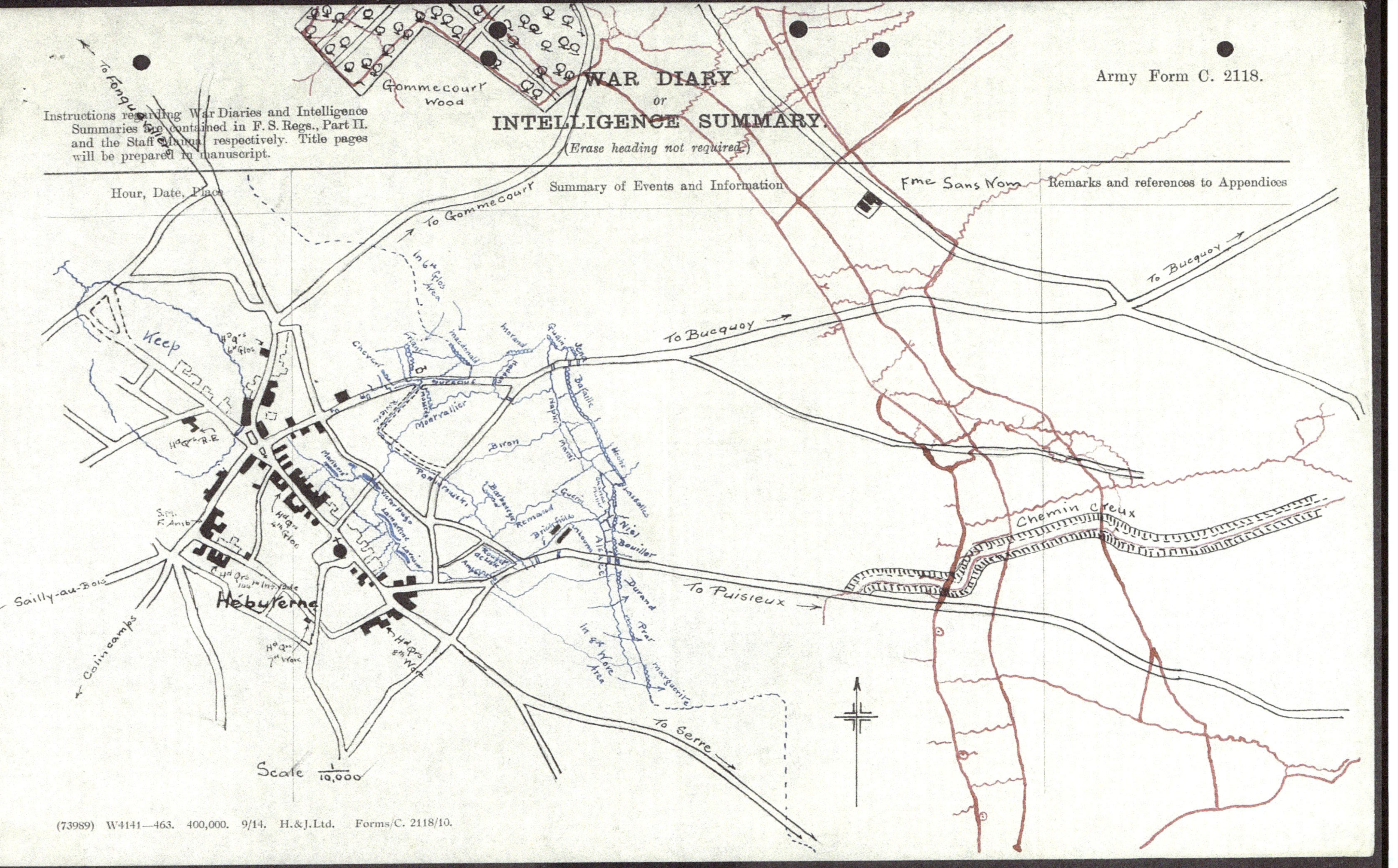

Army Form C. 2118.
WAR DIARY
or
INTELLIGENCE SUMMARY.
(Erase heading not required.)
Instructions regarding War Diaries and Intelligence Summaries are contained in F. S. Regs., Part II. and the Staff Manual respectively. Title pages will be prepared in manuscript.
Hour, Date, Place
Summary of Events and Information
Remarks and references to Appendices
Gommecourt Wood
Fme Sans Nom
To Fonquevillers
To Gommecourt
To Bucquoy
To Bucquoy
To Puisieux
To Serre
Chemin Creux
Keep
Hébuterne
Saiily-au-Bois
Colincamps
In 6th Glos Area
In 8th Worc Area
Scale 1/10,000
(73989) W4141—463. 400,000. 9/14. H.&J.Ltd. Forms/C. 2118/10.

144th Inf.Bde.
48th Div.

WAR DIARY

1/4th BATTN. THE GLOUCESTERSHIRE REGIMENT.

D E C E M B E R

1 9 1 5

WAR DIARY
or
INTELLIGENCE SUMMARY. 1/4th GLOUCESTER REGt.

(*Erase heading not required.*)

Army Form C. 2118.

Instructions regarding War Diaries and Intelligence Summaries are contained in F. S. Regs., Part II. and the Staff Manual respectively. Title pages will be prepared in manuscript.

Hour, Date, Place	Summary of Events and Information	Remarks and references to Appendices
1.12.15. AUTHIE	Battalion in Reserve at Authie. Battalion paraded for Route March at 9.40 A.M. – C. Company finding Advance Guard – Route AUTHIE – VAUCHELLES – LOUVENCOURT – BUS – AUTHIE – Main body moving in order C. A. B. D. Companies – [Packstores – M.G. Sectn. – 1st Line Transport [illegible]] In the afternoon A. Coy. practised Drill in tube smoke helmets – Cabinet shop opened in Billet in village – Work going on in billets making wood and wire beds for men – 4 Carpenters sent to ROSSIGNOL FARM to be attached to R.E. as Carpenters – 7 men returned from leave – No. 7 Pte. ERRICK – A. Coy. to LOUVENCOURT for postal work – 1 man returned from C.C.S. – 1 man to C.C.S. No. 19 – 2 men to C.C.S. No. 4 – 5 men to Field Ambulance. Strength 34. Officers and 802. O.R.	
2.12.15 . .	Battalion in Reserve at AUTHIE – A.B.C and D Companies provide 100 men each for R.E. and Corps working parties – Bn. Grenade class (2 men per platoon), Bn. Reserve M.G. Section – Snipers and Reserve Signallers paraded for instruction at 9.0 A.M. – 3 N.C.O.s & Men detailed from each Company to attend Brigade Grenadier Course at COUIN – Three men already attending this Course returned to their Companies this evening – 2/LIEUT. A.B. SELMAN was appointed M.G. Officer from 29/11/15 vice Capt. H. WADE. B. Company had Baths – 4 men to Field Ambulance – 1 man returned from Field Ambulance and 1 man from C.C.S. Strength 34. Officers and 808. O.R. – Rain most of the day & night.	
3.12.15 . . .	Battalion in Reserve at AUTHIE – All Companies paraded at 9.0 A.M. under Company arrangements for Musketry and organization of Platoons as Bombing parties in attack and defence – B. C and D Companies practised Drill in Smoke (tube) helmets under M.O. who arranged for sterilization of the helmets – practice helmets being used & not the men's own – Bn. Grenadier Class, Snipers, Reserve M.G. Section and Reserve Signallers paraded as yesterday at 9.0 A.M. – C. Company had Baths – 2 Officers and 22 O.R. proceeded on leave to ENGLAND from 5/12/15 to 12/12/15 inclusive – 8 men at present attached to 178 Tunnelling Coy. off strength – 1 man to C.C.S. + 1 man to Field Ambulance – 1 man returned from Field Amb. and 1 from C.C.S. Strength. 34. Officers and 796. O.R. Weather very wet –	
4.12.15 . . .	Battalion in Reserve at AUTHIE. A B. C and D. Companies had orders to find 100 men each for Corps and R.E. working parties – but owing to the heavy rain these were cancelled when the Companies paraded – Companies under Company arrangements organizing platoons and half-platoons in Bombing formations – and at work in Billets forming beds and tables – but this work is much hampered by lack of scantling timber – only boards available – Grenade Class, Snipers, Reserve M.G. Section and Signallers parade as	

(73989) W4141—463. 400,000. 9/14. H.&J.Ltd. Forms/C. 2118/10.

Instructions regarding War Diaries and Intelligence Summaries are contained in F. S. Regs., Part II. and the Staff Manual respectively. Title pages will be prepared in manuscript.

WAR DIARY
or
INTELLIGENCE SUMMARY.
(*Erase heading not required.*)

Army Form C. 2118.

Hour, Date, Place	Summary of Events and Information	Remarks and references to Appendices
4.12.15 – AUTHIE	as usual. 3 men to No 4. C.C.S. 3 men to Field Ambulance. Strength 34 Officers & 793 O.R.	
5.12.15 – " "	Battalion in Reserve. Church parade in Field on MARIEUX Road at 11.45 A.M. – Orders for Relief tomorrow detailed by C.O. to Company Commanders – 4 Carpenters return from R.E. and 1 Officer and 14 Bombers return from Class at COIN – Work on beds and tables in billets. 3 men to No 4 C.C.S. 5 men to Field Ambulance. – 1 man returned from C.C.S and 2 from Field Ambulance. Strength 34 Officers and 791 O.R. [initials]	
6.12.15 – HEBUTERNE	Battalion relieved 4. Royal Berks Regt in trenches at HEBUTERNE. Companies left AUTHIE in following order. viz – A Coy at 8.0 A.M. D Coy 8.15 A.M. C Coy 8.30 A.M. B Coy 8.45 A.M. – M.G. Section and [illegible] and Transport at 9.0 A.M. Relief completed without casualty by 4.0 P.M. – Owing to recent very wet weather the trenches are in very bad condition and M.G. emplacements are all very bad. Enemy fairly quiet during relief and all the day – Rain continues – 2 men to Field Ambulance & 1 man returned from Field Ambulance & 1 man from C.C.S. – Sergt NICHOLLS returned from M.G. Course – A Company hold right of our line and D Company left of line. C Company to Chateau and B Coy to Keep – 8/Worcester Regt on our Battalion Right and 6/Gloucesters on our left. IV Division on our Divisional Right immediately to right of 7/Worcesters and XXXVII Division on Divisional left to left of WARWICK Brigade which is on left of 6/Gloucester Regt. – positions same as shown on map attached to Diary for November – Strength 34 Officers and 792 O.R. [initials]	
7.12.15 " "	Battalion in the Trenches. Night 6–7 Dec. rather fine and enemy quiet – Men hard at work baling and pumping and removing fallen sides of trenches – pumping out sumps and repairing same. The shelters for Officers and men are untenable as most have fallen in owing to the wet and are half full of mud and water. The Communication trenches are especially bad – [illegible] for the last 500 yards towards the firing line is practically impassable and [illegible] in same condition from [illegible] to firing line – "Napier" Central is closed and also [illegible] – The right Company's post in "Hoche" could only be relieved [illegible] at dusk and had to remain for 24 hours at a time and the listening post for [illegible] and the left Company's post in "Bataille" could only be relieved by night along the parapet – Continuous baling and pumping is being kept up & sleeping – Another trench [illegible] kept free but very bad by Barricade and Remand is impassable at [illegible] – 2 Officers and 10 men returned from leave. 2 men to Field Ambulance – Strength 34 Officers and 792 O.R. [initials]	

Instructions regarding War Diaries and Intelligence Summaries are contained in F. S. Regs., Part II. and the Staff Manual respectively. Title pages will be prepared in manuscript.

WAR DIARY
or
INTELLIGENCE SUMMARY.

(Erase heading not required.)

Army Form C. 2118.

Hour, Date, Place	Summary of Events and Information	Remarks and references to Appendices
8.12.15. HEBOTERNE	Battalion in the Trenches - Night 7/8 quiet & wet - Trenches still very bad - HEBOTERNE was heavily shelled by Enemy at 12 Noon with 4" and 8" shells - this interfered with the arrival of the 16/Manchester Regt - which was coming into the Village for instruction and had two of its Officers wounded - H^d Q^rs of the Regt and A Company are attached to us for instruction. HEBOTERNE was shelled again at 4.0pm. with Field Guns and 8" shells - Several men of 16/Manchester and 6/Glouc. Regts were hit and two horses and 2 mules - one man of ours was slightly wounded. One shell struck out building immediately in front of Barricade at Batt. H^d Qrs & several fell in Keep on striking H^d Q^rs then. 22 men returned from Rest. 2/LIEUT. HAWKINS returned from Course - 1 man from Field Ambulance and 7 from C.C.S. 2 men to Field Ambulance and 1 on Command. Strength 34. Officers and 793. O.R.	
9.12.15 . . .	Battalion in the Trenches - Night 8/9 wet and quiet. HEBOTERNE shelled again by enemy between 8.0 A.M. and 8.30 A.M. Our artillery active all the time, especially the heavy batteries. Continuous work going on in baling and pumping and revetting as far as material will go but there is not nearly enough of it - 1 man to No 4 C.C.S. 3 men to Field Ambulance. Sergt OLIVER to R.E. for map making by Div^n Orders. Strength 34. Officers and 792. O.R.	
10.12.15 . . .	Battalion in the Trenches - Night 9/10 quiet - day also quiet but rain during day and heavy rain in morning and night - Work continuing on trenches - but the rain makes things nearly as bad as they were when we came in - 1 man to R.F.C. on probation. 1 man to base for dental treatment. 1 man to No 4 C.C.S. 2 men returned from Field Ambulance. Our Artillery active all day - Very little reply from enemy guns. Strength 34. Officers and 790. O.R.	
11.12.15 . . .	Battalion in the Trenches - Night 10/11 quiet and day also quiet - Trenches wetter and generally worse owing to heavy rain last night. Work still continues. It would not be possible to provide the posts in firing line [illegible] and do the continuous work necessary on trenches if it were not for having the Manchester Company attached - 1 man to No 19. C.C.S. and 1 man to Field Ambulance. Strength 34. Officers & 790. O.R.	
12.12.15 . . .	Battalion in Trenches - Night 11/12 quiet - Some rain - Enemy fired several shells into Keep End of Hebuterne - Our artillery fired at intervals throughout the night and all day - About 9.50 A.M. Enemy put twenty shells into Keep and Keep End of Hebuterne. Divine Service in Keep at 10.0 A.M. - Voluntary attendance.	

Instructions regarding War Diaries and Intelligence Summaries are contained in F. S. Regs., Part II. and the Staff Manual respectively. Title pages will be prepared in manuscript.

WAR DIARY
or
INTELLIGENCE SUMMARY.
(Erase heading not required.)

Army Form C. 2118.

Hour, Date, Place	Summary of Events and Information	Remarks and references to Appendices
12.12.15 HEBUTERNE	Capt NEWTH and Servant to School of Instruction at FLIXECOURT and also Sergt SHART - 2 Men to 7th Corps workshops & [illegible] Cookers - 1 Officer and 70 O.R. from Base - 2 Men to No 4. C.C.S. 4 Men to Field Ambulance. 1 Man back from Field Ambulance - Strength 34. Officers and 786. O.R. [initials]	
	Work continued as before on trenches - there are evidences that the Enemy's line is full of water as continuous streams of water are seen issuing from them - it is thought that their pumps are worked by a small engine - Weather frosty and very cold to evening - [initials]	
13.12.15 " "	Battalion in the Trenches. Night of 12/13 frosty and fine and quiet - Our Artillery (heavy guns) [illegible] fire at intervals - and M.G. are fired according to programme - LIEUT. WOOKEY and Patrol approached to within 50 yards of German Trenches advancing by 16 Poplars. Concluded that the trenches were strongly held at this point on account of sound of many men in it - Patrol returned safely. The trenches are slightly better owing to work done & cessation of rain - but water still continues and is [illegible]. 2/LIEUT. HAWKINS and 5 men gone back to ENGLAND - 2/LIEUT. DOWN returned from instructional course at FLIXECOURT - 2 Men to Field Ambulance. Strength - 34. Officers and 786. O.R. [initials]	
14.12.15 " "	Battalion in Trenches - Night 13/14 very cold with sharp frost but quiet - Our Artillery still firing at intervals - 16/Manchester Regt left HEBUTERNE by 8.30 AM. - Our Battalion relieved in trenches by 4/Royal Berks Regt. - Relief began about 11.0 AM. but owing to the state of the trenches and the time occupied by Platoons in the line changing gum-boots the relief took much longer than usual - but was completed without casualty and Battalion proceeded to Billets at AUTHIE by 6.15 p.m. - 2 Officers and 10 men returned from Base - 2 men returned from M.G. Course - 1 Man from C.C.S. and 3 Men from Field Ambulance. Strength. 34. Officers and 787. O.R. [initials]	
15-12-15 AUTHIE	Battalion in Reserve at AUTHIE in usual billets - The Brigadier-Genl. went round the billets with the C.O. in the morning - Companies had free day for inspection of Kits, Equipment, Arms, [illegible] billets and repairs generally [illegible] - Bath [illegible] allotted to C. Company - 1 Officer and 13 men to Brigade Grenadier Class - 4 Carpenters to R.E. at ROSSIGNAL FARM. - 7 men gone on leave and 12 men returned from leave - No 1786 Sergt. STOCKES to Base - time expired - Two men to Field Ambulance - 5 men returned from Field Ambulance - 1 Man to C.C.S. - Strength 34 Officers and 785. O.R. [initials]	

Instructions regarding War Diaries and Intelligence Summaries are contained in F. S. Regs., Part II. and the Staff Manual respectively. Title pages will be prepared in manuscript.

WAR DIARY
or
INTELLIGENCE SUMMARY.
(Erase heading not required.)

Army Form C. 2118.

Hour, Date, Place	Summary of Events and Information	Remarks and references to Appendices
16.12.15 AOTHIE	Battalion in Reserve at Authie – A.B.C. & D. Companies and M.G. Section find 425 men for Corps and R.E. Working parties. Snipers, Signallers, Bombers and Reserve M.G. Section paraded for instruction at 9.0 A.M. under their respective Officers – also Stretcher bearers under M.O. at Medical Inspection Room. Work on billets, making beds and tables. Transport Section and No 2 details had Baths – All Officers, except those on Working parties – attended lecture at Brigade Headquarters at Couin on Artillery Co-operation with Infantry by Major BOWLES. Brigade Major to C.R.A. 48th Division at 5.30. p.m. 1 man returned from leave – 1 man from C.C.S. – 3 men from Field Ambulance – 3 men sent to Field Ambulance – Strength 34. Officers and 786. O.R. [initials]	
17.12.15 " "	Battalion in Reserve at AOTHIE. Companies paraded at 9.0 A.M. for Tube Helmet Drill – practice in the use of the rifle wire breaker – and Company training – formation of platoons and sections as Bombing parties – Bn Grenadier Class, Reserve M.G. Section, and Signallers and Snipers parade as usual. Baths allotted to A and D Companies – Entertainment for N.C.Os & Men by Varlets' Variety Troupe at Café Nationale at 5.30 pm – 1 man to Div. Train as driver for Bde M.G. Transport. 2 men to Field Ambulance – 1 man returned from Ambulance – Strength 34. Officers and 788. O.R.	
18.12.15 " "	Battalion in Reserve at AOTHIE. A.B.C. and D Companies & M.G. Section provide 425 men for Corps and R.E. Working parties – Bn Grenadier Class, Snipers, Signallers & Reserve M.G. Section parade as usual. Baths cannot be used on account of shortage of coal – No 1186. Sergt. KERSLAKE to Base time expired – No 16. Sergt GREGORY to Base for trial on Munition work – 1 man to 3rd Army H.Q. for Wood cutting – 2/LIEUT. BIRD and 9 O.R. to WISQUES for LEWIS Gun Course – 1 Officer and 18 O.R. return from Bde Grenadier Course. 4 men to Field Ambulance – 8 men return from Field Ambulance – Strength 34. Officers and 787. O.R. 2 Officers and 18 men on leave to ENGLAND. [initials]	
19.12.15 " "	Battalion in Reserve at AOTHIE, – Divine Service parade in field on MARIEUX Road, and Celebration of Holy Communion in Sergts Room at Café Nationale afterwards. – Baths still unusable for lack of fuel – Stretcher Bearers paraded at Medical Inspection Room at 10.0 A.M. – A draft of 25. O.R. arrived from No 1. Entrenching Battalion and were inspected by C.O. and allotted to Companies. 1 man to C.C.S. No 4, & 1 man returned from C.C.S. – 2 men to Field Ambulance – and 2 men returned from Field Ambulance. Strength 34. Officers and 812. O.R. [initials]	

(73989) W4141—463. 400,000. 9/14. H.&J.Ltd. Forms/C. 2118/10.

Instructions regarding War Diaries and Intelligence Summaries are contained in F. S. Regs., Part II. and the Staff Manual respectively. Title pages will be prepared in manuscript.

WAR DIARY
or
INTELLIGENCE SUMMARY.
(Erase heading not required.)

Army Form C. 2118.

Hour, Date, Place	Summary of Events and Information	Remarks and references to Appendices
20.12.15. AOTHIE	Battalion in Reserve at AUTHIE. - A.B. C and D. Companies and M.G. Section find 425 men for Corps and R.E. Working parties - Bn. Grenadier Class, Snipers, Reserve M.G. Section and Signallers parade as usual at 9.0 A.M. Extract from London Gazette. 2/LIEUTS: R.F. IRVING and A.D. ANDERSON to be Temp: LIEUTS dated 2/10/15 and 2/LIEUT A.B. SELLMAN to be Temp: LIEUT. dated 12/11/15. 2 men to No. 4. C.C.S. 2 men to Field Ambulance & 2 men returned from Field Ambulance. Strength 34. Officers and 810. O.R. A.C.T.	
21.12.15. " "	Battalion in Reserve at AUTHIE. C & D Companies doing Tube Helmet drill and practised in the use of Wire breakers - from 9.0 AM till 11.0 AM. Snipers and Reserve Signallers parade as usual. Baths and Disinfector allotted to 'B' and 'A' Coys up to 12 Noon and C & D. Coys after 12 Noon. - M.O. examined all Smoke Helmets. Orders for relief [illegible] detailed by C.O. to Company Commanders - Practice alarm ordered by [illegible] at 6.0 pm. - 2 men returned from Corps Workshop - 2 men to C.C.S. and 1 man return from C.C.S. Strength 34. officers and 809. O.R. A.C.T.	
22.12.15. HEBUTERNE	Battalion relieved 4/Royal Berks. Regt. in the Trenches. A Coy left AUTHIE at 8.0 A.M. and other Companies followed at quarter of an hour intervals. M.G. and Transport at 9.0 A.M. Relief completed without casualty at 12.45 pm. Weather rainy and misty but warm. Trenches very wet and [illegible] owing to recent rains. Dispositions in trenches and billets as previously. - A. Coy and H.Q. of 18 Bn. King's Liverpool Regt. attached for instruction - at present in Reserve. - 2 Carpenters from R.E. rejoined the Battalion. 4 men to C.C.S. and 3 men to Field Ambulance. Enemy shelled our trenches in afternoon. Strength 34. officers and 805. O.R. A.C.T.	
23.12.15. " "	Battalion in the Trenches - Dispositions as usual. No. 1. Coy. 18. King's Liverpool Regt. in reserve and used as working party - Night 22/23 quiet. Rather more German rifle fire during day. Enemy shelled trenches in afternoon in response to our shelling of their positions and again in evening. - No. 2322 Pte. NASH. W. Killed in Action and Pte. GRANT. G. (No. 2689) seriously wounded - 3 men to Field Ambulance & 1 man returned from C.C.S. - 1 officer and 10 men return from leave. - Strength 34. Officers and 804. O.R. A.C.T.	

(73989) W4141—463. 400,000. 9/14. H.&J.Ltd. Forms/C. 2118/10.

Instructions regarding War Diaries and Intelligence Summaries are contained in F. S. Regs., Part II. and the Staff Manual respectively. Title pages will be prepared in manuscript.

WAR DIARY
or
INTELLIGENCE SUMMARY.

(Erase heading not required.)

Army Form C. 2118.

Hour, Date, Place	Summary of Events and Information	Remarks and references to Appendices
24.12.15. HEBUTERNE.	Battalion in the Trenches – Night 23/24 quiet but very wet and in consequence the trenches are again in a very bad condition. 18th King's Liverpool Regt left HEBUTERNE at 7.0 a.m. G.O.C. Division visited the Battalion & wished all Ranks a Happy Christmas and New Year and expressed his satisfaction with the work, the musketry and the interior economy of the Battalion – Usual shelling from our own guns and enemy replied – 1 Officer and 4 men back from leave – 1 Officer and 3 men back from LEWIS Gun Course – Capt W. LEWIS and 4 men to Field Ambulance. Strength 34 Officers + 804 O.R. [initialled]	
25.12.15 "	Battalion in the Trenches – Night 24/25 quiet but raining – A great deal of shelling on both sides which started early in the morning and continued at intervals throughout the day – H.Q. of Reserve Company at Chateau had seven direct hits on it – LIEUT. COOTE from Hampshire Regt attached to us – No 2082 Pte WILKINS wounded in action and also No 2416 Pte GARDNER slightly wounded but remaining at duty – 6 men return from LEWIS Gun Course – Between 4.0 pm and 5.0 pm the Germans sent over about 200 shells in direction of SAILLY. – 2 men to C.C.S. and 3 men to Field Ambulance – Strength 34 Officers and 801 O.R. [initialled]	
26.12.15 "	Battalion in the Trenches – Night 25/26 quiet but raining – Enemy Artillery quiet. Trenches better but very sticky – Large German flag was put up during night outside their wire (Red, White and Black). 1 man to Brigade [illegible] only at pigeon flyer – our guns shelled German positions as usual but reply slight – except in afternoon when a few shells fell in HEBUTERNE and the Keep – 2 Officers and 36 men go on leave to ENGLAND – Capt W. LEWIS and 7 men to C.C.S. 1 man to Field Ambulance – 8 men return from Field Ambulance, Strength 34 Officers and 800 O.R. [initialled]	
27.12.15 "	Battalion in the Trenches – Night 26/27 fine and quiet – during the day our Artillery were fairly active and the Enemy replied with a few small shells and 4.2 Hows. Some of the latter were blind – Trenches better – 7 men to Field Ambulance – 1 man to C.C.S. and 1 man returned from C.C.S. Strength – 34 Officers and 798 O.R. [initialled]	
28.12.15 "	Battalion relieved in the Trenches by 4/Royal Berks Regt – relief began about 11.0 a.m. and Battn all present in billets at AUTHIE at 6.15 pm without casualty. 4 or 5 Enemy Aeroplanes over during relief and on a bombing expedition, bombs being dropped at COURCELLES, AUTHIE and MARIEUX. 1 man to C.C.S. – 2 men to Field Ambulance – Strength 34 Officers and 798 O.R. [initialled]	

(73989) W4141—463. 400,000. 9/14. H.&J.Ltd. Forms/C. 2118/10.

Instructions regarding War Diaries and Intelligence Summaries are contained in F. S. Regs., Part II. and the Staff Manual respectively. Title pages will be prepared in manuscript.

WAR DIARY
or
INTELLIGENCE SUMMARY.
(Erase heading not required.)

Army Form C. 2118.

Hour, Date, Place	Summary of Events and Information	Remarks and references to Appendices
29.12.15. AOTHIE	Battalion in reserve at AOTHIE. Day fine - Baths allotted to B & C Companies. Companies had free day for rest and cleaning equipment arms, kit and repairs generally & work in billets. C.O. inspected billets - C.O. met all officers at Orderly Room at 5.30 pm. about Lecture recently delivered on fighting of [illegible] and about arrangements for Christmas festivities - 1 man returned from base. 3 men returned from Field Ambulance - 2 men to C.C.S and 1 man to Field Ambulance. Strength 34. officers and 797 O.R. [initials]	
30.12.15 " "	Battalion in reserve at AOTHIE. day fine - G.O.C. 144 Infantry Brigade inspected the Batt. in Marching Order on Grenadiers football field at 10 A.M. - Tube helmets are inspected by M.O. afterwards - 3 officers & 18 men returned from leave - 1 officer and 14 O.R. to Brigade Grenadier Class at COUIN. 1 man returned from C.C.S. and 5 men from Field Ambulance. Strength 34. Officers and 798. O.R. [initials]	

1/1/16

A. Davenport Lt Col
1/4th Glouces Regt

Army Form C. 2118.

Instructions regarding War Diaries and Intelligence Summaries are contained in F. S. Regs., Part II. and the Staff Manual respectively. Title pages will be prepared in manuscript.

WAR DIARY
or
INTELLIGENCE SUMMARY
(Erase heading not required.)

1/4. Glouc. Regt.

Hour, Date, Place	Summary of Events and Information	Remarks and references to Appendices

Bois de Gommecourt
To Fonquevillers
To Gommecourt
Fme Sans Nom
To Bucquoy
To Bucquoy
Keep
H^d Q^rs 6th Glos
In 6th Glos Area
Chevert
Frian
McDonald
Morand
Gudin
Jena
Hodden
Surcouf
Bataille
Monrvallier
Napier
Biron
Marai
Hoche
Bareancyre
Remaud
Guerin
Charles Muller
Lassalle
Brickfields
Niel
Bouiller
Alsace
Durand
Prar
Marguerite
In 48th Div. Area
Chemin creux
To Puisieux
To Serre
H^d Q^rs R.E.
Héburterne
S.M. F. Amb
H^d Q^rs 4th Glos
H^d Q^rs 144th Inf. Bde
H^d Q^rs 6th Worc
H^d Q^rs 7th Worc
To Sailly-au-Bois
To Colincamps
Scale 1/10,000

1247 W 3299 200,000 (E) 8/14 J.B.C. & A. Forms/C. 2118/11.

144th Brigade.

48th Division.

Note The entry for 31st is in Diary for February 1916.

1/4th BATTALION

GLOUCESTERSHIRE REGIMENT

JANUARY 1 9 1 6

Instructions regarding War Diaries and Intelligence Summaries are contained in F. S. Regs., Part II. and the Staff Manual respectively. Title pages will be prepared in manuscript.

WAR DIARY
or
INTELLIGENCE SUMMARY. 1/4th GLOUCESTER REGT.
(Erase heading not required.)

Army Form C. 2118.

Hour, Date, Place	Summary of Events and Information	Remarks and references to Appendices
31.12.15 AUTHIE	Battalion in billets at AUTHIE. Weather dull in morning and afternoon wet. A.B.C. & D Companies find 350 men and 7 officers for working parties - road making. Snipers, [illegible] Machine [illegible] recruit signallers and Bombers paraded as usual in morning - Sergts. Xmas dinner in evening at Café Nationale, extension allowed by A.P.M. till 10 o'clock - 1 man to C.C.S. 2 men to Hospital - Strength 34. Officers and 797. O.R. H.T.	
1.1.16	Battalion in Reserve at AUTHIE. Day [illegible] of the time. Holiday throughout the Battalion by special permission. Football matches between Companies during the morning and [illegible] officers [illegible] and men in afternoon - Cinema performances during afternoon. Company Xmas dinners to all Companies in the evening. Authority granted for Cafés [illegible] open till 10.0 p.m. Captain GUTERBOCK and 18 men go on leave to ENGLAND. 1 man to C.C.S. - 1 man to Field Ambulance - 1 man from [illegible] Strength 34. Officers and 796. O.R. H.T.	
2.1.16	Battalion in Reserve at AUTHIE. Day fairly fine. Battalion paraded for Divine Service at 10.0 AM in field on road AUTHIE - MARIEUX and Service for Wesleyans [illegible] same time in village - Celebration of Holy Communion at 10.30 AM. Baths allotted to A Coy. in the afternoon - 1 man to C.C.S. - LIEUT. GRAVELLE R.A.M.C. and 5 men to Field Ambulance. Strength 34. Officers and 776. O.R. O.C. visited all officers at 5.0 pm -	
3.1.16 HEBUTERNE	Battalion relieved 1/4 Royal Berks Regt. in the Trenches without casualty - A Company left AUTHIE at 6.0 AM and other Companies at [illegible] intervals - Relief completed by 12.30 noon - A & B Companies in fire trenches. C Company in [illegible] and D Comp.y in Keep - [illegible] Artillery active during early part of afternoon, also the Enemy who fired about 400 shells into our Right Sector - Especially [illegible] on front trench HOCHE which is considered in parts - 75 of these shells were blind - Positions of Divisions and Battalions on our Right and left the same as previously - 2 men to the [illegible] - 3 men to Field Ambulance - including Capt. REX (R.A.M.C. att.d). Capt. Mansfield to No. 3 Coy Train (vice Capt. BARTLETT to [illegible]). Strength 35 Officers and 794. O.R. LIEUT. COOTE (from Hants Regt.) taken on strength from 2/1/16. H.T.	
4-1-16	Battalion in the Trenches - night [illegible] quiet - Day fine during morning, wet afternoon. Artillery on both sides very quiet - Work on trenches draining - [illegible] and clearing dug outs - Especially Headquarters of left sector - Men from 5th SUSSEX Regt. fired 5 rounds from our trenches. [illegible] men to C.C.S. 2/LIEUT. SYMES and 6 men to Field Ambulance. Strength 35. Officers and 792. O.R. H.T.	

Instructions regarding War Diaries and Intelligence Summaries are contained in F. S. Regs., Part II. and the Staff Manual respectively. Title pages will be prepared in manuscript.

WAR DIARY
or
INTELLIGENCE SUMMARY.
(Erase heading not required.)

Army Form C. 2118.

Hour, Date, Place	Summary of Events and Information	Remarks and references to Appendices
5-1-16 HEBUTERNE	Battalion in the Trenches at HEBUTERNE. Night 4/5 quiet – Day fine – Enemy fired 3 or 4 [illegible] Shrapnel [illegible] Brickfields, Keep and Village at 7.45 A.M. – 4th [illegible] B. Coy [illegible] of [illegible] and Pte Botrall [illegible] about 10.15 A.M. Work on trenches as usual – Trenches in much better condition – 5th Sussex Regt and Brigade fired some new 5 Rounds from our trenches – [illegible] in Keep [illegible] by Brigade to C.O. for Regimental working party on trenches – 3 men to Field Ambulance. Strength 35 Officers and 792 O.R. [initials]	
6.1.16 ..	Battalion in the Trenches – Night 5/6 quiet – Day [illegible] and very misty – Artillery quiet on both sides – [illegible] from 5th Sussex Regt and from Brigade fired 5 Rounds from our Trenches – Work on trenches as usual. A & B Companies relieved in Trenches by C & D Companies – A Company to Chateau and B Coy to the Keep – 3 Men to C.C.S. – 1 Man to Field Ambulance – Strength 35 Officers and 787 O.R. [initials]	
7.1.16 ..	Battalion in the Trenches – Night 6/7 quiet – Day fine but dull – Our Artillery active during day – Work on trenches for maintenance as usual. [illegible] from 5th Sussex Regt fired 5 Rounds from our trenches [illegible] Patrol under Lieut. POLACK brought in PRUSSIAN flag which had been [illegible] by the Germans [illegible] our trench JENA for some days – 2 Officers and [illegible] men returned from leave – 3 Men to C.C.S. (including [illegible] RAMC attached) 3 Men to Field Ambulance – Strength 35 Officers and 784 O.R. [initials]	
8-1-16 ..	Battalion in the Trenches – Night 7/8 quiet – Day fine – Work on our trenches as usual – Enemy shelled SAILLY heavily during the morning and [illegible] in afternoon – Our Artillery shelled enemy trenches round LA LOUVIERE Fm in afternoon and [illegible] on fire – Patrol under Lieut. WOKEY [illegible] German wire near 16 Poplars – Capt. LEWIS to England (31.12.15) Major W.S. [illegible] at Base off strength (2.1.16) Q.M.S. BEER to C.C.S. – Sergt GREGORY to England on Munition Work. 1 Man [illegible] from [illegible] – Strength 33 Officers and 782 O.R. [initials]	
9-1-16 ..	Battalion in the Trenches – Night 8/9 quiet – Battalion relieved by 1/[illegible] Royal Berks in the trenches – Relief commenced at 11.0 A.M. [illegible] reported all present in Billets at AUTHIE without casualty at 5.20 p.m. – Weather colder and very fine with bright sunshine – Capt. NEWTH and [illegible] rejoined Battn from 3rd Army School of Instruction – 4 O.R. to Base time expired – 2 Men to C.C.S. 2 Men to Field Ambulance – 1 Man from Field Ambulance – Strength 33 Officers and 776 O.R. [initials]	
10-1-16 AUTHIE	Battalion in Reserve at AUTHIE. No detailed parades, but companies inspected by their Officers. Baths [illegible] – [illegible] Battn beat [illegible] R.F.A. in Fanshawe Cup Competition (Association Football) 3 goals to nil – C. in C. (Sir Douglas HAIG) visited Divisional Area – Capt. NEWTH to [illegible] as Brigade Grenadier Officer – 2/Lieut. [illegible] and 15 O.R. to [illegible] for Brigade Grenade Course – 2 Officers + 30 O.R. [illegible] to ENGLAND. 2 Men to Field Ambulance – 4 Men [illegible] from Field Amb. – Q.M.S. BEER 1 O.R. from C.C.S. Strength 33 Officers and 778 O.R. [initials]	

(73989) W4141—463. 400,000. 9/14. H.&J.Ltd. Forms/C. 2118/10.

Instructions regarding War Diaries and Intelligence Summaries are contained in F. S. Regs., Part II. and the Staff Manual respectively. Title pages will be prepared in manuscript.

WAR DIARY
or
INTELLIGENCE SUMMARY.
(Erase heading not required.)

Army Form C. 2118.

Hour, Date, Place	Summary of Events and Information	Remarks and references to Appendices
11.1.16. AUTHIE.	Battalion in Reserve at AUTHIE. All Companies paraded 9.0 AM to 12.30 pm – Arrow drill instruction of platoons as bombing parties – Wire making and Company work – Reserve M.G. Section paraded for instruction in LEWIS GUN. Bn Grenadier Class, Snipers and Reserve Signallers paraded at same hours as Companies. 2/LIEUT. E.L. REED joined Battn from 3/4 Glouc. Regt & posted to C. Company. 1 man to Base – [illegible] 3 men to Field Ambulance – 2 men returned from Field Ambulance – 34 Officers and 777 O.R. [initials]	
12.1.16 . .	Battalion in Reserve at AUTHIE. – B. C. & D Companies and M.G. Section found working parties or [illegible] Pde instruction. Reserve M.G. Section, Signallers, Snipers & Bn Grenade Class and A Company paraded for instruction as yesterday from 9.0 AM to 12.30 Noon. LIEUT. BEAVEN posted to A Company. 4 men to Bde to join 13th M.G. Company – 2 men to 7th Corps Workshops to assist in repairs – [illegible] to C.C.S. 4 men to Field Ambulance – 2 men returned from Field Ambce Strength 34 Officers & 772 O.R. [initials]	
13.1.16 . .	Battalion in Reserve at AUTHIE. Companies and details paraded 9.0 AM to 12.30 Noon as for Tuesday (11.1.16) – Major YOUNG (LEICESTER Regt) and Experts examined possible [illegible]. 2 out of 12 men were selected for further [illegible]. 1 Officer and 16 O.R. returned from leave – 2/LIEUT. BRADFORD joins from 3/4 Glouc. Regt and is posted to A Coy. – 3 men to C.C.S. 2/LIEUT. BIRD to Field Ambulance. 1 man returned from Field Ambulance – Strength 35 Officers and 769 O.R. [initials]	
14.1.16 . .	Battalion in Reserve at AUTHIE. M.O. inspected feet [illegible] of the Battalion in morning and remainder of parade devoted to preparation for trenches [illegible] feet [illegible] – O.C. detailed Orders for relief [illegible] to O.C. Companies. – 2/LIEUT. CHATTOCK and 2/LIEUT. RUSSELL joined us from 3/4 Gloucester Regt and a reinforcement of 25 men from Entrenching Battn (18 of these men had been with Battn previously) – 4 men sent to Base – C.Q.M.S. [illegible] to C.C.S. – LIEUT. BEAVEN and 3 men to Field Ambulance – LIEUT. SYMES and 2 men [illegible] from Field Ambulance – Strength 37 Officers and 789 O.R. [initials]	
15-1-16 HEBUTERNE.	Battalion relieved 4/Royal Berks Regt in the trenches. [illegible] left AUTHIE at 8.0 AM and remaining Companies at ¼ hour intervals – Relief completed by 12.30 Noon without casualty – [illegible] Companies & [illegible] and Battalion and [illegible] in front line – Trenches in fair condition – [illegible] to [illegible] Companies – 3 men [illegible] of Strength –	

Instructions regarding War Diaries and Intelligence Summaries are contained in F. S. Regs., Part II. and the Staff Manual respectively. Title pages will be prepared in manuscript.

WAR DIARY
or
INTELLIGENCE SUMMARY.
(Erase heading not required.)

Army Form C. 2118.

Hour, Date, Place	Summary of Events and Information	Remarks and references to Appendices
15.1.16 HEBUTERNE	1 man to C.C.S. – 8 men to Field Ambulance – 1 man returned from Field Ambulance – Strength 37 Officers and 785 O.R. J.C.T.	
16.1.16 " "	Battalion in the Trenches – Night 15/16 very fine & bright – No patrols out – About 11 a.m. the enemy put a few shrapnel along barricade at Orchard, and at 3 p.m. about 15 shells near top of REMAND trench and also shelled 8/[illegible] trenches – No damage done – Work going on on all trenches, clearing & pumping out sumps, [illegible] & [illegible] trenches and general maintenance – Sergt GARRAWAY went on one month's course to School of Instruction at FLIXECOURT – 2 men to Field Ambulance. Capt NEWTH to [illegible] as [illegible] officer and [illegible] 1 man returned from Field Ambulance – 1 officer & [illegible] O.R. from leave ENGLAND. Strength 37 Officers and 785 O.R. J.C.T.	
17-1-16 " "	Battalion in the Trenches – Night 16/17 fine – Patrol under Lieut. [illegible] examined hedge running towards enemy lines from M. Sap – Two of the men report hearing a buzzer such as is used on a telephone – but information not confirmed – Enemy fairly quiet [illegible] – Enemy aeroplane dropped 2 bombs in Keep at 9 a.m. – [illegible] aeroplanes (about 20 in all) passed over our trenches from German line at 10.30 A.M. Captain WADE and 1 man to Field Ambulance – and 1 man from Field Ambulance – Strength 37 Officers and 785 O.R. J.C.T.	
18-1-16 " "	Battalion in the Trenches – Night of 17/18 cloudy and [illegible] rain – Patrols out from both A & B Companies – Patrol from A Coy [illegible] [illegible] and [illegible] [illegible] and [illegible] [illegible] [illegible] BUCQUOY Road and found [illegible] muffler and German grenade – Patrol from [illegible] [illegible] German cartridge cases in shell hole [illegible] – At 12.30 p.m. enemy put [illegible] shells [illegible] [illegible] [illegible] [illegible] from the road [illegible] in the village – [illegible] sandbag barricade – 1 man at [illegible] [illegible] off strength – 2 men to C.C.S. – 2 men to Field Ambulance and 1 man returned from Field Ambulance. Strength 37 Officers and 782 O.R. J.C.T.	
19-1-16 " "	Battalion in the Trenches – Night 18/19 quiet – No patrols out – Work on trenches daily [illegible] as usual – 5 German aeroplanes passed over our lines [illegible] [illegible] – Artillery [illegible] – Weather very clear & fine –	

(73989) W4141—463. 400,000. 9/14. H.&J.Ltd. Forms/C. 2118/10.

WAR DIARY
or
INTELLIGENCE SUMMARY.
(Erase heading not required.)

Army Form C. 2118.

Instructions regarding War Diaries and Intelligence Summaries are contained in F. S. Regs., Part II. and the Staff Manual respectively. Title pages will be prepared in manuscript.

Hour, Date, Place	Summary of Events and Information	Remarks and references to Appendices
19-1-16 HEBOTERNE	Captain C.C.S. TILLY to ENGLAND off strength (16.1.16) 2 men to No 4 C.C.S. and 1 man to Field Ambulance – Strength 36 officers and 780 O.R. J.G.T.	
20-1-16 . . .	Battalion in the trenches – Night 19/20 very wet with heavy rain – Lieut WOOKEY on patrol [illegible] from right Company (C Company) at 4.30 a.m. and examined ground around the [illegible] – found small trenches which showed no signs of recent occupation – [illegible] [illegible] – Situation and artillery [illegible] – [illegible] 800 [illegible] [illegible] [illegible] as usual. J.G.T. Brigade [illegible] [illegible] –	
21-1-16 . . .	Battalion relieved by 4/Royal Berks Regt in the trenches – Night 20/21 fine and quiet. Details of relief done as usual – Relief began at 11 a.m. and Battalion reported present in Billets at AUTHIE without casualty at 5.30 p.m. 2 officers and 50 men detailed from leave – 1 man to Field Ambulance – Capt WADE and 6 men returned from Field Ambulance. Strength 36 officers and 778 O.R. J.G.T.	
22.1.16 AUTHIE	Battalion in Reserve at AUTHIE. Day devoted to cleaning [illegible] kits and equipment and work on billets – Inspections by Company Commanders – Battn allotted to [illegible] [illegible] companies – 2 officers and 29 men taken off strength on joining Brigade M.G. Company – 2 [illegible] [illegible] 1.C. met all officers in Orderly Room & detailed training [illegible] [illegible] – 6 men [illegible] from time expired – Sergt LESSIMORE to C.C.S. 2 men to Field Ambulance. Field Ambulance – Strength 34 officers and 746 O.R.	
23.1.16 . . .	Battalion in reserve at AUTHIE – Battalion paraded for Divine Service at 10.0 a.m. in field on road to MARIEUX – Celebration of Holy Communion afterwards in [illegible] – Inspections of arms and of [illegible] Helmets by M.O. [illegible] [illegible] – 2 men to [illegible] for [illegible] – Lieut SELLMAN and 2/Lieut BIRD to Brigade M.G. Company – 2 men to C.C.S. and 1 men to Field Ambulance – 1 man returned from C.C.S. and 1 man from Field Ambulance – Strength 34 officers and 745 men O.R. J.G.T.	
24.1.16 . . .	Battalion in Reserve at AUTHIE. A C + D Companies found 100 men each for R.E. working parties – B Company paraded from 9.15 a.m to [illegible] noon.	

(73989) W4141—463. 400,000. 9/14. H.&J.Ltd. Forms/C. 2118/10.

Instructions regarding War Diaries and Intelligence Summaries are contained in F. S. Regs., Part II. and the Staff Manual respectively. Title pages will be prepared in manuscript.

WAR DIARY
or
INTELLIGENCE SUMMARY.
(Erase heading not required.)

Army Form C. 2118.

Hour, Date, Place	Summary of Events and Information	Remarks and references to Appendices
24.1.16 AUTHIE	Morn – Battⁿ Grenadiers, Snipers, Lewis Gunners and Reserve Signallers paraded for instruction 9.0 A.M. to 12.30 noon. 1 man to C.C.S. – 1 man to Field Ambulance. – Sergᵗ LESSIMORE returned from C.C.S. & 2 men from Field Ambulance – Strength 34 Officers + 745 O.R. J.C.	
25.1.16 . . .	Battalion in Reserve at AUTHIE – All companies, Grenadier Coy, Snipers, Reserve Signallers and Lewis Gun Section paraded as usual from 9.0 A.M. to 12.30 noon – 7 German aeroplanes passed over AUTHIE in [illegible] direction about 11.30 A.M. 2 performances in the Cafe [illegible] were given by the 48ᵗʰ Division "Follies" at 4 p.m. + 6.0 p.m. – 1 man returned from Field Ambulance. – Strength 34 Officers and 745 O.R. J.C.	
26.1.16 . .	Battalion in Reserve at AUTHIE. Battalion paraded in full Marching Order [illegible] and [illegible] inspected by G.O.C. Brigade at 11 o'clock – All Officers attended Divisional Conference at BUS at 3.0 p.m. – address delivered by G.O.C. Division (Maj: Gen! Sir FANSHAWE K.C.B.) Pᵗᵉ WESTLAKE, R.A.M.C. attached – LIEUT. BIRD and 1 man to C.C.S. 1 man to Field Amb. 1 man returned from Field Ambulance. Strength 34 Officers + 746 O.R. J.C.	
27.1.16 HEBUTERNE	Sergᵗ SMART returned from 3ʳᵈ Army School – + 2 men from Command – & 1 man from C.C.S. Battalion relieved the 4/Royal Berks Regᵗ in the Trenches at HEBUTERNE – Relief carried out as usual. A + B Companies in the Line, C. Company in [illegible], D. Company in KEEP. Weather mild + fairly misty – Relief completed without casualty by 12.20 noon – Trenches in fair condition – 2/LIEUT. STEGER and 1 servant to 3ʳᵈ Army Gas School. 1 officer and 13 O.R. return from leave – Q.M. Sergᵗ BEER and 4 O.R. to Field Ambulance – Strength 34 officers and 746 O.R. J.C.	
28.1.16 . . .	Battalion in the Trenches – Troops on our right and left as on previous occasions. Night 27/28 quiet and normal except that about 7.20 p.m. an alarm of Gas was started in 7/Warwicks line owing to the action of a damp mist on Some Chloride of Lime thrown down for disinfecting purposes near the Cemetery – The alarm spread very rapidly and all the arrangements to meet same worked satisfactorily – The alarm reached Divisional H^d Q^rs in 3 minutes from its inception – At 2.30 A.M. the 1ˢᵗ + 2ⁿᵈ WARWICK Batteries fired about 190 shells into GOMMECOURT Wood – Work on trenches for maintenance as usual – Day quiet, weather very mild and rather misty – 1 man returned from leave and 2 men from Field Ambulance – Strength 34 Officers and 746 O.R. J.C.	
29.1.16 . .	Battalion in the Trenches – Night 28/29 quiet and fine – Patrol from B. Company, on our left, [illegible] Sap in front of German Line on N. side of BUCQUOY Road (in front of Fmᵉ Sans Nom) where 4 Germans were seen in Sap – Patrol returned without casualty – 2 men wiring in front of Trench NIEL (A Company) wounded by bomb or rifle grenade – Work on trenches as usual for maintenance	

Instructions regarding War Diaries and Intelligence Summaries are contained in F. S. Regs., Part II. and the Staff Manual respectively. Title pages will be prepared in manuscript.

WAR DIARY
or
INTELLIGENCE SUMMARY
(Erase heading not required.)

Army Form C. 2118.

Hour, Date, Place	Summary of Events and Information	Remarks and references to Appendices
29.1.16 HEBOTERNE	Situation normal - Our Artillery fairly active but German reply slight - 2 men wounded - 1 man to	
	C.C.S. - LIEUT: POLACK and 3. O.R. to Field Ambulance - 2 O.R. returned from Field Ambulance - 2 Men	
	returned from Field Ambulance - Draft of 61. O.R. arrived from Base - Strength 34 Officers and 800 O.R.	
	Wind changed to N.N.E. Artillery active - J.T.	
30.1.16 " "	Battalion in the trenches - Night 29/30 fine but very misty in the valleys - At 1.5 A.M. Germans put	
	about 12 shells on our right Sector - A Bombing raid on the S.W. Corner of GOMMECOURT WOOD was arranged	
	to take place under Brigade arrangements - The three Battalions on the right (7/Glouc. 8/Worcs & 6/Glouc.) making	
	demonstrations on various points & covering the raid by the left Battalion (1/6 Glouc. Regt.) at about	
	3. A.M. the 6/Glouc. sent out bombing parties (total about 110 men) to Raid S.W. Corner of WOOD but	
	the operation failed owing to the thick fog - Our patrols under LIEUT. COTE and LIEUT. BRIGGS (3 men	
	in all) left Trench BATAILLE at 2.30 A.M. accompanied by 3 Telephonists with lines - Reached	
	German Wire on left of BUCQUOY Road 2.55. A.M. & reported in position - On commencement of Shelling	
	by our Artillery supporting the Raiding parties, at 4.0 A.M. patrol bombed German Sap and at	
	4.20 A.M. reported that they were about to return when our Artillery support dropped to German	
	front line trenches - 2 men slightly wounded (at duty) - Day very misty but fine - Work on trenches	
	as usual - Our Artillery quiet - Germans dropped Shrapnel on our right Sector in morning -	
	3 men to Base, time expired - 2 men to Field Ambulance - Strength 34 Officers & 801 O.R.	
	J.T.	
	30/1/16 J. Davenport Lt. Col. 1/4 Royal Berks Regt	

1247 W 3299 200,000 (E) 8/14 J.B.C. & A. Forms/C. 2118/11.

144th Brigade

48th Division.

NOTE The entry for 29th is in diary for March

1/4th BATTALION

GLOUCESTERSHIRE REGIMENT

FEBRUARY 1 9 1 6

Instructions regarding War Diaries and Intelligence Summaries are contained in F. S. Regs., Part II. and the Staff Manual respectively. Title pages will be prepared in manuscript.

WAR DIARY
or
INTELLIGENCE SUMMARY

(Erase heading not required.)

Army Form C. 2118.

1/4 GLOUCESTER REGT.

Hour, Date, Place	Summary of Events and Information	Remarks and references to Appendices
31.1.16. HEBOTERNE	Battalion in the Trenches – Night 30/31 quiet and misty but not so foggy as preceding night. Dry and colder in day time – Morning quiet on both sides – Artillery rather active in afternoon. Situation normal. Work as usual on trenches for maintenance – 6 men from one month's leave to ENGLAND [illegible] – 2 Officers and 73 men gone leave to ENGLAND – ([illegible] M.O.). No 3638 Pte STEVENS on command at 1/S.M.F.A. as dental mechanic – 1 man to C.C.S. 2 men to Field Ambulance – Strength 34 Officers and 796 O.R. – [illegible] fired on German [illegible] J.G.T.	
1.2.16 . .	Battalion in the Trenches – Night of 31/1 fine and clear – Some shelling on the [illegible] and Warwick lines to our left at 12.30 A.M. including [illegible] – day fine and dry with sunshine in morning – Enemy fired [illegible] village in morning & usual artillery on both sides during afternoon, and our heavy [illegible] battery fired during afternoon – Trenches in very good condition considering the wet state they were in lately – Usual work of maintenance [illegible] on day & night. [illegible] Regt on our left sent a patrol down to German wire which [illegible] – while our trench mortars fired – No 2. Q.M.S. BEER to C.C.S. 1 man to Field Ambulance – and 1 man returned from Field Ambulance – Strength 34 Officers and 795 O.R. J.G.T.	
2.2.16 . . .	Battalion in the Trenches – Field Artillery fired 30 shells at [illegible] front of GOMMECOURT WOOD and patrol of 6/Gloucesters afterwards reconnoitred the wire & found it exceptionally strong – [illegible] German sap – Night 2/3 fine & [illegible] – Batt. relieved in the Trenches by 4/Royal Berks Regt [illegible] arrangements as usual and Batt. [illegible] in Billets at AUTHIE without casualty, at 5.0 p.m. KEEP handed over by Major THOMPSON to Major WALLER (5th Gloucester Regt) – No 2315 Pte BARNETT returned from Base [illegible] in Munition [illegible] – 1 man to ENGLAND on special leave – [illegible] to Battalion by G.O.C. for good bombing work – 1 man to C.C.S. 4 men returned from Field Ambulance. Strength 34 Officers and 794 O.R. J.G.T.	
3.2.16 AUTHIE	Battalion in Reserve at Authie in Billets – day fine & night – frost at night. Inspection of all Companies by Company Commanders. Billets inspected by C.O. & Major Thompson. Batt. Baths allotted to C & D Coys. C.O. went on leave to ENGLAND – Work on billets and general cleaning of Kits, arms & Equipment. LIEUT BEAVEN and 4 men returned from Field Ambulance – Strength 34 Officers and 794 O.R. J.G.T.	
4.2.16 . .	Battalion in Reserve at AUTHIE. A B and D Companies provide R.E. and Corps Working parties – [illegible] notice rec. from Brigade for working parties to stand by. Stood by till 11.0 A.M. and then proceeded to Rendezvous. Except A Coy which worked all the morning – C Coy paraded for Company Training 9–12.30 a.m. Snipers, Bombers, Lewis Gun teams and [illegible] paraded as usual at same time – Lieut FOLLEY off strength on selection as munition worker.	

Instructions regarding War Diaries and Intelligence Summaries are contained in F. S. Regs., Part II. and the Staff Manual respectively. Title pages will be prepared in manuscript.

INTELLIGENCE SUMMARY

(Erase heading not required.)

1/4 GLOUCESTER REGT.

Hour, Date, Place	Summary of Events and Information	Remarks and references to Appendices
4.2.16 AUTHIE	Sergt BAKER and 3 O.R. to Field Ambulance – LIEUT. POLACK and 1 man returned by Field Ambulance and 1 man from C.C.S. Strength 34. Officers and 794 O.R. – 2nd SEAFORTH Highlanders and the ARGYLE and S. Highlanders marched through AUTHIE on their way to MONDICOURT and marched past the G.O.C. 7th Corps (Sir T. D'O. SNOW. K.C.B.) Strength 34. Officers and 794 O.R. J.G.T.	
5.2.16 . . .	Battalion in reserve at AUTHIE. Weather dry fine & sunny – All Companies paraded for Company training 9.0 AM till 12.30 Noon – Company drill – Rapid loading & firing – Platoons, bombing parties & Lewis Gun team. Reserve Signallers & Snipers paraded as usual – 1 man returned from [illegible] – 2 officers and 22 men returned from leave – Sergt. [illegible] and Cpl. MARSH returned from 1 months leave to ENGLAND. 2/LIEUT. CLARK and 1 man returned from Field Ambulance – & 1 man from C.C.S. – 2 men sent to Field Ambulance & 1 to C.C.S. Strength 34. Officers and 796 O.R. A & C Companies had Baths – J.G.T.	
6.2.16 . . .	Battalion in Reserve at AUTHIE. A, B, C and ½ D Company found working parties for R.E. and Corps parties – Church parade at 10.0 AM. in old Ordnance Store. Major Thompson attended Brigade Conference at 10 AM at BUS – G.O.C. Brigade explained new line to be taken over from 111 & 112th Brigades in about a weeks' time & proposed dispositions – 2 men returned from leave – 1 man to C.C.S. and 1 man returned from Field Ambulance. O.C. explained proposed dispositions in new line to Company Commanders – Football (Rugby) match in afternoon against 6/Glouc. Regt. ended in a draw – Strength 34. Officers and 795. O.R. – B and D Companies had Baths – J.G.T.	
7.2.16 . . .	Battalion in reserve at AUTHIE. Parades from 9.0 to 12.30 Noon for Companies, Lewis Gun Team, Snipers, Reserve Signallers and Grenade Class as usual – Major THOMPSON and Adjutant visit [illegible] to 112th Brigade and inspected H.Q. BIENVILLERS, HANNESCAMP, and ST. AMAND and SOUASTRE – new line of trenches to be taken over – 3 men and Billets at BIENVILLERS and H.Q. at HANNESCAMPS [illegible] Strength 34. Officers & 795. O.R. – C.O. explained to Field Ambulance – & 2 men returned from 7th Amb. new positions as seen today, to Officers at 6.0 pm – Baths for H.Q. details & Transport. J.G.T.	
8.2.16 . . .	Battalion in reserve at AUTHIE. B. C. & D Coys. found 100 men each and A. Coy. 50 men for Corps and R.E. working parties – Company Commanders visited HANNESCAMP and inspected Trenches 62 to 76 inclusive. (37th Division) – O.C. attended Brigade Conference at BUS at 3.0 pm – Snipers and Reserve Signallers and bombers parade as usual – No 2539 Pte HOBBS to Base underage – Capt. SLADE and LIEUT. POLACK – and 21 O.R. go on leave to ENGLAND. – Sergt BAKER and 1 O.R. to C.C.S. 2 O.R. to Field Ambulance – Strength 34 Officers and 793. O.R. J.G.T.	

1247 W 3299 200,000 (E) 8/14 J.B.C. & A. Forms/C. 2118/11.

Instructions regarding War Diaries and Intelligence Summaries are contained in F. S. Regs., Part II. and the Staff Manual respectively. Title Pages will be prepared in manuscript.

or

INTELLIGENCE SUMMARY 1/4 GLOUCESTER REGT

(Erase heading not required.)

Place	Date	Hour	Summary of Events and Information	Remarks and references to Appendices
AUTHIE	9.2.16	—	Bn in divisional reserve. Companies inspected in marching order by C.O. Strength 34 offs 792 O.R.	
"	10.2.16	—	" " " " . Orders received to move to SOUASTRE on 11th. C.O. and Company officers went to SOUASTRE to see billets. Strength 34 offs 790.	
SOUASTRE	11.2.16	–	Bn. moved to SOUASTRE (6 miles). Moved off 12.15 pm. Weather bad - heavy rain and strong wind. Reached SOUASTRE 2.30 pm. Bn. present in billets 3pm. 34 offs 795 O.R.	
"	12.2.16	–	Bn. in divisional reserve Souastre. Strength 34 offs 795 O.R.	
"	13.2.16	–	Bn. in divisional reserve Souastre. Improvement of billets. Strength 34 offs 794	
"	14.2.16	–	Bn. in divisional reserve Souastre. Major Thompson to 3rd Army School. C.O back from leave. Strength 34 offs 794	
"	15.2.16	–	Bn in divisional reserve Souastre. C.O., Adjt, Company Commanders visited headquarters of opposite Batts at HANNESCAMPS. Strength 793 O.R. 34 offs	
"	16.2.16	–	Bn in divisional reserve Souastre. Brigade conference on relief at Brigade HQ Bienvillers 34 offs 793.	
" and HANNESCAMP TRENCHES	17.2.16	–	Bn relieved 6 Glosc. Regt in trenches. Companies left Souastre commencing 2pm. Relief complete 6pm. Dispositions of Brigade in trenches are as follows. In right Sector 8 Worcs. (relieved by 7 Worcs). In left Sector 4 Glosc (relieved by 6 Glosc). Brigade reserve at BIENVILLERS. Batts in divisional Reserve at SOUASTRE. On right of Brigade Warwick Brigade (143rd). On left of Brigade 37th Division	

2449 Wt. W14957/M90 750,000 1/16 J.B.C. & A. Forms/C.2118/12.

Instructions regarding War Diaries and Intelligence Summaries are contained in F. S. Regs., Part II. and the Staff Manual respectively. Title Pages will be prepared in manuscript.

WAR DIARY
or
INTELLIGENCE SUMMARY 1/4 GLOUCESTER REGT.

(Erase heading not required.)

Army Form C. 2118.

Place	Date	Hour	Summary of Events and Information	Remarks and references to Appendices
HANNESCAMP TRENCHES	17.2.16		When in trenches battalion holds roughly from HANNESCAMPS – ESSARTS road (inclusive) to HANNESCAMPS – MONCHY road (inclusive). Two companies are in the line, and two in reserve around the village. Battalion headquarters in HANNESCAMPS. The trenches are wide and partly revetted.	
"	"	8.45pm	Germans put rifle grenades, mortar bombs, and shells on trenches of our left company (C) opposite MONCHY, accompanied by bursts of rifle fire. This ceased 11pm. At 1.30pm several German Batteries opened simultaneously on the right of our right Battn (8 Worcs) and on left of Warwick Brigade (143rd). Over 1000 shells were fired. During bombardment a party of enemy entered 8 Worcs. trenches. Our casualties 1 killed 2 wounded. Strength 34 offrs 784	
"	18.2.16		In HANNESCAMPS trenches. Weather very wet. Situation normal. Strength 34 offrs 785	
"	19.2.16		In HANNESCAMPS trenches. Weather very wet. Situation normal. Strength 34 offrs 785	
"	20.2.16		In HANNESCAMPS trenches. Enemy shelled right Brigade (12th) of our Division and entered trenches, but were immediately driven out by counter attack.	
		10.30pm	Four aeroplanes passed over our lines flying Westward. Although bright moonlight none of the aeroplanes could be seen. Four bombs were dropped around HANNESCAMPS and near our trenches but did no damage. 50 Germans approached to within 200 yards of trench 67 but were seen and dispersed by Lewis Gun fire. Casualties O.R. One wounded. Strength. 34 offrs 781	

2449 Wt. W14957/M90 750,000 1/16 J.B.C. & A. Forms/C.2118/12.

Army Form C. 2118.

Instructions regarding War Diaries and Intelligence Summaries are contained in F. S. Regs., Part II. and the Staff Manual respectively. Title Pages will be prepared in manuscript.

WAR DIARY or INTELLIGENCE SUMMARY

(Erase heading not required.)

1/4 GLOUCESTER REGT.

Place	Date	Hour	Summary of Events and Information	Remarks and references to Appendices
HANNESCAMPS TRENCHES	21.2.16		Night 20-21 cold and fine. Own artillery shelled GOMMECOURT 10.30 PM. Battn relieved by 6 Glosr. Relief commenced 4pm. Battn present in Brigade Reserve Billets BIENVILLERS 9pm. Second blanket per man brought from transport at SOUASTRE. Strength 34 off 780	
BIENVILLERS	22.2.16		Battn in reserve at BIENVILLERS. Weather cold. Snow. Working parties on HANNESCAMPS defences and communication trenches. Strength 34 off 900. Draft of 121 O.R. arrived from Base.	
BIENVILLERS	23.2.16		Bn in Brigade reserve. Draft inspected. Fair standard. Health good. Strength 34 off 899.	
BIENVILLERS	24.2.16		Bn in Brigade reserve. Weather cold. Snow. Strength 34 offs 899.	
BIENVILLERS and HANNESCAMPS TRENCHES	25.2.16		Bn in Brigade reserve until 3pm when commenced to relieve 6 Glouc Regt. Weather very cold and snowing. Trenches frozen and no gum boots required. This facilitated relief which was completed by 5.30pm. Enemy quiet. Strength 34 off 895.	
HANNESCAMPS TRENCHES	26.2.16		Bn in trenches. Thaw commenced. A few odd shells fell in our area. 34 off 895	
"	27.2.16		Bn in trenches. Snow during night 26th - 27th. Enemy quiet. Trenches in fair condition. Strength 34 offs 893	
"	28.2.16		Bn in trenches. Frost during night. Enemy quiet. Strength 34 offs 888	J. Davenport Lt Col 1/4 Glouc Regt

2449 Wt. W14957/M90 750,000 1/16 J.B.C. & A. Forms/C.2118/12.

144th Brigade

48th Division.

1/4th BATTALION

GLOUCESTERSHIRE REGIMENT

MARCH 1 9 1 6

Instructions regarding War Diaries and Intelligence Summaries are contained in F. S. Regs., Part II. and the Staff Manual respectively. Title Pages will be prepared in manuscript.

WAR DIARY
or
INTELLIGENCE SUMMARY
(Erase heading not required.)

1/4 GLOUCESTER REGT

Army Form C. 2118.

Place	Date 1916	Hour	Summary of Events and Information	Remarks and references to Appendices
HANNESCAMPS	29.2.16		Battalion in the Trenches at HANNESCAMP. Weather cold and wet. Orders received that 112th Infty Bde will relieve us at 7.0pm. this evening - XI R. Warwick Regt relieved us in the trenches. Relief began at 7.0pm and was completed by 9.25pm. Battn present in Billets at SOUASTRE at 1.30 A.M. - 8/Worcesters moved to BUS - 6/Gloucesters to SAILLY - 7/Worcesters to COURCELLES. Bde Hd Qrs to SOUASTRE. 2/Lieut. CHATTOCK & Sergeant and Corpl MAY went to Divisional School on 27.2.16. 1 Man to C.C.S. 2 Men to Field Ambce. Strength 34 officers and 887 O.R.	H.T.
SOUASTRE	1.3.16		Battalion in Billets at SOUASTRE. Companies cleaning up and inspected at Billets. 1 Man to C.C.S. and 1 Man returned from Field Ambulance. 3 Men to Field Ambce. Strength 34 officers 882 O.R.	H.T.
"	2.3.16		Battn in Billets at SOUASTRE. Training of Companies and Special Section 9.5 am to 12.30. 1 Man to C.C.S. 6 O.R. to F. Ambce and 1 Man returned from Field Ambce. Strength 34 officers and 881 O.R.	H.T.
"	3.3.16		Battalion left SOUASTRE and moved to COURCELLES. Paraded at 3.0pm and reported present in Billets at COURCELLES at 5.03pm in Divisional Reserve. Bde Hd Qrs and Bde Reserve at COLINCAMPS. Battn Q.M. Stores and Transport at BUS. The Brigade now hold trenches in front of SERRE and the Division is now in 10th Corps 4th Army. 1 Man returned from leave. 1 from C.C.S, 3 from Field Ambce and 2 men sent to Field Ambulance. Strength 34 officers and 882 O.R.	H.T.
COURCELLES	4.3.16		Battn in Divisional Reserve at COURCELLES. Very heavy fall of snow. 2 officers and 2 men returned from leave. 1 Man to C.C.S, 1 Man to Field Ambulance. G.O.C. Division visited Battn Hd Qrs. Strength 34 officers and 880 O.R.	
"	5.3.16		Battalion relieved 6/Glouc: Regt in trenches 87 to 95 (from front of SERRE to TOUVENT FARM) C and D Companies left COURCELLES at 2.30pm. - 2 platoons of D. Compy to COLINCAMPS - remainder of Coy & C. Company to support trenches. A and B Compys left at 5.30pm and 6.15pm to relieve front Line. Relief completed at 11.30pm. To Base 4 men time expired. 3 men to C.C.S, 6 men to Field Ambulance, 2 men returned from Field Ambce and 1 from Hospital and 6 O.R. from 1 Months leave. Strength 34 officers and 880 O.R.	
SERRE TRENCHES	6.3.16		Battalion in the Trenches - A Coy on Right - B Coy on left. C Company in Support in MONK TRENCH and D. Coy in Reserve in The TROSSACHS. Dispositions on our Right and left. On Right the 36th Division and 145th Brigade (48th Divn) on our left. Trenches very wet and in many places impassable for mud. 4 posts	

2449 Wt. W14957/M90 750,000 1/16 J.B.C. & A. Forms/C.2118/12.

Instructions regarding War Diaries and Intelligence Summaries are contained in F. S. Regs., Part II. and the Staff Manual respectively. Title Pages will be prepared in manuscript.

WAR DIARY
or
INTELLIGENCE SUMMARY

(Erase heading not required.)

Army Form C. 2118.

Place	Date	Hour	Summary of Events and Information	Remarks and references to Appendices
SERRE TRENCHES	6.3.16		4 posts on the left of B. Coy. are completely isolated and can only be relieved at night – Weather very cold with snow and frost and conditions very trying – Much work required everywhere to restore fallen in trenches and maintain those still existing – 1 man to Brigade repairing Gumboots – 1 man to 3rd Army police intelligence School – 2 O.R. to C.C.S., 5 O.R. to Field Amb^ce – 3 men returned from Field Ambulance –	
		2.30 pm	Pte Gay (3360) and Pte Pickford (4891) wounded in Trenches by Rifle bullets –	J.T.
		3.0 pm	Pte HOTCHINS (1500) wounded in Trenches by Rifle bullets – Strength 34 Officers and 874 O.R.	
" "	7.3.16		Battalion in Trenches – Weather still very bad – Work on trenches continuously clearing and pumping – Batt. relieved by 6/Glouc. Regt – Relief began at 4.30 pm and was completed by 10.0 pm. – Battalion proceeded to billets at COURCELLES without Casualty, at 1.0 A.M. – 2 men to C.C.S. 5 men to Field Ambulance – 1 man returned from Field Ambulance – Strength 34 Officers and 872 O.R.	J.T.
COURCELLES	8.3.16		Battalion in Billets at COURCELLES in DIVISIONAL RESERVE – Companies cleaning up and inspected – 3 men to R.E. as Carpenters – 6 men to C.C.S. 7 men to Field Ambulance – 1 man returned from C.C.S. + 2 men from Field Ambulance – Strength 34 Officers and 867 O.R.	J.T.
" "	9.3.16		Battalion in Reserve at COURCELLES – C.O. attended Brigade Conference at 11.0 A.M. and had meeting of Officers at 2.15 pm. Companies and Special Sections paraded 9.0 A.M. till 12.0 Noon – Instruction in Mills Grenade fitted as Rifle Grenade by Bombing Officer at 12.15 pm. – Football Match between A + B. Coys in afternoon – A Coy won 5 goals to nil – 1 man to C.C.S. 6 men to Field Amb^ce – Strength 34 Officers + 866 O.R.	J.T.
" "	10.3.16		Battalion in Reserve at COURCELLES – Companies and Lewis Gun Sections, Snipers, Grenadiers and Reserve Signallers paraded 9.0 A.M. till 12.0 Noon. Inspection of billets by C.O. & 2nd in C. A Company had Baths at COLINCAMPS – Officers paraded under Adjutant for Communication Drill at 11.30 A.M. – 2 performances by the 48th Div^l "Cinema" arranged to take place at 4.30 pm + 6.30 pm in Recreation Room had to be abandoned as the troupe could not attend – G.O.C. 10th Corps visited Battalion H^d Q^rs at 10.30 A.M. 2 men to Field Amb^ce and 1 man returned from Field Amb^ce Strength 34 Officers and 866 O.R.	J.T.
" "	11.3.16		Battalion in Reserve as before – Relieved 6/Glouc. Regt in trenches. Reserve Coys (A + B.) left COURCELLES at 3.0 pm. – Two Trench Companies (C + D) left at 5.0 pm. Relief completed – without Casualty at 9.50 pm. Left Reserve Company (Coy) has two 2 platoons in TROSSACKS – 1 platoon in LA SIGNY and 1 platoon in COLINCAMPS – 24 Sick men also left in COLINCAMPS – 2/Lieut CHATTOCK and Servant to Field Ambulance from Command – 2 men to Base time – Weather still very cold with snow on ground –	

2449 Wt. W14957/M90 750,000 1/16 J.B.C. & A. Forms/C.2118/12.

Instructions regarding War Diaries and Intelligence Summaries are contained in F. S. Regs., Part II. and the Staff Manual respectively. Title Pages will be prepared in manuscript.

WAR DIARY
or
INTELLIGENCE SUMMARY
(Erase heading not required.)

Army Form C. 2118.

Place	Date	Hour	Summary of Events and Information	Remarks and references to Appendices
			time expired. 3 men to C.C.S. 3 men to Field Ambulance. Strength 34 Officers and 861 O.R.	J.C.T.
SERRE TRENCHES	12.3.16	11.0pm	Battalion in the Trenches opposite SERRE. Weather much finer. Enemy quiet. Rather more Machine Gun fire from enemy at 8.0pm than usual. Work as usual on trenches and clearing Jones Trench and CABER Trench also front line and communication trenches. Excavating for Left Company H^d Q^{rs} in CABER & Batt^n. H^d Q^{rs} in OBSERVATION WOOD. P^{te} STARKEY slightly wounded by M.G. bullet in Trench 91 but remained on duty. L/Cpl TAYLOR to Div^l Anti-Gas School. 5 men to C.C.S and 1 man to Field Amb^{ce} [illegible] O.R. returned from Field Amb^{ce}. Strength 34 Officers and 858 O.R.	J.C.T.
	13.3.16		Battalion in the Trenches. Night 12/13 quiet. Weather during day very fine & warm but with thunder at night. Artillery activity more than usual all day but especially in morning. British Aeroplane forced to descend between German front line and SERRE at 12.15 noon. [illegible] men from B^{de} Grenadier Class returned to duty and [illegible] Grenade Course [illegible]. 1 N.C.O and 2 men sent to SUCRERIE for Trench Railway repairs. 1 O.R. returned from Div^l School and 2 to Field Amb^{ce}. Strength 34 Officers and 858 O.R.	J.C.T.
	14.3.16		Battalion in the Trenches. Night 13/14 very bright Moonlight. A & B Companies relieved C & D Companies in fire trenches. Relief of isolated posts on LEFT observed by the Germans opposite who opened heavy firing. 2/Lieut: CHATTOCK (who had this day returned from Field Ambulance) killed by rifle bullet. Relief could not be completed until 3.30AM when moon went down. Considerable Artillery activity during day and several [illegible] bombs on our trenches during afternoon. Our Trench Mortar Battery and Heavy Guns replied. 2/Lieut: RUSSELL and Serg^t DARR to Div^l School. 2/Lieut: SMITH and 26 O.R. to Brigade [illegible] Company. L/Cpl GIBSON wounded in action. 3 men to C.C.S. 5 men to Field Ambulance. and 3 men returned from Field Amb^{ce} and 1 man from C.C.S. 2/Lieut: CHATTOCK buried in Military Cemetery by SUCRERIE at 6.0pm. Strength 33 Officers and 855 O.R. 2 men smothered by falling earth in right trenches caused by [illegible] [illegible] but [illegible] alive. [illegible] [illegible] (trenches [illegible] with C.O. [illegible])	J.C.T.
	15.3.16		Battalion in the Trenches. Night 14/15 normal. Artillery, Trench Mortars and Rifle Grenades more active than usual during the whole day.	
	16.3.16		Battalion in Brigade Reserve at Colincamps. Working parties provided by C & D Coys. Strength 33 officers 838 O.R.	
	17.3.16		Battalion in Brigade Reserve at Colincamps. Practice taking up Bde Reserve Alarm position in evening. Strength 35 officers 864 O.R.	

2449 Wt. W14957/M90 750,000 1/16 J.B.C. & A. Forms/C.2118/12.

Instructions regarding War Diaries and Intelligence Summaries are contained in F. S. Regs., Part II. and the Staff Manual respectively. Title Pages will be prepared in manuscript.

WAR DIARY
or
INTELLIGENCE SUMMARY
(Erase heading not required.)

Army Form C. 2118.

Place	Date	Hour	Summary of Events and Information	Remarks and references to Appendices
SERRE	18.3.16		Battalion in Brigade Reserve at Colincamps. [illegible] for sleeping on duty. Strength 35 officers 863 O.R.	
TRENCHES	19.3.16		Battalion in Brigade Reserve at Colincamps. At 2 am Germans shelled left Coy of the 6th Glosters heavily, Gas shells and lachrymatory shells being used. Battalion 'stood to Arms' at 2.10 am. A & C Coys moved to Brigade Reserve positions at 2.20 am. Strength 35 officers 862 O.R.	
	20.3.16		Battalion relieved the 6th Glosters in the trenches. Our Howitzers & Field Guns bombarded enemy's 1st & 2nd lines. 3365 Pte Upton, 4479 Pte Morton, 1654 Pte Britton wounded. Draft 26 O.R. Strength 35 officers 885 O.R.	
	21.3.16		Battalion in trenches. Night 20 & 21 normal. 3799 Pte White, & 1854 Cpl Avery killed. 2919 Pte Turner, 4770 Pte Wagner, 2622 Pte Eves, 8567 L/Cpl Abraham, 4805 Pte Sampson wounded. Strength 35 officers ~~875~~ 878 O.R.	
	22.3.16		Battalion in trenches. Enemy very quiet all day. 5 officers & 20 NCOs & men 13 E York. attached for instruction. Strength 32 officers 870 O.R.	
	23.3.16		Battalion in Trenches. Enemy quiet until 4 pm when they put over some Canister Bombs. Battalion relieved by 6th Glos Regt. L/Cpl Jenkins & 2896 Pte Pegrum killed. 4391 Pte Gillop suffering from shell shock. Strength 34 officers 877.	
	24.3.16		Battalion in billets at Courcelles. Divisional Reserve. Strength 35 officers 875 O.R.	
	25.3.16		Battalion in billets at COURCELLES. Companies paraded at 9 am for training. Strength 35 officers 872 O.R.	
	26.3.16		Battalion in billets at COURCELLES. Divine Service in Recreation Room at 11.30 am attended by G.O.C. Division. Strength 35 officers 874 O.R.	
	27.3.16		Battalion in billets at COURCELLES. Relieved 6th Glos Regt in trenches. Strength 35 off 870 O.R.	
	28.3.16		Battalion in trenches. Night quiet. Strength 35 officers 869 O.R.	
	29.3.16		Battalion in trenches. Enemy quiet. 2/Lt Russell, Sgts Dark & Johnston returned from Div School. Strength 35 officers 865 men.	

Army Form C. 2118.

Instructions regarding War Diaries and Intelligence Summaries are contained in F. S. Regs., Part II. and the Staff Manual respectively. Title Pages will be prepared in manuscript.

WAR DIARY
or
INTELLIGENCE SUMMARY
(Erase heading not required.)

Place	Date	Hour	Summary of Events and Information	Remarks and references to Appendices
SERRE TRENCHES	30.3.16		Battalion in trenches. Enemy quiet, but for a few rifle grenades. Day very fine. Aeroplanes very active. One of our planes was brought down near PUISIEUX by hostile plane.	

J. Cecil Thompson, Major
1/4th Glouc. Regt.
31/3/16.

2449 Wt. W14957/M90 750,000 1/16 J.B.C. & A. Forms/C.2118/12.

144th Brigade.

48th Division.

1/4th BATTALION

GLOUCESTERSHIRE REGIMENT

APRIL 1 9 1 6

12. P.
6 sheets

Confidential

War Diary
of

1/4th Battn Gloucestershire Regiment.

From 31-3-16 to 30-4-16

Volume 13.

Instructions regarding War Diaries and Intelligence Summaries are contained in F. S. Regs., Part II. and the Staff Manual respectively. Title Pages will be prepared in manuscript.

WAR DIARY
or
~~INTELLIGENCE SUMMARY~~
(Erase heading not required.)

1/4th Battalion Gloucestershire Regt.

Army Form C. 2118.

Place	Date	Hour	Summary of Events and Information	Remarks and references to Appendices
SERRE TRENCHES	31.3.16		Battalion in the trenches. Enemy very quiet. Weather very fine & warm. 1 officer and 13 O.R return from leave	
	1.4.16		Battalion in the trenches. Enemy quiet. C.O & officers 14th Yorks & Lancs Regt visited trenches. 2 officers and 5 O.R. per platoon for our two right Companies. Lt Colonel S Davenport & 2/Lt Reed to C.C.S.	
	2.4.16		Battalion in trenches. Enemy quiet. Relieved by 6th Glos Regt. Relief complete by 8.15 pm. Battalion present in billets at COUIN at 12 midnight. 2/Lt Simmonds to Divisional School of Instruction.	
COUIN	3.4.16		Battalion in Divisional Reserve in the hut billets at COUIN. No parades. Divisional Conference at SAILLY-AU-BOIS.	
	4.4.16		Battalion in Divisional Reserve at COUIN. Instructional parades at 9 am. Divisional Conference at SAILLY-AU-BOIS.	
	5.4.16		Battalion in Divisional Reserve at COUIN. Marching order inspection by C.O. followed by instructional parades. About 9 pm the Battalion had the order to "Stand by", owing to heavy German bombardment. Battalion fell in on Alarm Post, & was ready to move off at 9.15 pm. Battalion moved off at 9.30 pm & got as far as COIGNEUX, when the order came to return to billets. Battalion all in billets at 11.15 pm.	
	6.4.16		Battalion in Divisional Reserve at COUIN. Instructional parades at 9 am.	

2449 Wt. W14957/M90 750,000 1/16 J.B.C. & A. Forms/C.2118/12.

Instructions regarding War Diaries and Intelligence Summaries are contained in F. S. Regs., Part II. and the Staff Manual respectively. Title Pages will be prepared in manuscript.

WAR DIARY or ~~INTELLIGENCE SUMMARY~~

(Erase heading not required.)

1/4 Battalion Gloucestershire Regt.

Place	Date	Hour	Summary of Events and Information	Remarks and references to Appendices
COUIN	6.4.16		Battalion in Divisional Reserve at COUIN. Company Training 9 to 12 30	
	7.4.16		" " " " " "	
HEBUTERNE TRENCHES	8.4.16		Battalion relieved the 6th Glos in trenches near Hebuterne. Relief complete 10.45 pm Dispositions B Coy in the line A Company in Trossacks and JEAN BART. C+D Company H.Q.s at HEBUTERNE. Night quiet	
	9.4.16		Battalion in the trenches. Night normal. Casualties 3 killed 11 wounded by Canister Bombs. 20 oR reinforcements arrive.	
	10.4.16		Battalion in trenches. Normal.	
	11.4.16		" " " " A Coy relieve B Coy in front line. Divisional conference at Divisional HQ at COUIN at 2 30 pm	
	12.4.16		Battalion in trenches. Very wet, all work considerably hindered.	
	13.4.16		" " " " Everything Normal.	
	14.4.16		Battalion relieved by 6 Glouc Regt Relief commenced about 5 pm Battalion present in Billets at 11 30 pm. A+C Coys in COIGNEUX, B+D Coys +HQrs at SAILLY-AU-BOIS	
SAILLY AU BOIS	15.4.16		Battalion in Bde Reserve at SAILLY + COIGNEUX	
	16.4.16		" " " " " " Early morning parades + Church service. G.O.C. Brigade inspected billets.	
	17.4.16		Battalion in Bde Reserve at SAILLY and COIGNEUX. Early morning parade, usual Company parades	

2449 Wt. W14957/M90 750,000 1/16 J.B.C. & A. Forms/C.2118/12.

Instructions regarding War Diaries and Intelligence Summaries are contained in F. S. Regs., Part II. and the Staff Manual respectively. Title Pages will be prepared in manuscript.

WAR DIARY or ~~INTELLIGENCE SUMMARY~~

(Erase heading not required.)

4th Battalion Gloucestershire Regt.

Place	Date	Hour	Summary of Events and Information	Remarks and references to Appendices
SAILLY AU BOIS	18.4.16		Battalion in Bde Reserve. Company instructional parades.	
	19.4.16		" " " " "	
COIGNEUX	20.4.16		" " " at COIGNEUX	
	21.4.16		" " " in huts. Company parades 9 to 11.30 Divine Service 12.45 pm. Divisional Conference at Div H.Q. COIGN	
	22.4.16		Battalion in Div Reserve at COIGNEUX All Companies Lewis Gunners + Snipers paraded from 9am to 12.30. Very wet all day. Camp in a fearful state.	
	23.4.16		Battalion in Div Reserve at COIGNEUX Major Slade to Course at Flexecourt	
	24.4.16		Battalion in Div Reserve at COIGNEUX	
J SECTOR HEBUTERNE TRENCHES.	25.4.16.		Battalion relieved the 4th Royal Berks in the trenches. Enemy Artillery + trench Mortars fairly active.	
	26.4.16		Battalion in the trenches. Enemy artillery active during the day, especially on New Trench + Communication Trenches near.	
	27.4.16		Battalion in trenches. Enemy heavily shelled our line with Minenwerfers and 5.9" shells for 10 mins at about 1 am. One of our patrols encountered a strong German Patrol at the 16 Poplars. We had 1 killed 6 wounded 2 missing.	
	28.4.16		Battalion in trenches. About 1000 shells fell in the vicinity during the day Night quiet.	

2449 Wt. W14957/M90 750,000 1/16 J.B.C. & A. Forms/C.2118/12.

WAR DIARY

or

~~INTELLIGENCE SUMMARY~~

(Erase heading not required.)

4th Battalion Gloucestershire Regt

Instructions regarding War Diaries and Intelligence Summaries are contained in F. S. Regs., Part II. and the Staff Manual respectively. Title Pages will be prepared in manuscript.

Place	Date	Hour	Summary of Events and Information	Remarks and references to Appendices
J SECTOR HEBUTERNE TRENCHES.	29.4.16		Battalion in trenches. Enemy artillery fairly quiet up till the time we started a heavy bombardment on the right near SERRE. Heavy Minnenwerfer fell in our lines no damage done. Rest of night calm. 1 man slightly wounded.	
	30.4.16		Battalion in trenches. Enemy fairly quiet during the day.	
			1/5/16 J. Davenport [illegible] 1/4 [illegible]	

2449 Wt. W14957/M90 750,000 1/16 J.B.C. & A. Forms/C.2118/12.

144th Brigade.

48th Division.

1/4th BATTALION

GLOUCESTERSHIRE REGIMENT

M A Y 1 9 1 6

9.D. 13. Pi
7 sheets

Vol 14

C O N F I D E N T I A L.

War Diary

of

1/4th Battalion Gloucestershire Regiment.

from 1/5/16 to 30/5/16.

Volume 14

Army Form C. 2118.

Instructions regarding War Diaries and Intelligence Summaries are contained in F. S. Regs., Part II. and the Staff Manual respectively. Title Pages will be prepared in manuscript.

WAR DIARY
or
INTELLIGENCE SUMMARY
(Erase heading not required.)

1/4 Battalion Gloucestershire Regt.

Place	Date	Hour	Summary of Events and Information	Remarks and references to Appendices
HEBUTERNE TRENCHES	1/5/16		Battalion in trenches in HEBUTERNE. Enemy artillery and Minenwerfer active during early part of the day. Strength 35 offrs 859	
"	2/5/16		Battalion in trenches in HEBUTERNE. Enemy normal. Relieved by 1/5 Glouc. Regt. Relief commenced 9am. Battalion in billets at AUTHIE by 4.30 pm. Strength 34 offrs 859	
AUTHIE	3/5/16		Battalion in billets at AUTHIE. Strength 34 offrs 859	
BEAUVAL	4/5/16		Brigade moved to corps reserve at BEAUVAL. Left AUTHIE 6.30 am. Battalion present in billets at BEAUVAL 10 am. Strength 34 offrs 859	
"	5/5/16		Battalion in Corps Reserve at BEAUVAL. Company training and instructional classes. Strength 34 offrs 856	
"	6/5/16		" " " " " " " " " " 34 offrs 855	
"	7/5/16		" " " " " " Brigade Church Parade. Strength 35 offrs 849	
"	8/5/16		" " " " " " Company training & instructional parades. 36 offrs 895	

2449 Wt. W14957/M90 750,000 1/16 J.B.C. & A. Forms/C.2118/12.

Army Form C. 2118.

Instructions regarding War Diaries and Intelligence Summaries are contained in F. S. Regs., Part II. and the Staff Manual respectively. Title Pages will be prepared in manuscript.

WAR DIARY
or
INTELLIGENCE SUMMARY

(Erase heading not required.)

1/4 Battn Gloucestershire Regt

Place	Date	Hour	Summary of Events and Information	Remarks and references to Appendices
BEAUVAL	9/5/16		Battalion in Corps Reserve at BEAUVAL. Instruction parades and Range Practise (100x) Strength 36 offs 899	
"	10/5/16		" " " " " " " " Strength 36 offs 898	
"	11/5/16		" " " " " " Route March. " 36 offs 895	
"	12/5/16		" " " " " " Instructional parades " 36 " 895	
"	13/5/16		" " " " " " Brigade Sports " 36 " 897	
"	14/5/16		" " " " " " Brigade Church Parade Reinforcement 4/O.R Strength 34 offs 899	
COUIN	15/5/16		" (with rest of Brigade) moved to COUIN and became divisional reserve with 7 Worcs. Regt. Day very bad for marching – heavy rain. Strength 34 offs 900	
"	16/5/16		Battalion in Divisional Reserve at COUIN in huts. Company training. Strength 34 offs 948	
"	17/5/16		" " " " " " " " " " " 34 offs 946	

2449 Wt. W14957/M90 750,000 1/16 J.B.C. & A. Forms/C.2118/12.

Army Form C.2118.

WAR DIARY
or
INTELLIGENCE SUMMARY 1/4 Battn Gloucestershire Regt

(*Erase heading not required.*)

Instructions regarding War Diaries and Intelligence Summaries are contained in F. S. Regs., Part II. and the Staff Manual respectively. Title Pages will be prepared in manuscript.

Place	Date	Hour	Summary of Events and Information	Remarks and references to Appendices
COUIN	18/5/16		Battalion in Divisional Reserve at COUIN. Working parties. Strength 34 offrs 944	
"	19/5/16		" " " " " " " " " 34 offrs 942	
"	20/5/16		" " " " " " " " " 34 offrs 942	
"	21/5/16		" " " " " " " " " 34 offrs 939	
"	22/5/16		" " " " " " " " " 34 offrs 936	
"	23/5/16		" " " " " " " " " 34 offrs 935	
" and Trenches HEBUTERNE	24/5/16		" " " " " " Relieved 6 Glouc. Regt in trenches section H. Boundaries held by us are from HEBUTERNE – SERRE road to HEBUTERNE – PUISIEUX road. 7th Worcs on our right are Right Bn of the Brigade with 31st Divn on right of 7th Worcs. 56th Division are on left of our Battalion – at present Kensington London Battn are in the trenches.	

2449 Wt. W14957/M90 750,000 1/16 J.B.C. & A. Forms/C.2118/12.

Instructions regarding War Diaries and Intelligence Summaries are contained in F. S. Regs., Part II. and the Staff Manual respectively. Title Pages will be prepared in manuscript.

WAR DIARY
or
INTELLIGENCE SUMMARY
(Erase heading not required.)

1/4 Batt. Gloucestershire Regt.

Army Form C. 2118.

Place	Date	Hour	Summary of Events and Information	Remarks and references to Appendices
HEBUTERNE TRENCHE	25/5/16		Battalion in HEBUTERNE trenches. C and D Companies in front line, A Company in Support in the village, B Company in reserve in SAILLY. Bn HdQrs on E. end of village. Enemy artillery active between 10 am and 11 am. Strength 31 offrs 939	
"	26/5/16		Battalion in HEBUTERNE trenches. Dispositions as on 25th. Day normal. Night 26-27 several minenwerfers and 5.9" on our new front line trench. ~~During the night 56th Div on our left~~ Strength 30 offrs 890+49	
"	27/5/16		Battalion in trenches. At 8am 5.9" shells on right company damaging trench and closing it and also damaging the wire, and destroying Lewis Gun Position. Trench cleared during the day. At 10.30 pm several minenwerfers were put on our new trench accompanied by M.G. Fire from direction of GOMMECOURT. At 11.30pm the fire increased and a salvo of minenwerfers at the same time was put on 56th Div. N. of BUISIEUX ROAD. Under cover of this a German Patrol cut our wire & attempted to enter our trench but were stopped by bombs from Cpl. Scott's post and by rifle fire. Casualties 3 killed and 3 wounded. A German killed by one of our post was of 66th Bavarian Regt. The action of the following men of D Company is commended for their coolness and energy - 1660 Sgt GILBERT, 2455 L/Cpl CANTLE, 4023 Pt ULLER, 4501 Pt WHITTOCK, 5238 Pt JENKINS.	

Army Form C. 2118.

Instructions regarding War Diaries and Intelligence Summaries are contained in F. S. Regs., Part II. and the Staff Manual respectively. Title Pages will be prepared in manuscript.

WAR DIARY
or
INTELLIGENCE SUMMARY
(Erase heading not required.)

1/4 Battn Gloucestershire Regt.

Place	Date	Hour	Summary of Events and Information	Remarks and references to Appendices
HEBUTERNE TRENCHES	28/5/16		Bn in trenches. A and B Companies change over with C and D companies. Day normal. At 11pm a very heavy burst of Minenwerfer - M.G. and artillery fire was opened on new trench N. of PUISIEUX ROAD. This was repeated at 12 midnight and several of the minenwerfer fell on our trenches - the left bays of the new front trench being blown in. The trench was cleared by dawn. Strength 32 o/r 935	
"	29/5/16		Bn in trenches. Enemy quieter than usual - 200 shells on our trenches at 11.30 am. Usual Minenwerfer and artillery activity from 11 pm to 1 pm. Strength 32 o/r 933	
"	30/5/16		Bn in trenches. Enemy quiet during day. Night 30-31 quieter than usual. 5.9" around Bn HQ and Support company between 5pm and 7.30pm - a little damage. Our artillery dispersed German working parties about 11pm between PUISIEUX and SERRE roads. Strength 32 o/r 933	

[signature] Major
4th Glosc Regt

2449 Wt. W14957/M90 750,000 1/16 J.B.C. & A. Forms/C.2118/12.

144th Brigade.

48th Division.

1/4th BATTALION

GLOUCESTERSHIRE REGIMENT

JUNE 1916

48

Vol 15

E.O.S.

14.P
8 sheets

1/4th Bn Gloucestershire Regt

Confidential

War Diary

of

1/4th Bn Gloucestershire Regt

from 31.5.16 to 30.6.16

Volume 15.

Instructions regarding War Diaries and Intelligence Summaries are contained in F. S. Regs., Part II. and the Staff Manual respectively. Title Pages will be prepared in manuscript.

WAR DIARY
or
INTELLIGENCE SUMMARY

(Erase heading not required.)

1/4 Bn Glouc Regt

Army Form C. 2118.

Place	Date	Hour	Summary of Events and Information	Remarks and references to Appendices
TRENCHES	31/5/16		Battalion in HEBUTERNE trenches. Boundaries of line held are HEBUTERNE - SERRE and HEBUTERNE - PUISIEUX roads. Day quieter than usual. Night 31 - 1st quieter than normal Strength 32 offs 934	
COUIN	1/6/16		Battalion relieved in trenches by 5th R Warwick Regt. Relief commenced 7am and completed 9.30 am. Battalion proceeded to bivouacs at foot of COUIN hill - all present in bivouacs 2.50 pm Strength 32 offrs 935	
GEZAINCOURT	2/6/16		Battalion moved to GEZAINCOURT at 5. 30 am. Reached GEZAINCOURT 9.30 am. Roads and weather good. Battalion in billets 10 am. Brigade now in CORPS RESERVE Strength 33 offs 935	
GEZAINCOURT	3/6/16		Battalion in billets at GEZAINCOURT. Orders received at 7.30 pm to move to ST. RIQUIER on 4th Strength 33 offrs 940	
MAISON ROLLAND	4/6/16		Battalion moved to MAISON ROLLAND at 4 am. In billets at MAISON ROLLAND at 11.15 am (This place is about 4 miles E of ST. RIQUIER). Marching very good. Brigade halted for breakfasts near BEAUMETZ at 7. am. Strength 33 offs 940	
	5/6/16		Battalion at MAISON ROLLAND for divisional training. Both 144 & 145 INF BDE'S are in neighbourhood for divisional training. Training ground is N. of ONEUX. Strength 34 offs 939	

J.H.G. Dobbin Major O.C. 1/4 Glosters

2449 Wt. W14957/M90 750,000 1/16 J.B.C. & A. Forms/C.2118/12.

Army Form C. 2118.

Instructions regarding War Diaries and Intelligence Summaries are contained in F. S. Regs., Part II. and the Staff Manual respectively. Title Pages will be prepared in manuscript.

WAR DIARY
or
INTELLIGENCE SUMMARY
(Erase heading not required.)

1/4 . Bn Glouc. Regt

Place	Date	Hour	Summary of Events and Information	Remarks and references to Appendices
MAISON ROLLAND	6/6/16		Battalion in billets MAISON ROLLAND for training. 144 and 145 INF BDE's are now in CORPS RESERVE. Strength 34 off. 926	
"	7/6/16		Training consists chiefly of open warfare attacks on defensive positions 34 off. 925	
"	8/6/16		34 off 926	
"	9/6/16		33 off 926	
"	10/6/16		33 off 926	
"	11/6/16		33 off 928	
YVRENCH	12/6/16		Battalion moved from MAISON ROLLAND to YVRENCH (4 miles). YVRENCH is at N.E. corner of the training ground. Billets good. Draft of 60 O.R. arrived consisting of 10th Glouc. A good type of man. 33 off 928	

H.G. Dobbin Major
O.C. 1/4 Glos. Regt

2449 Wt. W14957/M90 750,000 1/16 J.B.C. & A. Forms/C.2118/12.

Army Form C. 2118.

Instructions regarding War Diaries and Intelligence Summaries are contained in F. S. Regs., Part II. and the Staff Manual respectively. Title Pages will be prepared in manuscript.

WAR DIARY
or
INTELLIGENCE SUMMARY

(Erase heading not required.)

1/4 Bn Glouc. Regt.

Place	Date	Hour	Summary of Events and Information	Remarks and references to Appendices
YVRENCH	13/6/16		Battalion in Corps Reserve at YVRENCH. Training 33 off 989	
YVRENCH and OCCOCHES	14/6/16		Battalion in Corps Reserve. Orders received at 12 noon to move at 2pm. Bn moved at 2pm for OCCOCHES, near DOULLENS. Arrived in billets at 8·30pm. Distance marched 17 miles. Bn HQ at OUTREBOIS. Roads very bad owing to rain. Time was put forward 1 hour on night 14th–15th. Bn thus lost a valuable hours sleep. Detachment under 2/Lt Symes of 53 O. Ranks leave for FLESSELLES 33 off 989	
OCCOCHES and COUIN	15/6/16		Battalion paraded at 4·45 am and marched to COUIN. Halted for Breakfasts from 7am to 9am. Reached COUIN (14 miles) at 12·30pm. Battalion thus marched 31 miles in 21 hours. March was very steady and on the day no one fell out. Battalion went into bivouacs at bottom of COUIN hill. Bn HQ at COIGNEUX (The Mairie) 33 off 986	
COUIN	16/6/16		Battalion in bivouacs at COUIN. Working parties 33 off 986	
"	17/6/16		" " " " " " 34 " 986	

2449 Wt. W14957/M90 750,000 1/16 J.B.C. & A. Forms/C.2118/12.

H. G. Dobbin Major O.C. 1/4 Glosters.

Army Form C. 2118.

Instructions regarding War Diaries and Intelligence Summaries are contained in F. S. Regs., Part II. and the Staff Manual respectively. Title Pages will be prepared in manuscript.

WAR DIARY
or
INTELLIGENCE SUMMARY
(Erase heading not required.)

1/4 Bn Glouc. Regt

Place	Date	Hour	Summary of Events and Information	Remarks and references to Appendices
COUIN	18/6/16		Battalion in Corps reserve at COUIN. 48th Division is now division in reserve to VIII Corps. Warwick Bde have 2 Bns in line and 2 attached to 4th Division. Working parties 37 offrs 1007.	
"	19/6/16		Battalion in Corps reserve at COUIN. 35 offrs 1008	
"	20/6/16		" " " " 35 offrs 1006	
"	21/6/16		" " " " " " Two parties each of 2 officers, 4 NCOs and 82 men. 16 whole under command of Capt Guterbock proceed to HEBUTERNE and carry up 100 Gas Cylinders and place them in front line trench near HEBUTERNE–SERRE road. Work successfully carried out. Standing patrols were out in front of our wire to cover the work. No sign of the enemy. 35 offrs 1006	
COUIN and SAILLY	22/6/16		Battalion paraded at Bivouacs at pt. COUIN and moved by platoons to bivouacs at pt. 126 W of SAILLY. Bde HQ and 6 Glos at same place. 2 Warcs Battn at COIGNEUX. 143 MG Coy at COUIN. WARWICK Bde in trenches and in reserve. 56th Division is on left of Div: front. 31st Div, 4th Div, 29th div on right of Divisional front in that order. 35 offrs 1015	

[illegible] Major
O.C. 1/4 Glosters

2449 Wt. W14957/M90 750,000 1/16 J.B.C. & A. Forms/C.2118/12.

Instructions regarding War Diaries and Intelligence Summaries are contained in F. S. Regs., Part II. and the Staff Manual respectively. Title Pages will be prepared in manuscript.

WAR DIARY
or
INTELLIGENCE SUMMARY

(Erase heading not required.)

1/4 Glouc. Regt

Place	Date	Hour	Summary of Events and Information	Remarks and references to Appendices
SAILLY BIVOUAC (pt 126)	23/6/16		Battalion in Corps reserve 1 mile W. of SAILLY in bivouacs at pt 126. VIII Corps artillery commence preliminary bombardment in preparation for IVth Army advance. This is known as "U" day. 35 o/r 1014	
"	24/6/16		Battalion in Corps reserve as above. 2nd day of bombardment of enemy trenches or "V" day. 35 o/r 1014	
"	25/6/16		Battalion in Corps reserve as above. 3rd day of bombardment or W day. 35 o/r 1006	
"	26/6/16		Battalion in " " " 4th " " " X day. 35 o/r 1007	
	27/6/16		" " " 5th " " " Y " 35 o/r 1007	

H. G. Dobbie Major
O.C. 1/4 Glo'ster

2449 Wt. W14957/M90 750,000 1/16 J.B.C. & A. Forms/C.2118/12.

Army Form C. 2118.

Instructions regarding War Diaries and Intelligence Summaries are contained in F. S. Regs., Part II. and the Staff Manual respectively. Title Pages will be prepared in manuscript.

WAR DIARY
or
INTELLIGENCE SUMMARY

(Erase heading not required.) 1/4 Bn Glouc Regt.

Place	Date	Hour	Summary of Events and Information	Remarks and references to Appendices
SAILLY BIVOUACS (Pt 126)	28/6/16		Battalion in Corps Reserve at SAILLY BIVOUACS. Fifth day of preliminary Artillery Bombardment. Tools and shovels drawn to complete battalion fighting order tools. The weather is very bad. Operations are postponed for 48 hours. 35 offrs 1005	
"	29/6/16		Battalion moved bivouacs ½ mile West to J.16.a as pt. 126 seemed likely to be shelled. This is sixth day of preliminary bombardment or Y1 day. Weather improving. 35 offrs 1005	
"	30/6/16		Battalion in Corps reserve in bivouacs at J.16.a. Grenades drawn to complete to two per man. Companies inspected in fighting order. General Fanshaw Commanding the division addressed all officers. This is the last day of the preliminary bombardment. Orders received that Battalion must be ready to move at half an hours notice after 8am on 1st. 35 off 1002	

F. J. Dobbin Major
O.C. 1/4 Glosters

2449 Wt. W14957/M90 750,000 1/16 J.B.C. & A. Forms/C.2118/12.

144th Inf.Bde.
48th Div.

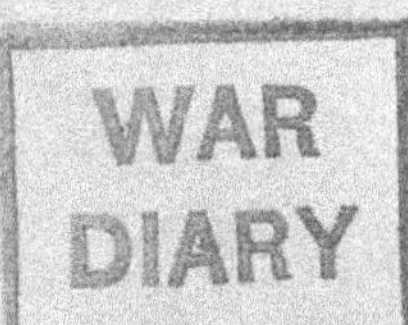

4th BATTN. THE GLOUCESTERSHIRE REGIMENT.

J U L Y

1 9 1 6

Instructions regarding War Diaries and Intelligence Summaries are contained in F. S. Regs., Part II. and the Staff Manual respectively. Title Pages will be prepared in manuscript.

or INTELLIGENCE SUMMARY

(Erase heading not required.)

1/4 Bn Glouc. Regt

Place	Date	Hour	Summary of Events and Information	Remarks and references to Appendices
P.12 G (S of SAILLY)	1/7/16		Battalion in bivouacs at pt 126 (S of Sailly). Divisions in reserve VIII Corps. Breakfast 6am. Operation orders received that Batt would be in readiness to pass the Brigade Starting point (J.15 c. 4.3) at 11 minutes after Zero and proceed to P.18 c (S.W. of MAILLY-MAILLET). At 8am message was received that zero time would be 8am. Battn paraded at once. When about to move an 8" shell fell within a few yards of the transport. 6 horses were put out of action, 1 man killed and 2 wounded. Bn eventually moved complete with transport to Bde starting point. Reached MAILLY-MAILLET via BERTRANCOURT and BEAUSSART at 11am & formed up in bivouac. 145 Bde joined bivouac at 3pm. Division was now behind the attack of the 29th Division. No further orders were received on this day but information of 4th Army attack showed that enemy had been very strong N of ANCRE and had counter attacked. SOUTH of the ANCRE the situation appeared more favourable. 34 off 945 (Ration strength)	
P.18 C (MAILLY-MAILLET)	2/7/16		Battalion with rest of Division (less 143 Bde who are attached to 4th Div) in position of readiness at pt P.18 c. Reveille 5am. 9am Brigade Conference. Orders received that 48th Divn would assault and capture German front line system of trenches from River Ancre on South to Y Ravine on North. 145 Bde are on right of attack, 144th in centre, and 87th Bde from 29th Divn on left. Of our Bde 6 Glos attack on left, 7 Worcs on right, 4 Glos Bde reserve, 8 Worcs Divnl reserve. 34 off. 943	

2449 Wt. W14957/M90 750,000 1/16 J.B.C. & A. Forms/C.2118/12.

H. G. Collins Lt Col.
Commanding 1/4 Gloster Regt

Instructions regarding War Diaries and Intelligence Summaries are contained in F. S. Regs., Part II. and the Staff Manual respectively. Title Pages will be prepared in manuscript.

INTELLIGENCE SUMMARY

(Erase heading not required.) 1/4 Bn. Glouc. Regt

Place	Date	Hour	Summary of Events and Information	Remarks and references to Appendices
P.18.c. (MAILLY-MAILLET)	2/7/16 (Cont'd)		At 8 pm Brigade marched from P 18 c. 8 Worcs remained in Div. reserve in their bivouac at P 18 c. Battn entered communication trench WITHINGTON AVENUE at 10.15 pm with a view to taking up position as Brigade Reserve at "KNIGHTSBRIDGE BARRACKS". Great delay was experienced in the communication trench. ~~Eventually reach~~ 33 off 943	
WITHINGTON AVENUE TRENCH	3/7/16	1 am	At 1 am 7 Worcs received orders that operations were cancelled and acting on this message the Battn returned to Bivouac.	
P.18.c.	3/7/16	4 am	Reached bivouac at P.18 c about 4 am. At 3 30 pm orders were received that Bde would leave bivouac at 5 pm. March orders received at 4.15 pm. Battalion moved at 5 pm to Bivouac at J.16 a (near	
J.16 a (S of SAILLY)	3/7/16	7.30 pm	(SAILLY) and reached there bivouac at 7.30 pm.) At 10 45 pm orders were received that Bn was to be ready to move at 5 minutes notice. No reason was given for this. Troops were known to be collecting behind GOMMECOURT.	
J.16 a (S of SAILLY)	4/7/16		Bn in bivouac. In afternoon 6 Glos and 8 Worcs relieved 92 and 94 Mr Bde (31st Div) respectively in trenches in front of SERRE. 4th Division on our right. 145 Bde on our left. Bde HQ moved to COURCELLES at 9.30 pm. 32 off 942	

2449 Wt. W14957/M90 750,000 1/16 J.B.C. & A. Forms/C.2118/12.

J.H.G. Dobbin Lt Col.

Commanding 1/4th Bn. Gloster Regt

Instructions regarding War Diaries and Intelligence Summaries are contained in F. S. Regs., Part II. and the Staff Manual respectively. Title Pages will be prepared in manuscript.

INTELLIGENCE SUMMARY

(Erase heading not required.) 1/4 Bn Glouc. Regt

Place	Date	Hour	Summary of Events and Information	Remarks and references to Appendices
COURCELLES	5/7/16		Battn paraded 8.30 am at Bivouacs at J 16 a and moved to COURCELLES. Reached billets at 10 am. In afternoon Battn commenced continuous working parties on Salvage work clearing material & stores etc from trenches and collecting and burying dead. Weather bad. 31 offrs 939	
"	6/7/16		Battn in Brigade Reserve at COURCELLES. Weather very bad. 27 offrs 937	
"	7/7/16		Battn in Brigade Reserve at COURCELLES. Weather very bad. 27 offrs 934	
COURCELLES to TRENCHES	8/7/16		Battn relieved 6 Glouc Regt in trenches. Boundaries MATTHEW COPSE on right or South to JOHN COPSE on North. Battn HQ junction of DUNMOW & EXCEMA (50x N. of Observation Wood). Front line is held by 10 posts (9½ platoons) found from 2 companies. Relief commenced 5.30 pm complete with exception of front posts at 7 pm. B Coy on right, D on left, A right reserve, C left reserve. Trenches found of MONK very bad full of mud & front line also full of dead. EXCEMA only communication trench open. During night enemy shelled our trenches heavily. 2/Lt Pollack on patrol examined German front line & found it held by posts. A stretch of 30x between posts was full of water. 30 offrs 931	

2449 Wt. W14957/M90 750,000 1/16 J.B.C. & A. Forms/C.2118/12.

H.G. Potter Lt Col.
Lieut. Col.
Commanding 4th Batt. Gloster Regt
1/4 Gloster Regt

Instructions regarding War Diaries and Intelligence Summaries are contained in F. S. Regs., Part II. and the Staff Manual respectively. Title Pages will be prepared in manuscript.

INTELLIGENCE SUMMARY

(Erase heading not required.) 1/4 Bn Glouc. Regt

Place	Date	Hour	Summary of Events and Information	Remarks and references to Appendices
TRENCHES in front of SERRE	9/7/16		At 12 30 am enemy shelled NORK and EXCEMA heavily with 5.9's obtaining several direct hits. Three shells fell on a working party killing 2/Lt H. P. FISHER (K.S.L.I. attached) and five men and wounding one man. They were buried in the SUCRERIE cemetery at 4 pm. 30 offrs 932 All quiet after morning stand to. Patrols from both front companies examined German wire at 11 pm and found it practically non-existent	
"	10/7/16		Intense bombardment of enemy trenches at K.23 b 1.8 and K.17.D.1.9 at 5 pm. Enemy very quiet during whole of day. Patrol from both companies at night located Germans working in their trenches. A few enemy shrapnel in afternoon wounded two men 30 offrs 916	
"	11/7/16		Enemy quiet all day. In evening M.G. fire increased slightly and half a dozen canister bombs fell on right company – no damage. Reinforcements 20 O.R. (14th Glouc.) arrived at Transport. Patrols from both front companies examined enemy wire which is slowly being improved. Our artillery shelled heavily several points opposite our front at 10 pm and 3 am. Enemy replied with a few small shells. 30 offrs 930	
"	12/7/16		Battalion in trenches. Enemy very quiet during day & night. Trenches are now very much improved – our work having been greatly assisted by the dry weather	

2449 Wt. W14957/M90 750,000 1/16 J.B.C. & A. Forms/C.2118/12.

H. G. Dobbin Lt Col
Lieut. Col. Commanding 4th Batt. Gloster Regt.
[illegible]

Instructions regarding War Diaries and Intelligence Summaries are contained in F. S. Regs., Part II. and the Staff Manual respectively. Title Pages will be prepared in manuscript.

INTELLIGENCE SUMMARY

(Erase heading not required.)

1/4 Battn Glouc. Regt.

Place	Date	Hour	Summary of Events and Information	Remarks and references to Appendices
COURCELLES	12/7/16 (Contd)		Battalion relieved in trenches by 6 Glosr Regt. Relief commenced 5pm. Morris trench relieved by 7pm. Relief very smooth and satisfactory. On return to COURCELLES 260 men were called out to carry smoke candles and "P" bombs from LA SIGNY and COLINCAMPS to 6 Glosr [illegible] & to place them in position in front line of the Brigade for use in demonstration on night 13th 14th. 30 offrs 929	
"	13/7/16		Battalion in Brigade Reserve Billets COURCELLES. 30 offrs 926	
COURCELLES and BOUZINCOURT	14/7/16		Battalion at COURCELLES. "Ready to move" order received. Orders received to be ready to move to BOUZINCOURT in motor lorries. Battalion paraded in marching order at 2pm. Battalion left COURCELLES in 39 lorries & buses at 2.45pm. In billets at BOUZINCOURT at 5.30pm. Transport also moved to BOUZINCOURT. BUCKS and BERKS moved to SENLIS. 31 offrs 919	
BOUZINCOURT and Trenches in front of OVILLERS	15/7/16		Battalion relieved 97th INF. BDE in trenches in front of OVILLERS-LA-BOISELLE. Northern limit X.7.B.2.8. Southern limit (X.7.B.5.1½ "THE POINT"). On our right are the 7 Worcs who extend across old German front line at X.8.B.½.2 & then along S.E. edge of OVILLERS. On our left are 49th Division. Dispositions B Coy front line and CONISTON (support line). A Coy in support at Quarries junction of X.7.A and W.12.B. C and D Companies in reserve at Quarries at W.11.C. Battalion commenced to leave BOUZINCOURT 5pm. Relief complete 9.15pm. 31 offrs 924	

H.T. [illegible] Lt Col
Lieut. Col. Commanding 4th Batt. Gloster Regt

2449 Wt. W14957/M90 750,000 1/16 J.B.C. & A. Forms/C.2118/12.

Instructions regarding War Diaries and Intelligence Summaries are contained in F. S. Regs., Part II. and the Staff Manual respectively. Title Pages will be prepared in manuscript.

INTELLIGENCE SUMMARY

(Erase heading not required.) 1/4 Battn Glouc. Regt.

Place	Date	Hour	Summary of Events and Information	Remarks and references to Appendices
TRENCHES neighborhood of OVILLERS	16/7/16		At 4 pm on 16th orders were received at Bde HQ to assault and capture the German front line trench from X.8.A.½.2 to X.7.B.9.9. This line is not visible from anywhere in our line owing to shape of ground. The artillery were therefore ignorant of state of wire, which was generally reported in good condition. It was therefore decided to reconnoitre the wire before the assault and decide actual formation of attack on receiving report as to gaps in wire. Zero time was also left unfixed until receiving this report. D and B Coys were detailed for the attack and it was decided that after dark about 10 pm, D Coy should be in readiness in the assembly trench 150x in front of our line with B Coy in readiness in communication trench leading to it, to wait in these positions until reconnaissance report was received. The right of the attack was to gain touch with 4 Oxfords who had advanced to X.8.A.½.2. At 10 pm D Coy were in position in assembly trench and at the same time 2/Lt C.F. HOLLAND with 6 NCOs and men from the attacking companies left to reconnoitre the wire. B Coy then moved into position in the communication trench. Each man carried four No 5 grenades and four sandbags and in addition one man in each platoon carried twelve No 5 grenades. 100 shovels and 100 picks were also taken. Lewis Guns accompanied companies. 2/Lt HOLLAND returned at 11.30 pm after a close reconnaissance of the German line to be attacked. He reported the trench held apparently strongly as he was several times	

2449 Wt. W14957/M90 750,000 1/16 J.B.C. & A. Forms/C.2118/12.

J.G. [illegible] Lieut. Col.
Commanding 4th Batt. Gloster Regt.

Instructions regarding War Diaries and Intelligence Summaries are contained in F. S. Regs., Part II. and the Staff Manual respectively. Title Pages will be prepared in manuscript.

INTELLIGENCE SUMMARY

(Erase heading not required.) 1/4 Battⁿ Glouc. Regt

Place	Date	Hour	Summary of Events and Information	Remarks and references to Appendices
TRENCHES near OVILLERS	16/7/16		fired at. He also reported that the wire was very much cut about and not much of an obstacle. The attack was to take the form of a surprise with 10 minutes bombardment to cover the approach of the two companies. Orders were issued for the two companies to attack in line, D Coy on left, and B on the right, and zero time was fixed for 2 am, allowing the minimum of time for B Coy to get in position.	
TRENCHES OVILLERS	17/7/16		The artillery barrage commenced 1.50 am and at same time M.G. Coy [illegible] covered our left flank. 31 offrs 926 About 2.30 am a wounded man returned from D Coy who reported that his company were in the trench. At 2.45 am a written report from Capt Castle commanding D Coy reached Bⁿ H.Q. by runner stated that all was well and owing to misunderstanding with a verbal report from right Company reported touch gained with the Warcs on our right. After this several wounded men returned through our lines At 5.25 am Capt Castle sent a message by a runner who worked his way across "no mans land". This reached Batt HQrs about 7 am and stated that the two companies were not in touch with Warcs and that they were being heavily bombed from both flanks. Orders were immediately issued to C Coy, who were in touch with Worcs at X.8.A.5.1, to work up by bombing attacks along	

2449 Wt. W14957/M90 750,000 1/16 J.B.C. & A. Forms/C.2118/12.

H.G. Dobbin Lt Col
Lieut. Col.
Commanding 4th Batt. Gloster Regt.

Instructions regarding War Diaries and Intelligence Summaries are contained in F. S. Regs., Part II. and the Staff Manual respectively. Title Pages will be prepared in manuscript.

INTELLIGENCE SUMMARY

(*Erase heading not required.*) 1/4 Bn Glouc. Regt

Place	Date	Hour	Summary of Events and Information	Remarks and references to Appendices
TRENCHES OVILLERS	17/7/16		front line German trench until touch was gained with B Coy. Major Slade and Lieut Fisher (OC. C Coy) personally supervised the bombing attacks which were eventually successful and about 12 noon communication was opened with the right flank of the attack. This operation was aided considerably by Stokes Mortars. It was found that each of the companies attacking had had about eighty casualties. Their supply of bombs had not run out, but several German bombs had been used with a view to saving the No 5s. About 3pm C Coy relieved B Coy, B Coy withdrawing to CRUCIFIX CORNER. At 7pm A Coy relieved D Coy, D Coy withdrawing to CONISTON. A Coy held line from X.8.A. 1.1 on left. 27 offrs 788	
TRENCHES OVILLERS	18/7/16		A Coy held line X.8.A.H. tonight until afternoon. Operation orders were then received (about 1pm) to push forward to X.8.A.3.7 – X.8.A.6.7. Worcesters pushing forward parallel with us on our right. A Coy commenced this operation about 5pm – pushing forward up German old front line – while C Coy pushed forward parallel with them up German old second line – C Coy keeping touch with Worcs. The line X.8.A.3.7 – X.8.A.6.7 was gained about 8pm with only a few casualties. During the afternoon Batt HQrs had moved to German original front line at X.8.A.0.8., D Coy moved to support near this pt & B Coy moved into CONISTON.	

2449 Wt. W14957/M90 750,000 1/16 J.B.C. & A. Forms/C.2118/12.

[signature] Lieut. Col. Commanding 4th Batt Gloster Regt.

Instructions regarding War Diaries and Intelligence Summaries are contained in F. S. Regs., Part II. and the Staff Manual respectively. Title Pages will be prepared in manuscript.

INTELLIGENCE SUMMARY

(Erase heading not required.) 1/4 Battn Glouc. Regt

Place	Date	Hour	Summary of Events and Information	Remarks and references to Appendices
TRENCHES OVILLERS	18/7/16		At 11 pm operation orders were received to push forward to X.8.A.3.9 – X.8.A.8.8 and beyond X.8.A.8.8 then line made by the original communication trenches – 7 Worcs advancing and prolonging the line on our right. Zero time was to be 1.30 am. Arrangements had to be made very hurriedly for this advance. A by & C by commenced it – each bombing up their own trench as previously. Each party was met by a very stubborn resistance. The left party was met by a machine gun in the trench and dug outs were set on fire in front of them to stop their advance & was found impossible to get forward. The ... on our right were turned back by M.G. fire. 28 offrs 765	
TRENCHES OVILLERS	19/7/16		In trenches in positions as above. Day was spent in consolidating our positions gained. 28 offrs 747	
TRENCHES OVILLERS and DONNET POST – RIBBLE STREET	20/7/16		Relieved by 6 Glouc. Regt. Relief commenced 11 am & completed by 2.30 pm. During relief enemy shelled all our trenches and ends of village heavily with 5.9s. Remarkably little damage was done. When relieved Battalion went to support at DONNET POST and Ribble Street, and took over carrying duties – water – grenades ammunition etc. 28 offrs 746	

H. T. Dobbin Lt Col
Lieut Col
Commanding 4th Batt Glouster Regt

2449 Wt. W14957/M90 750,000 1/16 J.B.C. & A. Forms/C.2118/12.

Instructions regarding War Diaries and Intelligence Summaries are contained in F. S. Regs., Part II. and the Staff Manual respectively. Title Pages will be prepared in manuscript.

INTELLIGENCE SUMMARY

(*Erase heading not required.*) 1/4 Battn Glouc. Regt

Place	Date	Hour	Summary of Events and Information	Remarks and references to Appendices
DORNETT POST and OVILLERS TRENCHES	21/7/16		6 Glouc took over line to pt. 47. This meant increased Brigade frontage. B and C Coys were therefore sent up in support to OVILLERS. Brigade is now practically working with 3 Battalions as 8 Worcs have been gassed while on working party and are out of action. 28 offrs 766	
OVILLERS TRENCHES	22/7/16		Battalion relieved 6 Glouc in trenches 6 Glouc being drawn out in order to attack line pt 90 to pt 40 which is at present on the immediate right of the line held by our brigade. Relief complete by 3.30 pm. B and C Coys in line 37-67-88-28-47. C Coy on right and B on left. D Coy is in support to B and A Coy in support to C. 6 Glouc attack was timed for 2.30 am and we were ordered to assist by bombing forward from pt 47 & pt 28. Attack commenced at time stated – 6 Glouc attacking with 3 companies and keeping one in reserve. Our companies worked hard to gain ground. C Coy found trench forward of 47 non-existent. In front of 28 enemy were in great strength and after bombing forward for a few bays wire was encountered. The bombing was continued throughout the night C Coy having about 30 casualties.	
OVILLERS TRENCHES	23/7/16		27 offrs 759 About 5 am on hearing that 6	

H.T. Dobbin Lt Col
Lieut. Col. Commanding, 4th Batt. Gloster Regt.

2449 Wt. W14957/M90 750,000 1/16 J.B.C. & A. Forms/C.2118/12.

Instructions regarding War Diaries and Intelligence Summaries are contained in F. S. Regs., Part II. and the Staff Manual respectively. Title Pages will be prepared in manuscript.

INTELLIGENCE SUMMARY

(Erase heading not required.) 1/4 Battn Glouc Regt

Place	Date	Hour	Summary of Events and Information	Remarks and references to Appendices
OVILLERS TRENCHES	23/7/16		Glouc attack had failed bombing attacks were stopped and A Coy relieved C Coy and Stokes Mortars were moved to fresh positions. 145 Bde at 7.30am attacked line between pts 37 and 79 on our right A Coy renewed bombing attacks. 145 Bde were successful and our bombing attacks were stopped. During these attacks 2/Lts Maclean and Fraser were severely wounded and 2/Lt Maclean could not be got at as he was just in front of German barricade. Remainder of the day was very quiet. 25 offrs 746	
OVILLERS TRENCHES and CRUCIFIX CORNER	24/7/16		About midnight 23rd 24th enemy made determined bombing attack on our barricade at pts 88 and 28. Our artillery immediately opened, also Stokes mortars & Lewis Guns. Enemy were easily kept back. Our casualties were about 10. 7 Warwicks relieved us in morning. Relief commenced 9.30am & was complete [illegible]. 1 Coy on relief went to RIBBLE STREET, remainder to CRUCIFIX CORNER	
OVILLERS TRENCHES and CRUCIFIX CORNER	25/7/16		145 Bde took line to go into [illegible] 22 offrs 689 B & D Coy relieve 5 Glouc. between pts 39 and 79 – D Coy in line and B Coy in support. D Coy are in touch with Warwicks on their right and 7 Worcs on their left. Night 25th 26th quiet. On this day Qr Master – transport officer was killed while on his way to Bn HQrs for orders. 21 offrs 659	

H. T. Dobbin Lieut Col
Commanding 4th Batt. Gloster Regt

2449 Wt. W14957/M90 750,000 1/16 J.B.C. & A. Forms/C.2118/12.

Summaries are contained in F. S. Regs., Part II. and the Staff Manual respectively. Title Pages will be prepared in manuscript.

INTELLIGENCE SUMMARY

(Erase heading not required.) 1/4 Bn Glouc. Regt

Place	Date	Hour	Summary of Events and Information	Remarks and references to Appendices
OVILLERS TRENCHES and CRUCIFIX CORNER	26/7/16		During morning D Coy attempted to push forward as reports had been received that Germans were retiring. This proved incorrect as D Coy met with strong opposition and M.G. fire. In afternoon C Coy relieved D Coy – B Coy remaining in support. During the day 145 Bde went to HEDAUVILLE – the division is now being relieved preparatory to going into rest. 22 offrs 652	
" and HEDAUVILLE	27/7/16		Brigade relieved by Brigade of 37th Division. 6th Battn the Queens Regt relieved our Battalion. Relief commenced about 10.15 am. B & C Coys were relieved by 12 noon. When relieved the Battn proceeded by companies to HEDAUVILLE – assembling for dinners outside BOUZINCOURT. Present in bivouacs at HEDAUVILLE about 5pm. 21 offrs 670	
HEDAUVILLE and ARQUEVES	28/7/16		Bn paraded at HEDAUVILLE at 7am and moved with Brigade (less 8 Wagons) to ARQUEVES. Present in billets at ARQUEVES at 10.30 am. 21 offrs 720	

H. G. Dobbin Lt. Lieut. Col.
Commanding, 4th Batt. Gloster Regt.

2449 Wt. W14957/M90 750,000 1/16 J.B.C. & A. Forms/C.2118/12.

Summaries are contained in F. S. Regs., Part II. and the Staff Manual respectively. Title Pages will be prepared in manuscript.

(Erase heading not required.) 1/4 Battn Glouc. Regt

Place	Date	Hour	Summary of Events and Information	Remarks and references to Appendices
ARQUEVES and BEAUVAL	29/7/16		Bn paraded at ARQUEVES at 7.15 am and moved with Brigade (less 8 waggons) to BEAUVAL. Present in billets at BEAUVAL at 10.15 am. Billets were same as when Battn was at BEAUVAL in May of this year.	
BEAUVAL and FRANQUEVILLE (Nr DOMART)	30/7/16		Bn paraded at BEAUVAL at 4.15 am to march via Candas to FRANQUEVILLE. Brigade halted at 7 am at FIENVILLERS for breakfasts and resumed the march at 8.30 am. Present in billets at FRANQUEVILLE at 10.30 am. The whole division is now in rest in neighbourhood of DOMART. Bde HQ are at FRANSU.	
			21 off. 734	
FRANQUEVILLE	31/7/16		Bn in rest at FRANQUEVILLE.	
			21 off. 758	

[illegible signature] Lieut. Col.
Commanding, 4th Batt. Glouster Regt.

2449 Wt. W14957/M90 750,000 1/16 J.B.C. & A. Forms/C.2118/12.

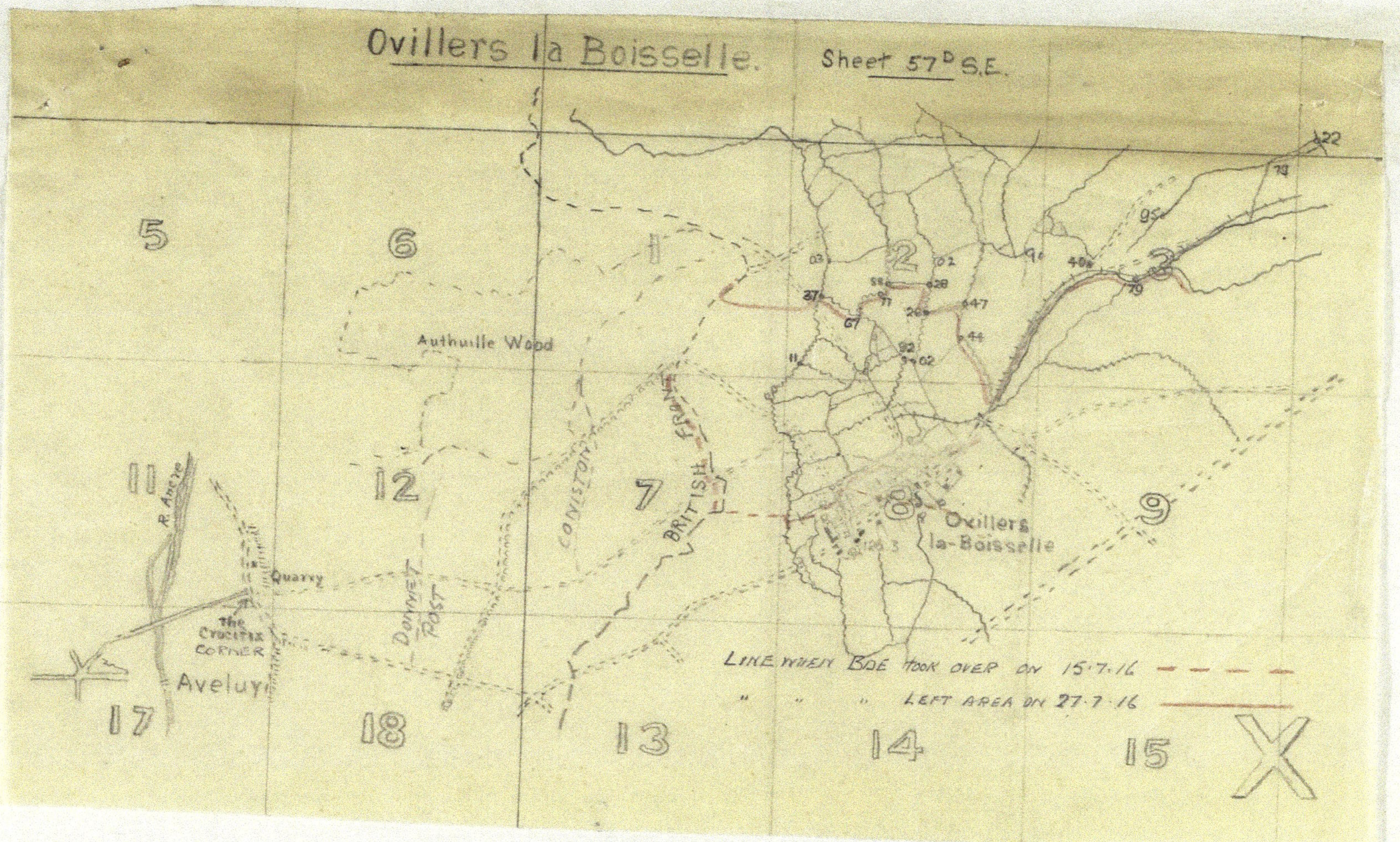

Ovillers la Boisselle.
Sheet 57D S.E.
Authuille Wood
R. Ancre
Quarry
The Crucifix Corner
Aveluy
Donnet Post
Coniston
British Front
Ovillers la-Boisselle
Line when Bde took over on 15.7.16
" " " Left area on 27.7.16

144th Brigade.

48th Division.

1/4th BATTALION

GLOUCESTERSHIRE REGIMENT

AUGUST 1 9 1 6

Instructions regarding War Diaries and Intelligence Summaries are contained in F. S. Regs., Part II. and the Staff Manual respectively. Title Pages will be prepared in manuscript.

or

INTELLIGENCE SUMMARY

(Erase heading not required.)

1/4 Battn Glous Regt

Place	Date	Hour	Summary of Events and Information	Remarks and references to Appendices
FRANQUEVILLE	1/8/16		Battalion in billets in FRANQUEVILLE. The 48th Division is now in rest in 9th Corps. Training is devoted to training bombers, Lewis Gun teams, and training new NCOs in their duties. The draft are trained daily under Sgt S.14.	Ration strengths Of. O.R 21. 457
"	2/8/16 to 7/8/16		Battalion remain in rest billets at FRANQUEVILLE (nr DOMART), for re-organisation of companies & training of specialists. Inspected by G.O.C. brigade on 6.8.16	22. 755 26. 741
AUTHEUX	8/8/16		Battalion moved from FRANQUEVILLE to AUTHEUX. Whole division is now moving from rest billets.	25. 743
FIENVILLERS	9/8/16		Battalion moved from AUTHEUX to FIENVILLERS.	" "
PUCHEVILLERS	10/8/16		Battalion moved from FIENVILLERS to PUCHEVILLERS. Bad roads necessitated transport moving on main road.	25. 743
"	11/8/16		Battalion remained in billets at PUCHEVILLERS.	25. 743

H. G. Dobbie

Lieut. Col.
Commanding 4th Batt. Glos'ter Regt.

2449 Wt. W14957/M90 750,000 1/16 J.B.C. & A. Forms/C.2118/12.

Instructions regarding War Diaries and Intelligence Summaries are contained in F. S. Regs., Part II. and the Staff Manual respectively. Title Pages will be prepared in manuscript.

or

INTELLIGENCE SUMMARY

(Erase heading not required.)

1/4 Battn Glouc Regt.

Place	Date	Hour	Summary of Events and Information	Remarks and references to Appendices
HEDAUVILLE	12/8/16		Battalion moved to HEDAUVILLE. ~~Bde and~~ 6 Glouc to BOUZINCOURT. 7 Worcs and Bde to FORCEVILLE.	Ration Strength OFF. O.R. 25. 762
HEDAUVILLE and Support to OVILLERS Sector in RIBBLE STREET	13/8/16		Battalion moved from bivouac at HEDAUVILLE at 1.15 pm, to relieve the battalion of 12th Division in brigade support to OVILLERS sector – A and D Coy. to OVILLERS, B and C Coys and HQ to RIBBLE STREET. 6 Glouc. move to take over line. Bde HQ to DONNET POST. 7 Worcs in Bde reserve at BOUZINCOURT. Our relief complete by 5 pm.	24. 751
OVILLERS Trenches & RIBBLE STREET	14/8/16		As for 13th. At 9pm A Coy move up to support to Glouc attack on line from 20–62. B Coy move from RIBBLE STREET to replace A Coy at 9pm. The attack did not succeed. B Coy return to RIBBLE STREET at 5am.	24. 768
OVILLERS TRENCHES	15/8/16		Relieved 6 Glouc in line, moving A & D Coys into front line and B & C from RIBBLE Street to support.	

H. G. Dobbin

Lieut. Col.

Commanding, 4th Batt. Gloster Regt.

2449 Wt. W14957/M90 750,000 1/16 J.B.C. & A. Forms/C.2118/12.

Instructions regarding War Diaries and Intelligence Summaries are contained in F. S. Regs., Part II. and the Staff Manual respectively. Title Pages will be prepared in manuscript.

INTELLIGENCE SUMMARY

(Erase heading not required.)

1/4 Batn Glouc. Regt

Place	Date	Hour	Summary of Events and Information	Remarks and references to Appendices
OVILLERS TRENCHES	15/8/16 cont^d		Dispositions as follows. A and D companies holding the line X.2.C 37-66-88 & X.2.B 28-47-90, where junction is made with the 145 Bde. Orders received to attack the line X.2.B. 20-62-90 with two companies. A and D were detailed, A to attack on right from 90 exclusive to 62 inclusive and D on left from 62 exclusive to 20 inclusive. After reconnoitring the ground it was decided that A Coy should start from the cross trench leading from X.2.D.47 to X.2.B.90, using the trench from X.2.D.47 to X.2.B.62 as a left guide. D Coy to start from the trench X.2.B.28.47. Two platoons of each company were to attack, two of D Coy being in reserve and one of A Coy, the remaining platoon of A Coy was to commence a simultaneous bombing attack from 90 towards 62. The artillery were to bombard intensely for 15 minutes before the attack. Heavies fired on the points to be attacked during afternoon and evening of 15th. Zero hour was fixed at 2am on 16th. During evening B Coy moved up from support and took over front line from X.2.C.37-66-88 to X.2.D.28 exclusive. C Company remained in support of A Coy, in 3rd Street.	Ration Strength OFF. OR. 24 768

H.G. Dobbin

Lieut. Col.
Commanding, 4th Batt. Glos'ter Regt.

2449 Wt. W14957/M90 750,000 1/16 J.B.C. & A. Forms/C.2118/12.

Instructions regarding War Diaries and Intelligence Summaries are contained in F. S. Regs., Part II. and the Staff Manual respectively. Title Pages will be prepared in manuscript.

INTELLIGENCE SUMMARY

(Erase heading not required.)

1/4 Battn Glouc Regt

Place	Date	Hour	Summary of Events and Information	Remarks and references to Appendices
			Diagram showing trenches to be attacked at 2am. 16.8.16 Scale 1:5,000	

2449 Wt. W14957/M90 750,000 1/16 J.B.C. & A. Forms/C.2118/12.

N.Y. Officer 1st Col

Instructions regarding War Diaries and Intelligence Summaries are contained in F. S. Regs., Part II. and the Staff Manual respectively. Title Pages will be prepared in manuscript.

INTELLIGENCE SUMMARY

(Erase heading not required.)

1/4 Battn Glouc. Regt

Place	Date	Hour	Summary of Events and Information	Remarks and references to Appendices
OVILLERS TRENCHES	16/8/16		The artillery barrage commenced 2 am and at this hour the assaulting platoons commenced to creep forward ready to assault when barrage lifted at 2 am. The night was very dark. The platoons were met with some rifle fire while moving out and when the barrage lifted and the assaulting troops got up to assault they were met with very heavy rifle and M G fire and a hail of bombs. It was found impossible to advance and the remainder of the assaulting platoons eventually withdrew to their original line. A Coy lost 2/Lt Down wounded (later died of wounds) and 2/Lts Bird, Baker, missing whilst in D Coy Lt Crump was badly wounded in the arm. In the ranks we lost about 70 killed wounded and missing. The enemy were evidently expecting an attack.	
			During morning orders were received that we were to be relieved by the E Warwicks Regt.	
			Guides met the relieving platoons at Crucifix Corner at 2 pm and companies when relieved assembled at the cookers at Crucifix Corner and then proceed to billets at BOUZINCOURT. Relief was completed about 4.20 pm and battalion was present in billets at BOUZINCOURT about 6.30 pm.	

2449 Wt. W14957/M90 750,000 1/16 J.B.C. & A. Forms/C.2118/12.

H. T. Dobbs [signature] Lieut. Col.
Commanding, 4th Batt. Glos'ter Regt.

Instructions regarding War Diaries and Intelligence Summaries are contained in F. S. Regs., Part II. and the Staff Manual respectively. Title Pages will be prepared in manuscript.

INTELLIGENCE SUMMARY

(Erase heading not required.)

1/4 Battn Glouc Regt

Place	Date	Hour	Summary of Events and Information	Remarks and references to Appendices
BOUZINCOURT	16/8/16 Contd		Enemy shelled BOUZINCOURT about 8.40 pm with 5.9's. Our casualties were 1 killed and 1 wounded.	Ration Strength OFF. O.R. 24. 768
BOUZINCOURT	17/8/16		Battalion in billets in BOUZINCOURT. At 11pm. enemy counter attacked on right of our Division & battalion received orders to be ready to move at short notice. Situation normal again 2.20 am on 18th	20. 685
BOUZINCOURT	18/8/16		Battalion in billets in BOUZINCOURT. From about 3pm Brigade was under orders to move at short notice to support attack by the 143 and 145 Brigades. About 11.40pm the Battalion received orders to move to RIBBLE STREET. The 144 M G Coy and 144 Stokes Mortar Battery accompanied the battalion. Battalion moved about midnight 18th 19th,	19. 696
RIBBLE STREET	19/8/16		and arrived RIBBLE STREET at 1.15am 19th. Accommodation for all the men was found in RIBBLE STREET, HODDER STREET and OVILLERS POST. Nothing happened during day. One company moved back to AVELUY to accomodate 2 companies of the Warwick who had moved back from OVILLERS.	18. 686
RIBBLE STREET	20/8/16		Battalion as for 19th. Orders were received that on 22nd battalion would attack the Southern face of the LEIPSIC REDOUBT from the trenches to left of NAB cross roads, at present held by the 7th Warwicks. During the day company officers ~~received~~ reconnoitred the 7 Warwick trenches.	18. 589

H.G. Dobbin. Lieut. Col.
Commanding, 4th Batt. Glos'ter Regt.

2449 Wt. W14957/M90 750,000 1/16 J.B.C. & A. Forms/C.2118/12.

Instructions regarding War Diaries and Intelligence Summaries are contained in F. S. Regs., Part II. and the Staff Manual respectively. Title Pages will be prepared in manuscript.

INTELLIGENCE SUMMARY

(Erase heading not required.)

1/4 Battn Glouc Regt

Place	Date	Hour	Summary of Events and Information	Remarks and references to Appendices
RIBBLE STREE	21/8/16		Further officers and NCO reconnoitred the 7 Warwick trenches in early morning. About 10 am orders were received that the battalion were to attack the German front and support line trenches on Southern face of the LEIPSIC REDOUBT, from X.1.B.59 ~~and~~ to X.1.A.98 and support trenches in rear R.31.C.90, R.31.D.30-62. At same time 6 Glouc were to attack from the right and by bombing past R.31.D.81 join with us at ~~R.31~~ X.1.B.59. C and B Companies were ordered to make the attack, A Coy in support and D in reserve. C and B Companies were each issued with 4 Mills Grenades, 2 Sandbags per man. 20 shovels per company, 50 red flares were also carried. The 1st Wilts Regt who already held the S.W. corner of the LEIPSIC REDOUBT were to attack or bomb simultaneously from the left and join with our left flank at X.1.A.98 and R.31.C.90. A grenade dump was prepared on the right of the position from which the Wilts were attacking which was to, and eventually did, supply our companies after the successful attack. C company moved from RIBBLE STREET about 1.15 pm, to allow time to get into position by the Zero hour which was notified as 6 pm. B, A, & D Companies followed in that order. Bn HQrs moved to Quarry BRAE at X.1.C.50, relieving the 7 Warwicks there	

H.T. Dobbin
Lieut. Col.
Commanding, 4th Batt. Glos'ter Regt.

2449 Wt. W14957/M90 750,000 1/16 J.B.C. & A. Forms/C.2118/12.

Instructions regarding War Diaries and Intelligence Summaries are contained in F. S. Regs., Part II. and the Staff Manual respectively. Title Pages will be prepared in manuscript.

INTELLIGENCE SUMMARY

(Erase heading not required.)

1/4 Battn Glouc Regt

Place	Date	Hour	Summary of Events and Information	Remarks and references to Appendices
TRENCHES LEIPSIC REDOUBT	21/8/16		B Company were to attack on the right from the Bank at X.1.B.4.2, covering half the frontage to the left from that point, C Company covering left half of the frontage. A company were in support at X.1.C.5.0 and D Coy in reserve at CONISTON X.7.C. The communication trenches leading to our front line had been very badly shelled for the past two days and were in many places practically destroyed. The companies thus found great difficulty in getting into position. However messages from Capt Wookey OC B Coy and Major Shellard OC C Coy were received about 5.15 pm to say they were ready. At 10 minutes to 6 o'clock B Coy commenced to move out into position & crawled forward for 100 yards under cover of the rising ground. About 6 pm C Coy also moved forward, each of the companies now being ready to assault, each company in two waves at 50 yards interval. The barrage was to be intense from 6 pm till 6.5 pm at which time it was to lift to second objective and infantry were to assault. The barrage was so excellent that the leading wave was able to get right up to the enemy parapet and waited there a few moments for it to lift, on which they rushed the trench, getting in before the enemy could leave their dugouts.	

H. T. Dobbin
Lieut. Col.
Commanding, 4th Batt. Glos'ter Regt.

2449 Wt. W14957/M90 750,000 1/16 J.B.C. & A. Forms/C.2118/12.

Instructions regarding War Diaries and Intelligence Summaries are contained in F. S. Regs., Part II. and the Staff Manual respectively. Title Pages will be prepared in manuscript.

INTELLIGENCE SUMMARY

(Erase heading not required.)

1/4 Battn Glouc Regt.

Place	Date	Hour	Summary of Events and Information	Remarks and references to Appendices
LEIPSIC REDOUBT	21/8/16	6pm	The Germans in the first trench were nearly all taken prisoners, the only ones offering any resistance being in the centre of the position, these were put out of action, their officer being sniped by Pte Bizley. A few were shot while retiring to the support line. The second wave of the attack passed through the first wave in the front trench and captured the support trench with very little opposition. This trench was very badly damaged. Communication trenches were non-existant between the two lines captured. Capt Wookey therefore took command in the original German support line, Major Shellard remaining in command of the whole. The 1st Wilts on our left also met with immediate success & touch was gained with them as intended, and also with the 6 Glosters on our right at R.31.D.81. Our casualties were slight. Immediately it was determined by observation & report that the position was taken A Coy under Lt Andrews were sent up in support & advanced over the open in lines of platoons at 50 yds interval	

[signature] Lieut. Col.
Commanding, 4th Batt. Glos'ter Regt.

2449 Wt. W14957/M90 750,000 1/16 J.B.C. & A. Forms/C.2118/12.

INTELLIGENCE SUMMARY

(Erase heading not required.)

1/4 Batt^n Glouc Regt

Place	Date	Hour	Summary of Events and Information	Remarks and references to Appendices
LEIPSIC REDOUBT	21/5/16	4pm	A Coy while advancing to the captured position had practically no casualties, and arrived at the position about 4.30 pm. The enemy were extremely slow in putting on any barrage.	Ration Strength
			All the prisoners taken were sent back across the open. They were about	OFF. O R
		10	150 in number, all of the 28th Infantry Regiment. They were passed through B^n H.Q^rs to CRUCIFIX CORNER.	18. 684
		12mt	After A Coy had moved, D Coy. were moved to replace them in support at X.1.C.50.	
			The trenches captured were very badly knocked about, especially on the right, where they were practically non existent.	
			The enemy shelled the captured position and our original front line intermittently	
LEIPSIC REDOUBT	22/5/16		The night 21-22 was spent in consolidating the position taken. Special Bd. working parties were also employed digging a communication trench from our original front line to the captured position about junction of X.1A and X.1.B.	
			During the night the enemy bombed down the communication trench	

2449 Wt. W14957/M90 750,000 1/16 J.B.C. & A. Forms/C.2118/12.

H. J. Dobbey [signature]
Lieut. Col.
Commanding, 4th Batt. Glos'ter Regt.

Instructions regarding War Diaries and Intelligence Summaries are contained in F. S. Regs., Part II. and the Staff Manual respectively. Title Pages will be prepared in manuscript.

INTELLIGENCE SUMMARY

(Erase heading not required.)

1/4 Batt. Glouc. Regt.

Place	Date	Hour	Summary of Events and Information	Remarks and references to Appendices
LEIPSIC REDOUBT	22/8/16		running N. from R.31.D.81 and drove them out of this point. We thus lost touch with the 6 Glouc. on our right about 1am.	Ration Strength
			The remainder of the night was quiet except for the usual shelling.	Off. O.R.
			A post was also established at R.31.D.81 at 4pm to keep touch with 6th Glouc.	17. 682.
			The 23rd passed quietly until 8pm when the shelling increased and became heavy, a barrage being placed along the original front line. This continued until 10pm. When enemy made a counter attack again on advanced points, both by bombing up communication trenches and attacking over the open. In all three counter attacks were made, they were all repulsed by bombing and Lewis Gun fire,	
LEIPSIC REDOUBT and BOUZINCOURT	23/8/16		the artillery also putting a slow barrage across our front. By 3.45am the situation was normal. During the night we took 15 prisoners, of the 15 Guards Reserve Division.	
			On the morning of the 23rd we were relieved by the 3rd Worcesters, 25th Division. Relief commenced 7am and was completed by 9.30am with exception of the isolated posts between R.31.D.81, and X.1.B.57. When relieved the Battalion moved to billets in BOUZINCOURT.	16. 543.

N. J. Dr[illegible]

Lieut. Col.
Commanding. 4th Batt. Glos'ter Regt.

2449 Wt. W14957/M90 750,000 1/16 J.B.C. & A. Forms/C.2118/12.

Summaries are contained in F. S. Regs., Part II. and the Staff Manual respectively. Title Pages will be prepared in manuscript.

(Erase heading not required.)

1/4 Battn Glouc. Regt

Place	Date	Hour	Summary of Events and Information	Remarks and references to Appendices
BOUZINCOURT	24/8/16		Battalion in billets in Bouzincourt. The whole of 144 INF-BDE is now relieved and is in BOUZINCOURT and in camp behind that place. In the afternoon the G.O.C. II Corps on battalion parade, presented Capt G.S. Castle with the CROIX de GUERRE for gallantry on 16-17 July 1916, after which the battalion marched past in column of route. The battalion was complemented on the excellent work done during the operations round OVILLERS etc.	Ration Str. OFF. O.R. 19. 531
"	25/8/16		Battalion in billets at BOUZINCOURT. Officers reconnoitred trenches of 71st Bde near AUCHONVILLERS	19. 533
FORCEVILLE.	26/8/16		Battalion moved to FORCEVILLE at 1.30 pm. Present in billets at FORCEVILLE at 3.15 pm. Bde HQ at FORCEVILLE. Orders received to relieve 2/SHERWOOD FORESTERS in right subsector 71st Bde on 27th inst. 144 INF Bde relieve 16 and 71 INF-BDES, putting all battalions in the line	18. 539

2449 Wt. W14957/M90 750,000 1/16 J.B.C. & A. Forms/C.2118/12.

A. J. Dobbs

Lieut. Col.

Commanding 4th Batt. Glos'ter Regt.

Summaries are contained in F. S. Regs., Part II. and the Staff Manual respectively. Title Pages will be prepared in manuscript.

(Erase heading not required.)

1/4 Batt^n Glouc. Regt.

Place	Date	Hour	Summary of Events and Information	Remarks and references to Appendices
TRENCHES 5.9 AUCHONVILLERS	27/8/16		Battalion left FORCEVILLE ~~at~~ by companies at 15 minute intervals in order D, A, C, B, companies. D Coy moved at 7.15 am. Packs were dumped en route for collection by transport at P.23.D 89. Transport proceed to P.17.D Q.M. Stores to billet ~~at~~ Mailly Mailly. Relief of 2/SHERWOOD FORESTERS 71st Bd. commenced about 9.30 am and was complete at 12.15 pm. Dispositions D Coy on right, A on left, C right support, B left support. Our front extends from the MARY REDAN on right to left at junction of N. ABBEY and WELLINGTON TRENCH. On our right are 1/1st CAMBRIDGESHIRE REGT, 39th Divn and on our left 1/6 Glouc. Regt. Trenches good by neither revetted or boarded. General situation is fairly quiet.	Ration Str. OFF. O.R. 18. 549
"	28/8/16		Battalion in trenches as above. Weather bad. Situation normal	18. 549

2449 Wt. W14957/M90 750,000 1/16 J.B.C. & A. Forms/C.2118/12.

H.G. Ottley [signature] Lieut. Col.
Commanding 4th Batt. Glos'ter Regt.

and the Staff Manual respectively. Title Pages will be prepared in manuscript.

(Erase heading not required.)

1/4 Battn Glouc Regt

Place	Date	Hour	Summary of Events and Information	Remarks and references to Appendices
TRENCHES S. of AUCHONVILLERS	29/8/16		Battalion in trenches as for 28th. Weather bad. Situation normal. Notification received of following awards. Major E. C. SLADE D.S.O. Capt G. S. CASTLE and 2/Lt. C. F. HOLLAND Military Cross. 2417 Cpl H. C. PERRY and 1736 Cpl. W. J. BIRD D.C.M's.	Ration Str. OFF. O.R. 22 564
"	30/8/16		Battalion in trenches as for 29th. Weather very bad. Owing to shortage of men and material trenches cannot be kept in decent repair. Situation normal	23 558
"	31/8/16		Battalion in trenches. C Coy relieved D Coy at 8 am. B Coy relieved A Coy at 12 noon. Weather much improved. Situation normal. Orders received to assist attack of 39th and 49th Divisions on our right (astride the R ANCRE) by Lewis Gun fire. Zero for the attack not yet fixed.	23 558

2449 Wt. W14957/M90 750,000 1/16 J.B.C. & A. Forms/C.2118/12.

H. J. Dobbin [signature] Lieut. Col.
Commanding, 4th Batt. Gloster Regt.

144th Brigade.

48th Division.

1/4th BATTALION

GLOUCESTERSHIRE REGIMENT

SEPTEMBER 1 9 1 6

Vol 18

17.P.
9 sheet

Confidential

War Diary

of

1/4th Batt. Gloucestershire Regiment

from 1. 9. 16 to 30. 9. 16

Volume. 18.

WAR DIARY
or
INTELLIGENCE SUMMARY
(Erase heading not required.)

Instructions regarding War Diaries and Intelligence Summaries are contained in F. S. Regs., Part II. and the Staff Manual respectively. Title Pages will be prepared in manuscript.

1/4 Battn Glouc Regt

Place	Date	Hour	Summary of Events and Information	Remarks and references to Appendices
				RATION STRENGTH
				OFFR. O. RANK
TRENCHES .17.A.5.3 to .10.D.5.2	1/9/16		Battalion in trenches from MARY REDAN on right to Y Ravine on left. Dispositions C company on right front, B company left front, D Company right support, A company left support. Battalion Headquarters at Q.16.B.3.3. On our right are the 39th Division and on our left the 6 Glous and ~~rem~~ the battalions of 144 Bde. Artillery covering us is 11th Div Artillery. The last two days wet weather has made trenches bad, owing to the fact that they are neither sumped or boarded	23 559
	2/9/16		Battalion in trenches. Dispositions as above. Weather dry and trenches improving. Situation normal and generally quiet except that enemy artillery activity has increased in the last 48 hours. Own artillery continuously active.	23 555
	3/9/16		In trenches dispositions as above. At 5.10 am the 39th Division on our immediate ~~front~~ Right attacked from the MARY REDAN to the RIVER ANCRE, their objective being German front line system of trenches. The attack was continued S. of the ANCRE by other divisions. Our Lewis Guns and Machine Guns assisted by putting barrage to cover left flank of the attack	23 542

[illegible signature]
Lieut. Col.
Commanding ~~1/4~~ 4th Batt. Glos'ter Regt.

2449 Wt. W14957/M90 750,000 1/16 J.B.C. & A. Forms/C.2118/12.

Instructions regarding War Diaries and Intelligence Summaries are contained in F. S. Regs., Part II. and the Staff Manual respectively. Title Pages will be prepared in manuscript.

WAR DIARY
or
INTELLIGENCE SUMMARY

(Erase heading not required.)

1/4 Battn Glouc Regt.

Place	Date	Hour	Summary of Events and Information	Remarks and references to Appendices
TRENCHES G.11.A.5.3 to G.10.D.5.2	3/9/16 (Cont'd)		Owing to the darkness and smoke from the barrage very little of the attack could be seen from our trenches. Germans sent up large numbers of very lights immediately the intense bombardment began and these did not cease throughout the attack until daylight. Enemy barrage was put on quickly and was intense consisting chiefly of 5.9's. Our trenches were badly damaged, the support lines being more damaged than the front line. Our casualties were very slight. The enemy barrage became normal about 1 pm, and remained normal from that time onwards. About 11 pm the enemy commenced to put phosgene gas shells immediately in rear of JOHN STREET and shortly afterward increased the range so that the shells fell behind Battn. H.Q. Q.rs. It was thought that the objective was the batteries still further in rear	RATION STR. OFFR. O.RKS
"	4/9/16		The wind being N. the effect of this gas was to drift across our battalion area. The men wore gas helmets and the gas shells continued without stopping until 4 a.m. No men showed definite signs of having been gassed.	23 529

[signature]
Lieut. Col.
Commanding 1/4th Batt. Glos'ter Regt.

2449 Wt. W14957/M90 750,000 1/16 J.B.C. & A. Forms/C.2118/12.

Army Form C. 2118.

Instructions regarding War Diaries and Intelligence Summaries are contained in F. S. Regs., Part II. and the Staff Manual respectively. Title Pages will be prepared in manuscript.

WAR DIARY
or
INTELLIGENCE SUMMARY

(Erase heading not required.)

1/4 Battn Glouc Regt.

Place	Date	Hour	Summary of Events and Information	Remarks and references to Appendices
TRENCHES Q.M.A.5.3 to Q.10.D.5.2	4/9/16 Contd		At 4 am gas shells ceased and from this time situation was normal. Division N of us put over gas during night 4th 5th	RATION STR. OFFR. O.RKS.
"	5/9/16		In trenches Situation normal. At 8.30pm our division from MAREYLEBONE to N put over Gas. Enemy after about 4 minute put up a Barrage.	24 529
" and Bois de WARMMONT	6/9/16		Situation normal. Relieved by 16th NOTTS and DERBY REGT. Relief commenced 9am and was complete at 12.20 pm. A very satisfactory relief. When relieved Companies were taken by motor Bus to hutments in BOIS de WARMMONT. Battalion present in BOIS de WARMMONT at 4.30pm.	24 544
"	7/9/16		In hutments BOIS de WARMMONT. Companies spend day cleaning and at BATHS at RIVER HOTHIE.	25 542
"	8/9/16		In hutments BOIS DE WARMMONT. - Company training in morning.	25 544

H Davenport
Lieut. Col.
Commanding 1/4th Batt. Glos'ter Regt.

2449 Wt. W14957/M90 750,000 1/16 J.B.C. & A. Forms/C.2118/12.

Instructions regarding War Diaries and Intelligence Summaries are contained in F. S. Regs., Part II. and the Staff Manual respectively. Title Pages will be prepared in manuscript.

WAR DIARY
or
INTELLIGENCE SUMMARY

(Erase heading not required.)

1/4 Batt.n Glouc: Regt.

Place	Date	Hour	Summary of Events and Information	Remarks and references to Appendices
				RATION STR. OFF. O.RKS
BOIS DE WARNIMONT.	9/9/16.		In hutments BOIS DE WARNIMONT. Inspection by G.O.C. 48th Division at 11 am	25 541
"	10/9/16.		In hutments BOIS DE WARNIMONT. Church parade 10am. A, B, C, & D Coys fired grouping practise on range, A company commencing at 10am. 79 Reinforcements arrived.	21 621
" & BUS	11/9/16		Battalion moved to huts at BUS. Move completed by 10.30 am. The remainder of the morning was devoted to Company training.	21 616
"	12/9/16.		Battalion found a working party of 500 men in 2 reliefs of 250 to dig a cable trench near BERTRANCOURT. A & D Cos worked from 8.45 - 12.30 PM B & C Cos from 12.30 PM - 5 PM.	19 620
" & ORVILLE	13/9/16		Battalion moved to billets in ORVILLE. Paraded at 8.15 am, & advance across country was practised as far as MARIEUX - THIEVRES road, when the Battalion was closed up & march continued by road to ORVILLE	19 618
"	14/9/16.		Battalion in billets at ORVILLE. Physical training before breakfast & Company training in morning. Reinforcements 6 Officers & 14 O.R arrived	24 629

2449 Wt. W14957/M90 750,000 1/16 J.B.C. & A. Forms/C.2118/12.

[signature] Davenport

Lieut. Col.
Commanding 1/4th Batt. Glos'ter Regt.

WAR DIARY
or
INTELLIGENCE SUMMARY
(Erase heading not required.) 1/4 Battn Glouc: Regt.

Instructions regarding War Diaries and Intelligence Summaries are contained in F. S. Regs., Part II. and the Staff Manual respectively. Title Pages will be prepared in manuscript.

Place	Date	Hour	Summary of Events and Information	Remarks and references to Appendices
				RATION STR. OFF. O.RKS.
ORVILLE	15/9/16.		In billets at ORVILLE. Physical training before breakfast. Company training in morning including musketry on range.	24 627
"	16/9/16.		In billets at ORVILLE. Physical training, & company parades in morning	24 622
"	17/9/16		In billets at ORVILLE. Church Parade in morning. Coys continued firing on range. 33 Reinforcements arrived.	21 637
" & AUTHEUX.	18/9/16		Battalion moved to billets in AUTHEUX. Paraded at 8.30 am. Present in billets at AUTHEUX about 12 noon. Weather was very bad and heavy rain made the march unpleasant.	22 639
"	19/9/16		In billets at AUTHEUX. Rain throughout day made training impossible	22. 636
"	20/9/16		In billets at AUTHEUX. Weather bad. Training commenced consisting chiefly of musketry, Lewis Gun and Grenadier classes	23 630
"	21/9/16		In billets at AUTHEUX. Training continued as above.	24 627

Davenport
Lieut. Col.
Commanding 1/4th Batt. Gloster Regt.

2449 Wt. W14957/M90 750,000 1/16 J.B.C. & A. Forms/C.2118/12.

Instructions regarding War Diaries and Intelligence Summaries are contained in F. S. Regs., Part II. and the Staff Manual respectively. Title Pages will be prepared in manuscript.

WAR DIARY or INTELLIGENCE SUMMARY

(Erase heading not required.)

1/4 BATTN GLOUC REGT.

Place	Date	Hour	Summary of Events and Information	Remarks and references to Appendices
AUTHEUX	22/9/16		Battalion in Billets at AUTHEUX. Training in morning. Weather fine. Brigade Conference at BOIS BERGUES in afternoon on Training.	RATION STR OFF. O. RKS. 24 632
"	23/9/16		Battalion in Billets at AUTHEUX. Company training	24 630
"	24/9/16		Battalion in Billets at AUTHEUX. Church services. Brigade Tour in afternoon preparatory to Brigade day arranged for 26th.	22 630
"	25/9/16		Brigade training. Battalion paraded 7.30 am. complete with transport and after route march carried out Brigade Scheme	22 701
"	26/9/16		Battalion in Billets Autheux. Company training	22 745
"	27/9/16		Battalion in Billets AUTHEUX. Preliminary reconnaissance preparatory to Divisional exercise set for 28th	22 781
"	28/9/16		Battalion in Billets AUTHEUX. Brigade exercise set by division. Route march advance guard and attack on village. Away from billets from 8.30 am till 6.45 pm.	22 780

H Davenport
Lieut. Col.
Commanding 1/4th Batt. Gloster Regt.

2449 Wt. W14957/M90 750,000 1/16 J.B.C. & A. Forms/C.2118/12.

Instructions regarding War Diaries and Intelligence Summaries are contained in F. S. Regs., Part II. and the Staff Manual respectively. Title Pages will be prepared in manuscript.

or

INTELLIGENCE SUMMARY

(Erase heading not required.)

1/4 Batt^n Glouc. Regt.

Place	Date	Hour	Summary of Events and Information	Remarks and references to Appendices
AUTHEUX	29/9/16		Battalion in billets at AUTHEUX. Orders received to move to SUS-ST-LEGER on 30th.	RATION STR. OFF. ORKS. 23 736
" and SUS-ST-LEGER	30/9/16		Battalion paraded 8 am and moved to Bde Starting point HEM & thence to SUS-ST-LEGER. Considerable movement of troops on road made march difficult. Weather fine. In billets SUS-ST-LEGER at 4.15 pm.	24 816

[signature]
Lieut. Col.
Commanding 4th Batt. Gloster Regt.

2449 Wt. W14957/M90 750,000 1/16 J.B.C. & A. Forms/C.2118/12.

144th Brigade.

48th Division.

1/4th BATTALION

GLOUCESTERSHIRE REGIMENT

OCTOBER 1 9 1 6

18. P
13 sheet

Vol 19

Confidential

War Diary

of

1/4th Battalion Gloucestershire Regiment.

From 1-10-16 To 31-10-16

Volume 19.

Instructions regarding War Diaries and Intelligence Summaries are contained in F. S. Regs., Part II. and the Staff Manual respectively. Title Pages will be prepared in manuscript.

INTELLIGENCE SUMMARY

(Erase heading not required.)

1/4 Batt^n Glouc. Regt

Place	Date	Hour	Summary of Events and Information	Remarks and references to Appendices
SUS-ST-LEGER and HALLOY	1/10/16		Battalion in billets at SUS-ST-LEGER. At 8.30 am orders were received that Brigade were to move to the area MONDICOURT-GRENAS-HALLOY. Battalion paraded at 10 am & moved with Brigade Group via IVERGNY and LUCHEUX to HALLOY. Present in huts at HALLOY at 2 pm. Weather good and favourable to marching. Bde HQ at HALLOY.	Present with Battn 25 offs. 830 O.R.
HALLOY	2/10/16		Battalion in hut billets at HALLOY. Inspection parades. Weather bad - steady rain. 8.30 pm orders received to move to ST. AMAND or SOUASTRE on 3rd.	24 offs 815 O.R
HALLOY and SOUASTRE	3/10/16		Battalion in huts at HALLOY. Paraded 11 am and moved via GRENAS, PAS and HENU to SOUASTRE. Present in hut billets at SOUASTRE at 2 pm. Weather bad and ground around huts very muddy. Huts are on low-lying swampy ground.	24 offs 806 O.R
SOUASTRE	4/10/16		Battalion in hut billets at SOUASTRE. Weather bad - steady rain.	24 offs 815 O.R

Havenport[?]

Lieut. Col.
Commanding, 4th Batt. Glos'ter Regt.

2449 Wt. W14957/M90 750,000 1/16 J.B.C. & A. Forms/C.2118/12.

Instructions regarding War Diaries and Intelligence Summaries are contained in F. S. Regs., Part II. and the Staff Manual respectively. Title Pages will be prepared in manuscript.

INTELLIGENCE SUMMARY

(Erase heading not required.)

1/4 Battn Glouc. Regt.

Place	Date	Hour	Summary of Events and Information	Remarks and references to Appendices
SOUASTRE	5/10/16		Battalion at SOUASTRE. Working parties digging cable trenches.	Present with Batt 25 off 802 O.R
SOUASTRE	6/10/16		Battalion at SOUASTRE. Working parties digging cable trenches.	26 off 792 O.R
SOUASTRE and Trenches.	7/10/16		Battalion at SOUASTRE. Orders received at 11 am to go to trenches to relieve 4 Bucks and 4 Warwicks. Companies moved at 20 minute intervals commencing 2pm in following order, D, C, A, B Companies. Guides met platoons at HQ of Bucks battalion in HEBUTERNE on Fonquevillers Road. Transport followed after dark. Battalion hold trenches immediately opposite S.W. face of Gommecourt Wood, from YANKEE STREET exclusive on right to YUS inclusive on left. Disposition D Coy hold left of line, C Coy hold centre, A Coy hold right. B Coy are in support on left and 2 Companies of Bucks remain in HEBUTERNE in support and reserve on Right.	26 off 791 O R

H Carrington(?)

Lieut. Col.
Commanding 4th Batt. Glo'ster Regt.

2449 Wt. W14957/M90 750,000 1/16 J.B.C. & A. Forms/C.2118/12.

Instructions regarding War Diaries and Intelligence Summaries are contained in F. S. Regs., Part II. and the Staff Manual respectively. Title Pages will be prepared in manuscript.

INTELLIGENCE SUMMARY

(Erase heading not required.)

1/4 Battn Glouc. Regt.

Place	Date	Hour	Summary of Events and Information	Remarks and references to Appendices
TRENCHES opposite GOMMECOURT	8/10/16		Battalion in trenches. During night 7th 8th patrols went out from D and A Companies to examine enemy wire, which Artillery had been cutting during the day. 2/Lts Wallace & Wakefield were in command of the patrols. Enemy wire was examined & reported to be very little damaged. At 9am 2 companies 4 Worcs. relieved D Coy and B Coy, who in turn relieved 2 companies of Bucks who had remained in support and reserve. Dispositions C Coy on left from YUSIF exclusive A Coy on right to YANKEE STREET exclusive. B Coy in support and D Coy in reserve. Enemy quiet weather very wet. The trenches are in excellent condition.	Present with Battn 28 offs 778 O.R
"	9/10/16		Battalion in trenches as above. During night 8th 9th. patrols under 2/Lts Wallace and Clark went out to examine enemy wire. Both met strong German covering parties, and were unable to reach the wire. Enemy quiet during the day.	28 offs 787 O.R

[signature]
Lieut. Col.
Commanding, 4th Batt. Gloster Regt.

2449 Wt. W14957/M90 750,000 1/16 J.B.C. & A. Forms/C.2118/12.

Instructions regarding War Diaries and Intelligence Summaries are contained in F. S. Regs., Part II. and the Staff Manual respectively. Title Pages will be prepared in manuscript.

INTELLIGENCE SUMMARY

(Erase heading not required.)

1/4 Battn. Glouc. Regt.

Place	Date	Hour	Summary of Events and Information	Remarks and references to Appendices
TRENCHES opposite GOMMECOURT	10/10/16		Battalion in trenches. During night 9th–10th patrols under 2/Lts Harrison and Wakefield examined German wire. Weather improving. Trenches excellent. Enemy quiet.	Present with Batt 30 offs 800 O.R
"	11/10/16		Battalion in trenches. Dispositions unchanged. B and D Coys each find 130 men daily for work under R.E. During night 10th 11th patrols under 2/Lts Thompson and Welsby went out to examine German wire. Owing to very bright moonlight they were only able to reach the outer belt, which was found to be fairly well cut. Enemy rather more active than usual. Orders received for relief	30 offs 797 O R
" and SOUASTRE	12/10/16		Battalion relieved by 4 Royal Berks Regt. Commenced at 10 am. Guides met platoons of Berks at pond in Hebuterne. Platoons as relieved proceeded independently to SOUASTRE via SOLFERINO and NAP trenches. Relief complete 12.35 pm. Present in billets SOUASTRE 3.30 pm. During night 11th–12th 2/Lts Leith and McClelland examined enemy wire.	31 offs 799 O.R

[signature] Lieut. Col.
Commanding 4th Batt. Glos'ter Regt.

2449 Wt. W14957/M90 750,000 1/16 J.B.C. & A. Forms/C.2118/12.

Instructions regarding War Diaries and Intelligence Summaries are contained in F. S. Regs., Part II. and the Staff Manual respectively. Title Pages will be prepared in manuscript.

INTELLIGENCE SUMMARY

(Erase heading not required.)

1/4 Batt^n Glouc. Regt.

Place	Date	Hour	Summary of Events and Information	Remarks and references to Appendices
				Present with Batt^n
SOUASTRE and WARLINCOURT	13/10/16		In billets at SOUASTRE. At 1.15 pm battalion ~~less~~ less B and D Companies paraded and moved to WARLINCOURT via HENU and PAS. Present in billets at WARLINCOURT at 4pm. B and D Companies under Major Slade remained at SOUASTRE	32 o/s 804 O.R.
LA HAIE and WARLINCOURT	14/10/16		Battalion less B and D Companies in billets at WARLINCOURT. B and D companies under Major Slade DSO MC. move from SOUASTRE to LA HAIE.	33 o/s 801 O.R
WARLINCOURT and LA HAIE	15/10/16		Battalion less B and D Companies in billets at WARLINCOURT. B and D Companies at LA HAIE.	29 o/s 796 O.R
"	16/10/16		As for 15th. A and C companies at WARLINCOURT find 250 men for fatigue at HENU digging in water pipe line.	29 o/s 795 O.R

[illegible] Lieut. Col.
Commanding, 4th Batt. Glos'ter Regt.

2449 Wt. W14957/M90 750,000 1/16 J.B.C. & A. Forms/C.2118/12.

Instructions regarding War Diaries and Intelligence Summaries are contained in F. S. Regs., Part II. and the Staff Manual respectively. Title Pages will be prepared in manuscript.

INTELLIGENCE SUMMARY

(Erase heading not required.)

1/4 Batt^n Glouc. Regt.

Place	Date	Hour	Summary of Events and Information	Remarks and references to Appendices
WARLINCOURT and LA HAIE	17/10/16		Battalion less B and D Companies at WARLINCOURT. B and D Companies under Major Slade D.S.O. M.C. at LA HAIE Chateau. Company parades 7-7.30 am and 9-12.30 pm. 9.30 pm warning order received that battalion would probably go to trenches on 18th	RATION STR. OFF. 30 O.R. 797
WARLINCOURT LA HAIE and Trenches	18/10/16		1.15 am orders received that battalion less B and D Coys was to move from WARLINCOURT in time to arrive at SOUASTRE for mid-day dinners. Batt^n less B and D Companies paraded WARLINCOURT at 10 am and moved via Gaudiempre and ST AMAND. Halted between ST. AMAND and SOUASTRE for dinners. Roads were very bad. Meanwhile Bde had issued orders that B+D Coys were to take over line from 4 E. YORKS (17th Div.) - boundaries YANKEE STREET inclusive on N. to WHISKEY STREET exclusive on S. Major Slade DSO MC in charge of B&D Coys at LA HAIE reconnoitred this line and made all necessary arrangements with O.C. 4 E. YORKS. B and D Companies moved from LA HAIE by platoons at 1.30 pm. Orders were received for A&C Coys. to replace B and D at LA HAIE, & Bn HQ to take over HQ from 4 E. YORKS at HEBUTERNE.	30 803

[signature]
Lieut. Col.
Commanding 4th Batt. Gloster Regt.

2449 Wt. W14957/M90 750,000 1/16 J.B.C. & A. Forms/C.2118/12.

and the Staff Manual respectively. Title Pages will be prepared in manuscript.

(Erase heading not required.)

1/4 BATTN GLOUC REGT

Place	Date	Hour	Summary of Events and Information	Remarks and references to Appendices
TRENCHES YANKEE ST. to WARRIOR ST. or K.10.B.1.5 to K.16.B.9.5-8	18/10/16		A & C Coys moved from dinner bivouac outside SOUASTRE at 2.30 pm for LA HAIE arriving latter place 3.15 pm. Orders were then received that these two companies were to relieve the 1/2 Bn 4 Yorks holding the line from WHISKEY street to WARRIOR ST. (SUNKEN ROAD).	Present with Batt 30 offs 793 O.R
			A & C Coys moved by platoons from LA HAIE 3.30 pm & were met by Guides of 4 YORKS. at entrance to HEBUTERNE at 4.30 pm.	
			H.Q. took over from HQ 4. E. YORKS at 4.30 pm.	
			Relief complete 7.15 pm.	
			Dispositions; B, D & A Companies each have 3 platoons in front line from YANKEE ST. to WARRIOR ST and 1 platoon in CROSS STREET. C Company in reserve in HEBUTERNE village.	
			Transport and Q.M. Stores at BAYENCOURT.	
	19/10/16		Battalion in trenches dispositions unchanged. Bad weather during the day. 70 men of C Coy during the day and 30 during the night working on the trenches which collapsed owing to the rain. During the night a patrol under Lieut. Phippen	29 offs 788 O.R

[signature]
Lieut. Col.
Commanding, 4th Batt. Gloster Regt.

2449 Wt. W14957/M90 750,000 1/16 J.B.C. & A. Forms/C.2118/12.

Instructions regarding War Diaries and Intelligence Summaries are contained in F. S. Regs., Part II. and the Staff Manual respectively. Title Pages will be prepared in manuscript.

INTELLIGENCE SUMMARY

(Erase heading not required.)

1/4 Batt Glosc Regt

Place	Date	Hour	Summary of Events and Information	Remarks and references to Appendices
			went out from WOMAN SAP towards enemy wire.	Present with Batt
		10·30pm	Orders received that Battalion was being relieved by 1/5th York & Lancs Regt on morning of 20th and would move to WARLINCOURT.	
WARLINCOURT + GRINCOURT.	20/10/16		Battalion relieved by 1/5th Y and L Regt commencing 9·30 am. Relief completed by 10·30 am. Companies as relieved proceeded independently to a field between SOUASTRE + ST AMAND for dinners. After dinner the Battalion moved into billets in WARLINCOURT and GRINCOURT arriving 4·45pm. Headquarters C and A Companies in WARLINCOURT B + D Companies in GRINCOURT	34 O/ffs 796 O.R
SUS-ST-LEGER.	21/10/16		Battalion paraded at 12·30 pm and moved into billets at SUS-ST-LEGER via MONDICOURT and LUCHEUX.	34 O/ffs 792 O.R
SUS-ST-LEGER	22/10/16		Battalion in billets. Physical training and company parades in the morning. Weather very fine.	34 O/ffs 792 O.R.
SUS-ST-LEGER	23/10/16		Battalion in billets. Physical training and company parades. Orders received for transport, Lewis guns to move to TALMAS on 24th inst. Remainder of Battalion to move to BREBLE in motor busses on 25th.	35 O/ffs 786 O.R

[signature] Lieut. Col.
Commanding, 4th Batt. Gloster Regt.

2449 Wt. W14957/M90 750,000 1/16 J.B.C. & A. Forms/C.2118/12.

Instructions regarding War Diaries and Intelligence Summaries are contained in F. S. Regs., Part II. and the Staff Manual respectively. Title Pages will be prepared in manuscript.

INTELLIGENCE SUMMARY

(Erase heading not required.)

1/4 Batt Glos Regt

Place	Date	Hour	Summary of Events and Information	Remarks and references to Appendices
SUS-St LEGER. Transport SUS-St-LEGER and TALMAS	24/10/16		Battalion in billets. The Transport, Lewis Gun Section and Billeting Party on cycles paraded at 9am and moved with remainder of Brigade Transport to TALMAS. Remainder of Battalion paraded 7am till 7.30am for Physical Exercises, 9am – 12.30 under Company arrangements. The night was very wet.	Present with Battn 35 Offs. 782 O.R
SUS-St-LEGER + BRESLE	25/10/16		The Battalion less Transport and Lewis Gun Section paraded at SUS-St-LEGER at 7.15 and proceeded to NERGNY where it embussed and proceeded in motor busses via DOULLENS and AMIENS to BRESLE arriving about 3pm. The whole Battalion in tents. Site of camp good. The Transport and Lewis Gun Section route marched from TALMAS arriving at BRESLE about 7.30pm. Some rain during the day.	35 offs 787 O.R
BRESLE	26/10/16		Battalion in camp. Parades 9am – 12.30 under Company arrangements. B+D Coys and a few details who did not have baths at WARLINCOURT went to BAISIEUX for baths and clean clothing. Orders were received from 144 Inf Bde for Battalion to move to ALBERT on 27th inst. These were cancelled at 10.30pm.	34 offs. 782 O.R

[signature] Lieut. Col. Commanding 4th Batt. Gloster Regt.

2449 Wt. W14957/M90 750,000 1/16 J.B.C. & A. Forms/C.2118/12.

Instructions regarding War Diaries and Intelligence Summaries are contained in F. S. Regs., Part II. and the Staff Manual respectively. Title Pages will be prepared in manuscript.

INTELLIGENCE SUMMARY

(Erase heading not required.)

14 Batt Glosr Regt.

Place	Date	Hour	Summary of Events and Information	Remarks and references to Appendices
				Present with Batt
BRESLE	27/10/16		Battalion in camp. Very wet day. Companies paraded between the storms and gave what instruction was possible in the tents. The Commanding Officer and Officers Commanding A + C. Coys reconnoitred the front of the 15th Division during the afternoon.	34 Offs 784 O.R
BRESLE	28/10/16		Battalion in camp. Weather showery. Parades 7am-7.30am Physical Exercises and 9am - 12.30pm under company arrangement. A Coy had the use of the Range. The Lewis Gun Teams and Reserve Teams paraded 9am - 12.30 under Lieut. Mathews.	34 Offs 778 O.R
BRESLE	29/10/16		Battalion in camp. Very wet day. Church Parade impossible owing to weather conditions.	34 Offs 780 O.R
BRESLE	30/10/16		Battalion in camp. Weather showery. Parades 7am - 7.30 Physical Exercises and 9am - 12.30pm under company arrangements. Major Slade and Company Commanders went in motor bus to CONTALMAISON VILLA to proceed from there to reconnoitre line to be taken over from 15th Division. Orders received for Battalion to move to ALBERT on 31st inst.	31 Offs 778 O.R

[signature]
Lieut. Col.
Commanding 4th Batt. Gloster Regt.

2449 Wt. W14957/M90 750,000 1/16 J.B.C. & A. Forms/C.2118/12.

Summaries are contained in F. S. Regs., Part II. and the Staff Manual respectively. Title Pages will be prepared in manuscript.

(Erase heading not required.) 1/4 Batt Glosc Regt

Place	Date	Hour	Summary of Events and Information	Remarks and references to Appendices
BRESLE + ALBERT.	31/10/16		The Battalion paraded at 7.50 am and marched via HÉNENCOURT and MILLENCOURT into billets at ALBERT. Reported all present at 12 noon.	Present with Batt.n 31 o/o 7?3 O R

[signature]
Lieut. Col.
Commanding, 4th Batt. Glos'ter Regt.

2449 Wt. W14957/M90 750,000 1/16 J.B.C. & A. Forms/C.2118/12.

144th Brigade.

48th Division.

1/4th BATTALION

GLOUCESTERSHIRE REGIMENT

NOVEMBER 1 9 1 6

a.D 19. P.
12 sheets

144/48

Vol 20

Confidential

War Diary

of

1/4th Battalion Gloucestershire Regiment.

from. 1/11/16 to 30/11/16

Volume 20.

Army Form C. 2118.

Instructions regarding War Diaries and Intelligence Summaries are contained in F. S. Regs., Part II. and the Staff Manual respectively. Title Pages will be prepared in manuscript.

WAR DIARY
or
INTELLIGENCE SUMMARY
(Erase heading not required.)

1/4 Batt Glouc Regt.

Place	Date	Hour	Summary of Events and Information	Remarks and references to Appendices
ALBERT	1/11/16		Battalion in billets. A working party of 400 OR under Captain E.E. Wookey M.C. paraded at 7am and worked until 1am clearing mud in the streets. Orders for the Battalion to move to CONTALMAISON on Nov 2nd were received at 7pm.	
BAZENTIN le PETIT + trenches	2/11/16		The Battalion moved to BAZENTIN-le-PETIT via CONTALMAISON, and relieved the 7th Batt Camerons. Platoons moved from ALBERT at 100x distance. The following dispositions were taken up. C and A coys in STARFISH TRENCH with both headquarters about M 33.d. 7.5. and B + D coys in SWANSEA TRENCH. B Coy HQ (S.2.b 1.8) D Coy HQ (S.2.d central) Battalion HQs N of BAZENTIN-le-PETIT (S 8 a 8.5.) All roads and approaches to the Companies were in a very bad condition and much difficulty was experienced in getting up rations. Transport about X.19.d.	
	3/11/16		Dispositions unchanged. Companies improving shelters in their trenches. Working party of 100 OR from D Coy at work under R.E's in MARTINPUICH	
	4/11/16		Dispositions unchanged. One party of 100 OR at work carrying grenades. Two other parties of 100 OR each worked under instructions of OC. 8th Worcesters. Orders received to relieve 6th Batt Glouc Regt on night of 5th/6th inst.	

E. Slade Major
Commanding 1/4th Batt Glos Regt.

2449 Wt. W14957/M90 750,000 1/16 J.B.C. & A. Forms/C.2118/12.

Army Form C. 2118.

WAR DIARY
or
INTELLIGENCE SUMMARY

(Erase heading not required.)

Instructions regarding War Diaries and Intelligence Summaries are contained in F. S. Regs., Part II. and the Staff Manual respectively. Title Pages will be prepared in manuscript.

Place	Date	Hour	Summary of Events and Information	Remarks and references to Appendices
BAZENTIN le PETIT and MARTINPUICH	5/11/16		The Battalion relieved the 6th Batt Glouc Regt in the support Trenches around MARTINPUICH the relief commencing at dusk. Dispositions B Company in O.G.1 about M.27 c. 2.0 D Company and HQ details in CRESCENT ALLEY about M.28 a 3.2 A+C Companies in PRUE TRENCH M 28 c and M 28 d All trenches in a very bad condition. At 8.30 pm B Company	
MARTINPUICH Support Trenches	6/11/16		Dispositions unchanged. Weather very bad.	
LE SARS and MARTINPUICH	7/11/16		The Battalion relieved the 6th Batt. Glouc. Regt. in Trenches at LE SARS. commencing relief at dusk. Guides met Companies at point where white posts track crosses MARTINPUICH – EAUCOURT L'ABBAYE Rd. Relief complete 8.30 pm. Dispositions. A+B Coys. in front line from M16 D77 to M16 a.5.8. D Coy. SUNKEN Rd. LESARS. C. Coy. in Trench O.G.2. B.H.Q. in O.G.2. C. Coy. carried rations for A+B Coys. from railhead S.W. of MARTINPUICH. Raining the whole time & conditions for men very bad. Enemy quiet during the night.	

G. Blad[illegible] Major
Commanding, 4th Batt. Gloster Regt.

Army Form C. 2118.

WAR DIARY
or
INTELLIGENCE SUMMARY

(Erase heading not required.)

Instructions regarding War Diaries and Intelligence Summaries are contained in F. S. Regs., Part II. and the Staff Manual respectively. Title Pages will be prepared in manuscript.

1/4th Batt. Glos. Regt.

Place	Date	Hour	Summary of Events and Information	Remarks and references to Appendices
LE SARS	8/11/16		Dispositions unchanged. Enemy artillery very active during the day. At 5pm enemy commenced very heavy bombardment on all of our positions continuing until 7 pm. Casualties very slight. LIEUT. E.M. MATTHEWS killed, Capt. E. HOOKEY & LIEUT PHIPPEN wounded. During the night situation normal. Trenches in a very bad condition	
LE SARS	9/11/16		Dispositions unchanged. Enemy artillery fairly active. Orders received for relief. Weather very much improved. Battalion relieved by the 5th Batt. Warwick Regt. Battalion goes back to NORTH CAMP PEAKE WOOD CONTALMAISON. LIEUT. CLARK killed & LIEUT LAUGLAND wounded during relief.	
CONTALMAISON	10/11/16		In camp. Men spend the day in drying & cleaning. Weather good. LIEUT. PHIPPEN died of wounds	
"	11/11/16		Battalion in camp. A,C & D Companies find working parties for road repairing & hutting.	

[illegible] Major

Commanding 1/4th Batt. Glouces. Regt.

2449 Wt. W14957/M90 750,000 1/16 J.B.C. & A. Forms/C.2118/12.

Army Form C. 2118.

WAR DIARY
or
INTELLIGENCE SUMMARY

(Erase heading not required.)

Instructions regarding War Diaries and Intelligence Summaries are contained in F. S. Regs., Part II. and the Staff Manual respectively. Title Pages will be prepared in manuscript.

Place	Date	Hour	Summary of Events and Information	Remarks and references to Appendices
CONTALMAISON	12/11/16		Battalion in NORTH CAMP, PEAKE WOOD. B&C. Companies find working parties (200 men) for road repairing & hutting. Brigade Church Parade 10.30 am. Weather good.	
CONTALMAISON	13/11/16		Battalion in NORTH CAMP, PEAKE WOOD. A&D. Companies find working parties (200 men) for road repairing & hutting. B&C. Companies inspections & find working parties for improving camp. Weather good.	
CONTALMAISON	14/11/16		Battalion in NORTH CAMP, PEAKE WOOD. B&C. Companies find working parties (200 men) for road repairing & hutting. A&D. Companies inspections & find working parties for improving camp. Weather good.	

E.H. Wade [signature]
Major
Commanding, 4th Batt. Gloster Regt.

2449 Wt. W14957/M90 750,000 1/16 J.B.C. & A. Forms/C.2118/12.

Army Form C. 2118.

WAR DIARY
or
INTELLIGENCE SUMMARY
(Erase heading not required.)

Instructions regarding War Diaries and Intelligence Summaries are contained in F. S. Regs., Part II. and the Staff Manual respectively. Title Pages will be prepared in manuscript.

Place	Date	Hour	Summary of Events and Information	Remarks and references to Appendices
CONTALMAISON	15/11/16		Battalion in NORTH CAMP, PEAKE WOOD. A.B & D Companies find working parties (300 men) for road repairing, hutting & R.E. fatigue. C. Company inspection & find working party for improving camp. Weather good.	
CONTALMAISON	16/11/16		Battalion in NORTH CAMP, PEAKE WOOD. C & D Companies find working parties (200 men) for road repairing & hutting. A & B Companies have baths at BECOURT. Weather good.	

[illegible] Major
Commanding, 4th Batt. Gloster Regt.

2449 Wt. W14957/M90 750,000 1/16 J.B.C. & A. Forms/C.2118/12.

Army Form C. 2118.

Instructions regarding War Diaries and Intelligence Summaries are contained in F. S. Regs., Part II. and the Staff Manual respectively. Title Pages will be prepared in manuscript.

WAR DIARY
or
INTELLIGENCE SUMMARY
(Erase heading not required.)

Place	Date	Hour	Summary of Events and Information	Remarks and references to Appendices
CONTALMAISON	17/11/16		Battalion in NORTH CAMP, PEAKE WOOD All Companies found Working Parties for Hutting + Road Repairing. Weather good.	
CONTALMAISON	18/11/16		Battalion in NORTH CAMP, PEAKE WOOD A+B. Companies found working Parties for Hutting + Road Repairing (200 men) C+D Companies have baths at BECOURT. Weather good.	
CONTALMAISON	19/11/16		Battalion in NORTH CAMP, PEAKE WOOD Voluntary Church Parades Battalion employed on improving Camp. Weather fair.	
CONTALMAISON + MARTINPUICH	20/11/16		Battalion in NORTH CAMP, PEAKE WOOD Orders for Battalion to proceed to MARTINPUICH received Battalion moved to MARTINPUICH Platoons at 100 yards distance and relieved the BUCKS.	

E. H. Slade Major
Commanding, 4th Batt. Glos'ter Regt.

2449 Wt. W14957/M90 750,000 1/16 J.B.C. & A. Forms/C.2118/12.

Army Form C. 2118.

Instructions regarding War Diaries and Intelligence Summaries are contained in F. S. Regs., Part II. and the Staff Manual respectively. Title pages will be prepared in manuscript.

WAR DIARY
or
INTELLIGENCE SUMMARY.
(Erase heading not required.)

Place	Date	Hour	Summary of Events and Information	Remarks and references to Appendices
MARTINPUICH	21/11/16		Dispositions unchanged. A + D Companies found working parties (200 men) for clearing road for Railway through MARTINPUICH. Weather good.	
MARTINPUICH	22/11/16		Battalion Received orders to relieve the 7th Worcesters at LE SARS. At dusk Platoons moved at 100 yards distance. Relief complete 9 P.M. Battalion subjected to heavy Enemy artillery fire and Tear Shells whilst approaching and entering LE SARS. Dispositions of Companies:- Battalion H.Q. in O.G.2 A. Company } In support. B COY → In trench OG2. A COY → In SUNKEN ROAD LE SARS. B. " C. " } In front line from M.16 d 77 to M16 a.58 D. B Company provided carrying parties for Rations for Companies in front line. Weather good. Enemy quiet during night.	

E Slade Major
Commanding 1/4th Batt. Glos'ter Regt.

A5834 Wt. W4973/M687 750,000 8/16 D. D. & L. Ltd. Forms/C.2118/13.

Army Form C. 2118.

Instructions regarding War Diaries and Intelligence Summaries are contained in F. S. Regs., Part II. and the Staff Manual respectively. Title pages will be prepared in manuscript.

WAR DIARY
or
INTELLIGENCE SUMMARY.
(Erase heading not required.)

Place	Date	Hour	Summary of Events and Information	Remarks and references to Appendices
LE SARS.	23/11/16.		Dispositions unchanged. Enemy quiet. orders received that the 5th ROYAL WARWICKS will relieve us on the evening of the 24th inst, Weather good.	
LE SARS + CONTALMAISON	24/11/16		Battalion relieved by 5th ROYAL WARWICKS. Relief completed by 10 P.M. Enemy artillery + machine gun fire fairly active as platoons moving at 100 yards distance leaving LE SARS + approaching O.G.2. 2nd LIEUT TAYLOR A COY slightly wounded in hip by shell fragment Weather good	
CONTALMAISON	25/11/16		Battalion in huts at GORDON CAMP (PIONEER CAMP) Weather bad. Day occupied in cleaning equipment etc.	
CONTALMAISON	26/11/16		Battalion in huts at GORDON CAMP (PIONEER CAMP) Voluntary Church Parades. Company Inspections. A+B Companies found working parties (200 men) at CONTALMAISON at POZIERES. Weather good.	

E. [illegible] Major
Commanding 1/4th Batt. Glo'ster Regt.

A5834 Wt. W4973/M687 750,000 8/16 D. D. & L. Ltd. Forms/C.2118/13.

Instructions regarding War Diaries and Intelligence Summaries are contained in F. S. Regs., Part II. and the Staff Manual respectively. Title pages will be prepared in manuscript.

WAR DIARY
or
INTELLIGENCE SUMMARY.
(Erase heading not required.)

Army Form C. 2118.

Place	Date	Hour	Summary of Events and Information	Remarks and references to Appendices
CONTALMAISON	27/11/16		Battalion in huts at GORDON CAMP (PIONEER CAMP) C Company provided working party (100 men) for work on Tramway Track at X16.B.24 CONTALMAISON D Company provided working party (100 men) for work on Tramway Track at X4 B93 POZIERES A + B Companies occupied on Camp improvements Weather good. Two officers + 1 N.C.O. from each Coy proceeded to SHELTER WOOD for Rapid wiring course.	
CONTALMAISON	28/11/16		A + B Companies provided working parties (200 men) for work at CONTALMAISON + POZIERES C Company + H.Q. details proceeded to BECOURT for Baths Two Officers + 1 N.C.O. from each Coy. proceeded to SHELTER WOOD for course in rapid wiring. Weather good.	
CONTALMAISON	29/11/16		Battalion in huts at GORDON CAMP (PIONEER CAMP) C + D Companies provided working parties (200 men) for work at CONTALMAISON + POZIERES. A + B Coys employed on improving Camp 2 Officers + 1 NCO from each Company proceeded to SHELTER WOOD for course in Rapid wiring. Weather good.	

[signature] Major
Commanding 4th Batt. Gloster Regt

A5834 Wt. W4973/M687 750,000 8/16 D. D. & L. Ltd. Forms/C.2118/13.

Army Form C. 2118.

Instructions regarding War Diaries and Intelligence Summaries are contained in F. S. Regs., Part II. and the Staff Manual respectively. Title pages will be prepared in manuscript.

WAR DIARY
or
INTELLIGENCE SUMMARY.
(Erase heading not required.)

Place	Date	Hour	Summary of Events and Information	Remarks and references to Appendices
CONTALMAISON	30/11/16		Battalion in huts at PIONEER CAMP,	
			A+B Coys found working Parties (200 men) at CONTALMAISON at POZIERES	
			C+D Coys Employed on improving Camp.	
			1 N.C.O. from each Coy + 2 Officers proceeded to SHELTER WOOD for course in rapid wiring	
			weather good.	

E C Slade Major
Commanding 1/4th Batt. Glos'ter Regt.

A5834 Wt. W4973/M687 750,000 8/16 D. D. & L. Ltd. Forms/C.2118/13.

144th Brigade.

48th Division.

1/4th BATTALION

GLOUCESTERSHIRE REGIMENT

DECEMBER 1 9 1 6

Confidential

Vol 21

War Diary

of

1/4th Gloucestershire Regiment

From 1st December 1916 to 31st December 1916

Volume 21.

D.P.
8 sheet

Instructions regarding War Diaries and Intelligence Summaries are contained in F. S. Regs., Part II. and the Staff Manual respectively. Title pages will be prepared in manuscript.

WAR DIARY
or
INTELLIGENCE SUMMARY.
(*Erase heading not required.*)

Army Form C. 2118.

1/4th Bn Gloucestershire Regt

Place	Date	Hour	Summary of Events and Information	Remarks and references to Appendices
CONTALMAISON	1/12/16		Battalion in Huts at PIONEER CAMP. Battalion provided working parties of 300 for work at POZIERES and CONTALMAISON. Orders received to Relieve BUCKS at MARTINPUICH. Weather good.	
CONTALMAISON & MARTINPUICH	2/12/16		Battalion proceeded at dusk - Platoons 100 yards interval - to MARTINPUICH to relieve BUCKS. Relief complete by 7.0 P.M. B.H.Q. & C & B Companies at MARTINPUICH. A & D Companies in 26th AVENUE. Weather good.	
MARTINPUICH	3/12/16		Battalion dispositions unchanged. D Coy provided working Party 100 men for carrying to LE SARS. A.B & C employed on improving Trenches and erecting new Shelters. Weather good	
MARTINPUICH	4/12/16		Battalion in Support at ~~[illegible]~~ MARTINPUICH. C & B Coys provide working parties 100 men for carrying - A & D employed in erecting new Shelters and improving 26th AVENUE.	
MARTINPUICH & CONTALMAISON	5/12/16		Battalion relieved by 6th ROYAL WARWICKS. Relief complete by 7.30 P.M. Battalion proceeded to huts in PIONEER CAMP. CONTALMAISON	

[signature]
Lieut. Col.
Commanding 1/4th Batt. Gloster Regt.

A5834 Wt. W4973/M687 750,000 8/16 D. D. & L. Ltd. Forms/C.2118/13.

Army Form C. 2118.

Instructions regarding War Diaries and Intelligence Summaries are contained in F. S. Regs., Part II. and the Staff Manual respectively. Title pages will be prepared in manuscript.

WAR DIARY
or
INTELLIGENCE SUMMARY.
(Erase heading not required.)

1/4th Bn Gloucestershire Regt

Place	Date	Hour	Summary of Events and Information	Remarks and references to Appendices
CONTALMAISON	6/12/16		Battalion in huts at PIONEER CAMP. Men employed in cleaning up equipment &c. Weather bad.	
CONTALMAISON	7/12/16		Battalion in huts at PIONEER CAMP. All Coys had inspections & lectures in huts. WORKING COMPANY formed (2nd Lt HIBBERD & 2nd Lt FOX) & 80 men. Weather bad	
CONTALMAISON	8/12/16		Battalion in huts at PIONEER CAMP. C Coy had baths. B & D Coys provided working Party of 100 men for carrying to LE SARS. Weather good.	
CONTALMAISON	9/12/16		Battalion in huts at PIONEER CAMP. Orders received to relieve 1/6 ROYAL WARWICKS in Trenches on 10th inst. A.B. & D Coys had baths. Weather bad.	
CONTALMAISON & LE SARS	10/12/16		Relief of 1/6 ROYAL WARWICKS complete by 7.30 PM. H.Q. ~~& D Coy~~ 26th AVENUE LE SARS. D RESERVE. C SUPPORT B LEFT FRONT. A RIGHT FRONT. Weather good.	

S. Davenport
Lieut. Col.
Commanding 4th Batt. Gloster Regt.

A5834 Wt. W4973/M687 750,000 8/16 D. D. & L. Ltd. Forms/C.2118/13.

Instructions regarding War Diaries and Intelligence Summaries are contained in F. S. Regs., Part II. and the Staff Manual respectively. Title pages will be prepared in manuscript.

WAR DIARY
or
INTELLIGENCE SUMMARY.
(Erase heading not required.)

Army Form C. 2118.

1/4th Bn Gloucestershire Regt

Place	Date	Hour	Summary of Events and Information	Remarks and references to Appendices
LE SARS.	11/12/16		Battalion in trenches. Dispositions unchanged weather bad.	
LE SARS.	12/12/16		Battalion in trenches. Dispositions unchanged. Weather good.	
LE SARS	13/12/16		Battalion in trenches C Coy Relieved A D Coy Relieved B. Weather good	
LE SARS + MARTINPUICH	14/12/16		Battalion Relieved by 1/8 WORCESTERS and proceeded to MARTINPUICH as Left Support Battalion Relief complete by 7.0c. Weather good	
MARTINPUICH + SCOTS REDOUBT SOUTH.	15/12/16		Battalion Relieved by 12 H.L.I. Relief complete by 6.45. P.M " In huts at SCOTS REDOUBT SOUTH. Weather bad	
SCOTS REDOUBT SOUTH	16/12/16		Battalion in huts at SCOTS REDOUBT SOUTH Men Employed in cleaning Equipment &c. Weather fair	

J Haverfield
Lieut. Col.
Commanding 1/4th Batt. Glos'ter Regt.

A5834 Wt. W4973/M687 750,000 8/16 D. D. & L. Ltd. Forms/C.2118/13.

Instructions regarding War Diaries and Intelligence Summaries are contained in F. S. Regs., Part II. and the Staff Manual respectively. Title pages will be prepared in manuscript.

WAR DIARY
or
INTELLIGENCE SUMMARY.
(Erase heading not required.)

Army Form C. 2118.

1/4th Bn Gloucestershire Regt

Place	Date	Hour	Summary of Events and Information	Remarks and references to Appendices
SCOTS REDOUBT SOUTH + MAMETZ WOOD	17/12/16		Battalion proceeded to MAMETZ WOOD + Relieved the 8/10 GORDONS Battalion under canvas. Conditions very bad	
Do	18/12/16		Battalion find daily working parties of 300 men for Road Repairing draining + unloading. Weather good	
Do	19/12/16		Do. Do. Do.	
Do	20/12/16		One working Party of 75 men Relieved by 8 WORCESTERS from to-day onwards. Weather good	
Do	21/12/16		Do Do Do. Weather bad.	

[signature]
Lieut. Col.
Commanding 1/4th Batt. Glos'ter Regt.

A5834 Wt. W4973/M687 750,000 8/16 D. D. & L. Ltd. Forms/C.2118/13.

Instructions regarding War Diaries and Intelligence Summaries are contained in F. S. Regs., Part II. and the Staff Manual respectively. Title pages will be prepared in manuscript.

WAR DIARY
or
INTELLIGENCE SUMMARY.
(*Erase heading not required.*)

Army Form C. 2118.

1/4th Bn Gloucestershire Regt

Place	Date	Hour	Summary of Events and Information	Remarks and references to Appendices
MAMETZ WOOD	22/12/16		Battalion found working parties (total 225 men) for Road repairing, Draining & unloading. Weather bad.	
MAMETZ WOOD & FRICOURT CAMP.	23/12/16		Battalion proceeded to FRICOURT CAMP & occupied unfinished huts. Working parties found as above. Weather bad.	
FRICOURT CAMP	24/12/16.		Battalion found working parties for Road repairing, Draining & improvement to Camp. Weather fair.	
do	25/12/16.		Battalion excused all working parties. Weather fair.	

Havenport
Lieut. Col.
Commanding 1/4th Batt. Glos'ter Regt.

A5834 Wt. W4973/M687 750,000 8/16 D. D. & L. Ltd. Forms/C.2118/13.

Instructions regarding War Diaries and Intelligence Summaries are contained in F. S. Regs., Part II. and the Staff Manual respectively. Title pages will be prepared in manuscript.

WAR DIARY
or
INTELLIGENCE SUMMARY.

(*Erase heading not required.*)

Army Form C. 2118.

1/4th Bn Gloucestershire Regt.

Place	Date	Hour	Summary of Events and Information	Remarks and references to Appendices
FRICOURT CAMP	26/12/16		Battalion found working parties of 225 men for Road repairing & training. Remainder improving Camp. Weather good.	
do	27/12/16		Battalion found working parties as above. Weather bad.	
do	28/12/16		Battalion found working parties as above. Orders received to move to BECOURT CAMP on the 29th inst & CONTAY on the 30th inst. Weather bad.	
do & BECOURT CAMP	29/12/16		Battalion proceeded to BECOURT CAMP. Working parties found as above. Weather bad.	
BECOURT CAMP & CONTAY.	30/12/16		Battalion proceeded to CONTAY. Men in billets. Weather good.	

[signature]

Lieut. Col.
Commanding 1/4th Batt. Glos'ter Regt.

A5834 Wt. W4973/M687 750,000 8/16 D. D. & L. Ltd. Forms/C.2118/13.

Instructions regarding War Diaries and Intelligence Summaries are contained in F. S. Regs., Part II. and the Staff Manual respectively. Title pages will be prepared in manuscript.

WAR DIARY
or
INTELLIGENCE SUMMARY.
(Erase heading not required.)

Army Form C. 2118.

1/4th Bn Gloucestershire Regt

Place	Date	Hour	Summary of Events and Information	Remarks and references to Appendices
CONTAY	31/12/16		Battalion in billets. The day spent cleaning arms, equipment & personnel. Weather good.	

[signature]
Lieut. Col.
Commanding 1/4th Batt. Glos'ter Regt.

A5834 Wt. W4973/M687 750,000 8/16 D. D. & L. Ltd. Forms/C.2118/13.

21. P
8 sheet

Vol 22

Confidential

War Diary

of

1/4th Bn Gloucestershire Regiment

from 1.1.17 to 31.1.17

Volume 22.

Instructions regarding War Diaries and Intelligence Summaries are contained in F. S. Regs., Part II. and the Staff Manual respectively. Title pages will be prepared in manuscript.

WAR DIARY
or
INTELLIGENCE SUMMARY.
(Erase heading not required.)

Army Form C. 2118.

1/4th Bn Gloucester Regt

Place	Date	Hour	Summary of Events and Information	Remarks and references to Appendices
CONTAY	1/1/17		Battalion Training. Weather fair.	
"	2/1/17		Battalion Training. Weather good.	
"	3/1/17		Ditto Weather bad.	
"	4/1/17		Ditto Weather fair.	
"	5/1/17		Battalion Route March (Less Transport) Weather good.	
"	6/1/17		Battalion Training. In the afternoon Battalion inspected by Corps Commander. Weather fair. Orders received to move. Transport 7/1/17 Battalion 8/1/17	

Havenport
Lieut. Col.
Commanding, 4th Batt. Gloster Regt.

A5834 Wt. W4973/M687 750,000 8/16 D. D. & L. Ltd. Forms/C.2118/13.

Instructions regarding War Diaries and Intelligence Summaries are contained in F. S. Regs., Part II. and the Staff Manual respectively. Title pages will be prepared in manuscript.

WAR DIARY
or
INTELLIGENCE SUMMARY.
(Erase heading not required.)

Army Form C. 2118.

1/4th Bn Gloucester Regt

Place	Date	Hour	Summary of Events and Information	Remarks and references to Appendices
CONTAY	7/1/17		Battalion Church Parade. Weather good. Transport left for HUCHENNVILLE.	
+ HUCHENNVILLE	8/1/17		Battalion marched to HEILLY & entrained to PONT REMY. Battalion marched to CAUMONT & HUCHENNVILLE. A & B Coys in CAUMONT. D, C & H.Q. in HUCHENNVILLE. also Transport 2 officers & 50 men left for fatigue at CONTAY. Weather bad.	
HUCHENNVILLE + CAUMONT	9/1/17		Battalion Training. Weather bad.	
Ditto	10/1/17		Battalion Training. Weather bad.	
Ditto	11/1/17		~~Battalion Training. Weather bad.~~	

[signature]
Lieut. Col.
Commanding 4th Batt. Gloster Regt.

A5834 Wt. W4973/M687 750,000 8/16 D. D. & L. Ltd. Forms/C.2118/13.

Instructions regarding War Diaries and Intelligence Summaries are contained in F. S. Regs., Part II. and the Staff Manual respectively. Title pages will be prepared in manuscript.

WAR DIARY
or
INTELLIGENCE SUMMARY.
(Erase heading not required.)

Army Form C. 2118.

1/4th Bn Gloucester Regt

Place	Date	Hour	Summary of Events and Information	Remarks and references to Appendices
[ ]ICHENNEVILLE & CAUMONT	11/1/17		Battalion Training. Weather bad.	
Ditto	12/1/17		Ditto Ditto	
Ditto	13/1/17		Battalion Training. Weather fair. 1st Round of "Fanshawe Cup" played. Result. 7th Worc. Regt. 5 goals 4th Glos. Regt. 3 goals. Splendid game.	
Ditto	14/1/17		Battalion Church Parade cancelled owing to bad weather.	
Ditto	15/1/17		Battalion Training. "B" "C" & "D" Cos at full strength. "A" Coy. find all employ & have use of the Range. Weather good.	
Ditto	16/1/17		Battalion Training. "B" "C" & "D" Cos at full strength. "A" Cy. find all employ. "A" Cy have use of Bath at Huppy in morning, "B" C in afternoon. Transport inspected by O.C. 48th Div. Train.	

S Harcourt
Lieut. Col.
Commanding, 4th Batt. Gloster Regt.

A5834 Wt. W4973/M687 750,000 8/16 D. D. & L. Ltd. Forms/C.2118/13.

Instructions regarding War Diaries and Intelligence Summaries are contained in F. S. Regs., Part II. and the Staff Manual respectively. Title pages will be prepared in manuscript.

WAR DIARY
or
INTELLIGENCE SUMMARY.
(Erase heading not required.)

Army Form C. 2118.

1/4th Bn Gloucester Regt.

Place	Date	Hour	Summary of Events and Information	Remarks and references to Appendices
HUCHENNVILLE + CAUMONT	17/1/17		Battalion inspected by G.O.C. 144th Bgde. Full marching order. A Coy have use of Range & C Coy have baths in afternoon. Weather - snowing hard all day.	
"	18/1/17		Battalion Training. A.B.C at full strength. D Coy find all employ & have use of range. D have bath in morning. Weather good.	
"	19/1/17		Ditto Ditto	
"	20/1/17		Battalion Training. A, B & D Coy at full strength. C Coy find all employ & have use of range. Weather good	

S Davenport
Lieut. Col.
Commanding, 4th Batt. Gloster Regt.

A5834 Wt. W4973/M687 750,000 8/16 D. D. & L. Ltd. Forms/C.2118/13.

Instructions regarding War Diaries and Intelligence Summaries are contained in F. S. Regs., Part II. and the Staff Manual respectively. Title pages will be prepared in manuscript.

WAR DIARY
or
INTELLIGENCE SUMMARY.
(Erase heading not required.)

Army Form C. 2118.

1/4th Bn Gloucester Regt

Place	Date	Hour	Summary of Events and Information	Remarks and references to Appendices
HUCHENNVILLE + CAUMONT	21/1/17		Battalion Church parade. Weather good.	
"	22/1/17		Battalion parade, fighting order, at 10 am for Brigade Training at HALLENCOURT. Weather good.	
"	23/1/17		Ditto Ditto. Transport inspected at HUPPY	
"	24/1/17		Battalion Training. A, C & D Coys at full strength. B Coy find all employ & have use of range. Weather good.	
"	25/1/17		Ditto Ditto Movement orders received.	

[illegible] Lieut. Col.
Commanding, 4th Batt. Gloster Regt.

A5834 Wt. W4973/M687 750,000 8/16 D. D. & L. Ltd. Forms/C.2118/13.

Instructions regarding War Diaries and Intelligence Summaries are contained in F. S. Regs., Part II. and the Staff Manual respectively. Title pages will be prepared in manuscript.

WAR DIARY
or
INTELLIGENCE SUMMARY.
(Erase heading not required.)

Army Form C. 2118.

Place	Date	Hour	Summary of Events and Information	Remarks and references to Appendices
HUCHENNVILLE & CAUMONT	26/1/17		Battalion Training. B. C. & D Coys full strength. A Coy find all employ & had use of range. Transport moved at 7 a.m. Weather good.	
"	27/1/17		Battalion Training. Weather good.	
"	28/1/17		Battalion marched to PONT REMY & entrained. Detrained at CERISY & occupied Camp at that place. Weather good.	
CERISY	29/1/17		Battalion in huts. Company inspections & general cleaning up. Weather good	
"	30/1/17		Ditto Ditto	
"	31/1/17		Ditto Ditto	

Hasenport
Lieut. Col.
Commanding 4th Batt. Glos'ter R.

A5834 Wt. W4973/M687 750,000 8/16 D. D. & L. Ltd. Forms/C.2118/13.

Vol 23

War Diary

of

1/4th Battalion Gloucestershire Regt.

from 1/2/1917 to 28/2/1917

Volume 23.

Instructions regarding War Diaries and Intelligence Summaries are contained in F. S. Regs., Part II. and the Staff Manual respectively. Title pages will be prepared in manuscript.

WAR DIARY
or
INTELLIGENCE SUMMARY.
(Erase heading not required.)

Army Form C. 2118.

1/4 Battn. Gloucester Regt.

Place	Date	Hour	Summary of Events and Information	Remarks and references to Appendices
CERISY & CAPPY.	1.2.17		Battalion left CERISY CAMP & moved to Camp 56 – CAPPY. Weather good.	
CAPPY	2.2.17		Battalion moved to trenches leaving Camp at 4.30 pm. 'C' & 'D' Coys in front line. C left front Coy. DOLLFUS. D right front Coy. NORD. A Coy in reserve STETTIN. B Coy working Company & remained with Q.M. Stores & Transport at Camp. Battalion relieved the 1st Battalion 135th FRENCH REGT. Relief complete at 10 pm. Quiet night. Weather good.	
	3.2.17		Battalion in trenches. Enemy quiet. Weather good.	
	4.2.17		Battalion in trenches. Enemy very active all day. Heavy bombardment commenced at 5.30 pm lasting until 7 pm. Battalions on our right & left raided. Enemy quiet during night. Weather good.	
	5.2.17		Battalion in trenches. Enemy active with Rifle Grenades & A. Torpedoes. Weather good.	
	6.2.17		Battalion in trenches. Enemy fairly quiet. Weather good. Relief orders received.	
	7.2.17		Battalion in trenches. Enemy fairly quiet. Our artillery more active. Hostile Aeroplanes active. Battalion relieved by 8th Worcs. Relief complete by 8.30 pm. Battalion moved back to MARLY Camp. Weather cold but good.	
MARLY CAMP	8.2.17		Battalion in camp. Day spent in general cleaning & Platoon inspections. Weather good.	
Do	9.2.17		Battalion in Camp. Company inspections & lecture by D.G.O. B Coy found working party. Weather good.	

Roger Wilkinson
Lieut. Col.
Commanding 4th Batt. Glosr. Regt.

A5834 Wt. W4973/M687 750,000 8/16 D. D. & L. Ltd. Forms/C.2118/13.

Instructions regarding War Diaries and Intelligence Summaries are contained in F. S. Regs., Part II. and the Staff Manual respectively. Title pages will be prepared in manuscript.

WAR DIARY
or
INTELLIGENCE SUMMARY.
(*Erase heading not required.*)

Army Form C. 2118.

1/4 Battn Gloucester Regt

Place	Date	Hour	Summary of Events and Information	Remarks and references to Appendices
MARLY CAMP	10.2.17		Battalion in Camp. Companies Training. Weather good.	
	11.2.17		Battalion in Camp. Companies Training. Weather good.	
	12.2.17		Battalion in Camp. Companies Training. Weather good. B. Coy working party FROISSY (1 off 340 R)	
Do	13.2.17		Battalion in Camp Companies Training Weather good ditto ditto	
Do	14.2.17		Battalion in Camp. Companies Training. Weather good.	
Do	15.2.17		Battalion have Baths at CAPPY. B Coy found working party (1 off 40 OR) LA FLAQUE. Orders received to move to Camp at 56 CAPPY Weather good.	
CAPPY	16.2.17		Battalion moved to Camp 56 CAPPY. Weather good. Orders received to relieve 4th R Berks.	
	17.2.17		Battalion moved to trenches & relieved 4th R Berks. C. A & B Companies front line FRONT LEFT } BURGER - Right NORD. D Company reserve in DESIRE. also Batt. HQ. Forward Batt HQ STETTIN Relief complete by 10 pm. 2Lt Young & 2Lt Tidd, did patrols but owing to extreme darkness could gather no information. Slight drizzle sets in.	
	18.2.17		Battalion in trenches. Enemy fairly quiet. Owing to thaw & rain trenches begin to get in bad condition. Patrols sent out but gathered little information owing to darkness etc.	
	19.2.17		Battalion in trenches. Trenches in very bad condition mud & water waist high in places. Patrol sent out but little information gathered owing to state of ground & darkness.	
	20.2.17		Ditto Ditto Ditto. 2nd Lt Young with 12 OR. attempted to raid German Sap. owing to German barrage & condition of ground etc this was not successful. No casualties. Relief orders received.	
	21.2.17		Battalion relieved by 8th Worc. Relief Complete by 3 am. but owing to state of trenches Companies were not Complete until late the next day. Some men were stuck in mud in trenches for over 2 hours. Battalion moved back to reserve C Coy at FLAUCOURT, A Coy at HERBIECOURT, HQ B & D at SOPHIE	

Roger [illegible]
Lieut. Col
Commanding 4th Batt. Glos [illegible]

A5834 Wt. W4973/M687 750,000 8/16 D. D. & L. Ltd. Forms/C.2118/13.

Instructions regarding War Diaries and Intelligence Summaries are contained in F. S. Regs., Part II. and the Staff Manual respectively. Title pages will be prepared in manuscript.

WAR DIARY
or
INTELLIGENCE SUMMARY.
(*Erase heading not required.*)

1/4 Batt Gloucester Regt

Army Form C. 2118.

Place	Date	Hour	Summary of Events and Information	Remarks and references to Appendices
SOPHIE TRENCH	22.2.17		Battalion in reserve. Clearing & working on own lines. Major R. Wilkinson took over Command of the Battalion. Weather fair.	
"	23.2.17		Battalion in reserve, clearing & working on own lines. Weather fair. Relief orders received.	
"	24.2.17		Battalion moved back to MARLY CAMP being relieved by 1/5 Glos. Regt. Relief complete by 2 am. Weather good.	
MARLY.	25.2.17		Battalion in Camp. Day spent cleaning, feet washing & inspection by C. Officer (Clean fatigues). Weather good.	
"	26.2.17		Battalion in Camp. Camp fatigues & inspections. Weather good. Training of specialists	
"	27.2.17		Battalion in Camp. Camp fatigues. Batt. found working party (ABD 250 men) for clearing communication trenches. Weather good. Training of specialists	
"	28.2.17		Battalion in Camp. C Coy find Camp fatigues. Batt. have Baths at CAPPY. Battalion moved to billets in CAPPY. Working party found (C & D 100 men). Weather good. Training of specialists	
CAPPY.				

Roger Wilkinson
Lieut. Col.
Commanding 4th Batt. Gloster Regt.

A5834 Wt. W4973/M687 750,000 8/16 D. D. & L. Ltd. Forms/C.2118/13.

Confidential

Vol 24

144/48

1/4th Bn Gloucestershire Regiment

WAR DIARY FOR MARCH 1917.

VOLUME. 24

23. P.
7 sheets

Instructions regarding War Diaries and Intelligence Summaries are contained in F. S. Regs., Part II. and the Staff Manual respectively. Title pages will be prepared in manuscript.

WAR DIARY
or
INTELLIGENCE SUMMARY.
(Erase heading not required.)

Army Form C. 2118.

1/4 Battn. Gloucester Regt.

Place	Date	Hour	Summary of Events and Information	Remarks and references to Appendices
CAPPY.	1.3.17		Battalion in billets. Companies Training. Training of Specialists. Working parties found. Weather good.	
	2.3.17		Ditto Ditto Ditto. Operation orders received.	
	3.3.17		Battalion moved to trenches & relieved Oxford & Bucks. Battn. A. B. D 2 platoons of each in front line & 2 support. C. Coy in reserve. Relief complete by 10.30 pm. 2/Lt Liddy & 2 O.R. patrolled at 10.30 pm. & reported gap in enemies wire. Quiet night. Weather good.	
	4.3.17		Battalion in Trenches. Enemy Artillery active paying special attention to STETTIN & DOUBLEMONT. 2/Lt Beadell patrolled at 10.30 pm & confirmed previous information. Weather fair.	
	5.3.17		Battalion in Trenches. Hostile Artillery, A. Torpedoes, & Rifle Grenades active, chiefly on right front Company & STETTIN. Patrol report as above.	
	6.3.17		Ditto Ditto. 2/Lt Beadell patrolled at midnight with 2 O.R. & found a large gap in enemies wire. Operation orders received. Weather fair.	
	7.3.17		Battalion relieved by 4th R. Berks Battn. & moved back to billets in CAPPY. All present by 12.30. Weather good.	

Roger W. Robinson [?] Lt. Col.
Comdg. 1/4 Glos. Regt.

A5834 Wt. W4973/M687 750,000 8/16 D. D. & L. Ltd. Forms/C.2118/13.

Instructions regarding War Diaries and Intelligence Summaries are contained in F. S. Regs., Part II. and the Staff Manual respectively. Title pages will be prepared in manuscript.

WAR DIARY
or
INTELLIGENCE SUMMARY.
(Erase heading not required.)

Army Form C. 2118.

Place	Date	Hour	Summary of Events and Information 1/4th Battn. Gloucester Regt.	Remarks and references to Appendices
CAPPY.	8.3.17		Battalion in billets. Inspections & cleaning up. Weather good.	
do	9.3.17		Battalion in billets. Training of specialists. Battalion have Baths at Cappy. Working parties found. Weather good.	
do	10.3.17		Battalion in billets. Demonstration of an attack by C & D Coys. Training of specialists. Working parties found. Respirator & M.O.'s inspection in afternoon. Weather good.	
do	11.3.17		Battalion in billets. Voluntary Church Services. Training of specialists. Working parties found. Weather fair.	
do	12.3.17		Battalion in billets. Demonstration of an attack by A.C. Training of specialists. Operation orders received.	
do SOPHIE	13.3.17		Battalion move to SOPHIE & relieve 2nd R. Berks. Bn. Hd. Qrs. A.D.C. SOPHIE, B.G. at VIRGIN WOOD.	
do	14.3.17		Battalion in SOPHIE. Training of specialists continued. Working party found. Weather stormy.	
SOPHIE	15.3.17		Battalion in SOPHIE. Training of specialists continued. Working parties found. Weather fair.	
do	16.3.17		Battalion in SOPHIE. Training of specialists continued. Working parties found. Weather fair. Operation orders received.	[illegible]

A5834 Wt. W4973/M687 750,000 8/16 D. D. & L. Ltd. Forms/C2118/13.

Instructions regarding War Diaries and Intelligence Summaries are contained in F. S. Regs., Part II. and the Staff Manual respectively. Title pages will be prepared in manuscript.

WAR DIARY
or
INTELLIGENCE SUMMARY.
(Erase heading not required.)

Army Form C. 2118.

Place	Date	Hour	Summary of Events and Information 1/4 Gloucester Regt.	Remarks and references to Appendices
	17-3.17.		Battalion moved to trenches & relieved the 8th Worcesters in our own front line & two companies of the 5th Glosters holding O.G.1.2&3. 'B.C.' Coys. two platoons of each in O.G.3 & two platoons of each in O.G.1&2. 'D' Coy in support. 'A' Coy in reserve. 2nd Lt Benson & 10 O.R. patrolled as far as the canal at LA CHAPELLETTE but saw no signs of the enemy. In the morning the enemy put a few shells on LA MAISONETTE. Weather good.	
	18.3.17.		'A' Coy went forward established an outpost line from east of BIACHES at I.32a.31.63. to O.3d.18.55. Three picquets were found who pushed forward sentry groups to watch the river crossings. A strong point was established at O.2.b.7.6. 'C' Coy. was in support in O.G.3. 'B & D' Coys. were in reserve. Patrols were sent out & reconnoitred FAUBERG DE PARIS FLAMICOURT & PERONNE, the latter was found to be held by the 8th WARWICKS. All bridges had been destroyed. Another patrol reconnoitred the ground on the east side of the river but saw no signs of the enemy.	
	19.3.17.		'D' Coy relieved 'A' Coy & pushed their outpost line across the SOMME. Two picquets were posted at I.35d. Central & O.6.a.3.2. at night they were moved to the Cross roads at DOINGT & the road junction at J.31.a.99. The strong point was at O.2.b.7.6. 'A' Coy was in support. 'C & B' Coys in reserve. Patrolling was carried out but no signs of the enemy were seen. Weather fair.	R.J. Wilkinson Lt Col Comdg 1/4 Gloucester R.

A5834 Wt. W4973/M687 750,000 8/16 D. D. & L. Ltd. Forms C.2118/13.

Instructions regarding War Diaries and Intelligence Summaries are contained in F. S. Regs., Part II. and the Staff Manual respectively. Title pages will be prepared in manuscript.

WAR DIARY
or
INTELLIGENCE SUMMARY.

(Erase heading not required.)

Army Form C. 2118.

Place	Date	Hour	Summary of Events and Information 1/4 Gloucester Regt.	Remarks and references to Appendices
	20.3.17		The Battalion moved across the SOMME & established its Headquarters at LITTLE FLAMICOURT. 'B' Coy relieved 'D' Coy on outpost line & took up dispositions as follows:- one picquet at J.33.a.2.0. & one picquet at P.3.a.9.8. with a strong point at J.32.c.3.6. "A & C" Coys were in support holding the line from DOINGT (inclusive) to road junction at O.6.a.4.9. 'D' Coy. was in reserve in LITTLE FLAMICOURT. CARTIGNY, BRUSLE & BUIRE were reconnoitred but no signs of the enemy were seen. Movement orders received. Weather fair.	
	21.3.17		Battalion was relieved by the 1/4 ROYAL BERKS moved back to SOPHIE. Weather good.	
SOPHIE	22.3.17		Battalion in SOPHIE. Training of specialists. Weather good.	
do.	23.3.17		Battalion in SOPHIE. Training of specialists. Two companies on working party. Weather good.	
do	24.3.17		Battalion in SOPHIE. Training of specialists. Two companies on working party. Weather good.	
SOPHIE & CARTIGNY	25.3.17		Battalion in SOPHIE. At 3pm. Battalion, Transport etc. moved to CARTIGNY. Weather good.	[illegible] Lt. Col. Comdg. 1/4 Gloucester Regt.

A5834 Wt. W4973/M687 750,000 8/16 D. D. & L. Ltd. Forms/C.2118/13.

Army Form C. 2118.

Instructions regarding War Diaries and Intelligence Summaries are contained in F. S. Regs., Part II. and the Staff Manual respectively. Title pages will be prepared in manuscript.

WAR DIARY
or
INTELLIGENCE SUMMARY.
(Erase heading not required.)

1/4 Gloucester Regt.

Place	Date	Hour	Summary of Events and Information	Remarks and references to Appendices
CARTIGNY	26.3.17.		Battalion at CARTIGNY. One company working on craters, & one company clearing roads in village. Weather rainy.	
CARTIGNY	27.3.17		Battalion at CARTIGNY 'A.B.& C' Coys training 'D' Company repairing roads in village & filling in craters.	
CARTIGNY.	28.3.17.		Battalion at CARTIGNY all companies on working parties. Weather fair.	
CARTIGNY VILLERS FAUCON.	29.3.17.		Battalion moved to VILLARS FAUCON relieved the Bucks 'A'B' Coys & Battalion H.Q. in the village, 'C' Coy holding the ROISEL - VILLERS FAUCON ROAD & 'D' Coy in reserve at K3.d.7.9. The latter sending two platoons into the village that night. 2nd Lt. [illegible] went out to reconnoitre STE. EMILIE & found it strongly held; on being reinforced by 2nd Lt. [illegible] & a Lewis gun team they endeavoured to advance further. Shortly afterwards they were observed & two red lights were sent up & the enemy's artillery fire on the entrances to VILLERS FAUCON. A patrol went out from E.28.d.2.5 & advanced as far as E.29.d.25.60, but as soon as they were observed two red lights were sent up & the enemy's artillery at once put shrapnel on them.	

[illegible signature] Lt. Col.
Comdg. 1/4th Gloucester Regt.

A5834 Wt. W4973/M687 750,000 8/16 D. D. & L. Ltd. Forms/C.2118/13.

Army Form C. 2118.

Instructions regarding War Diaries and Intelligence Summaries are contained in F. S. Regs., Part II. and the Staff Manual respectively. Title pages will be prepared in manuscript.

WAR DIARY
or
INTELLIGENCE SUMMARY.
(Erase heading not required.)

1/4 Gloucester Regt.

Place	Date	Hour	Summary of Events and Information	Remarks and references to Appendices
VILLARS FAUCON.	30.3.17		Battalion at VILLARS FAUCON. At 4 pm in the afternoon "A & B" Coys. attacked STE EMILIE & by 6 pm "B" Coy had occupied the village. "A" Coy having to retire owing to heavy machine gun fire. One prisoner & one machine gun were captured. Our casualties were heavy. At the same time two platoons of "C" Coy attacked PLEASANT HOUSE which they occupied & advanced to the ridge running through K.5.b & c & E.30.c. which they occupied at 5.45 p.m. & consolidated. That night our dispositions were as follows:- "A & B" Coys. holding STE. EMILIE, a cyclist post at E.24.c.7.2. Two platoons of "C" Coy holding the ridge from K.5.c.0.0. to E.30.c.1.9. & two platoons in support holding the line from K.5 central to E.29.a.3.4. One company of the 8th Worcesters holding VILLERS FAUCON & "D" Coy in the sunken road running through E.22.b & d. Battalion H.Q. in VILLERS FAUCON. Weather rainy	
VILLERS FAUCON.	31.3.17		Battalion holding VILLERS FAUCON, STE. EMILIE, ridge from K.5.c.0.0. to E.30.c.1.9. Dispositions the same as the previous night with the exception of one platoon of the 8th Worcesters having a Lewis gun post at E.24.c.6.2. & rifle post at E.24.c.4.4. The cyclists having moved their gun to E.30.a.3.6. The enemy shelled STE. EMILIE from 8 a.m. to 8.10 a.m. very heavily, but "B" Coy only had one casualty. At the moment of this bombardment the enemy advanced towards STE. EMILIE to a line running through E.13.d.5.4., E.19.b.6.5., E.19.d.7.3., F.25.b.4.6. F.25 central F.25.c.3.0. with a machine gun at F.25.c.3.0.	

Reginald [illegible] Lt. Col.
Comdg. 1/4 Gloucester Regt.

A5834 Wt. W4973/M687 750,000 8/16 D. D. & L. Ltd. Forms/C.2118/13.

Confidential

Vol 25

War Diary

of

1/4th Bn The Gloucestershire Regt. T.F

From 1/4/17 To 30/4/17

(VOL. XXIV)

24 P
6 sheets

Instructions regarding War Diaries and Intelligence Summaries are contained in F. S. Regs., Part II. and the Staff Manual respectively. Title pages will be prepared in manuscript.

Army Form C. 2118.

WAR DIARY
or
INTELLIGENCE SUMMARY.

(Erase heading not required.) 4th Battalion Gloucestershire Regiment.

Place	Date	Hour	Summary of Events and Information	Remarks and references to Appendices
	1-4-17		Battalion at LONGAVESNES At 6-30 a.m. they stood too in conjunction with the attack by the 144th Infantry Brigade on EPEHY. Weather Fair.	
	2-4-17		Battalion at LONGAVESNES. Weather Stormy.	
	3-4-17		do do do Moved to CARTIGNY.	
	4-4-17		Battalion at CARTIGNY Training of Specialists.	
	5-4-17		do do do do	
	6-4-17		Battalion moved at 2 a.m. to (K.5. central.) and stood too in conjunction with the attack by the 145th Brigade. Weather Fine.	
	7-4-17		Battalion moved up to front line and relieved "B" & "C" 4th Royal Berks Regt. in front line "D" Coy in Support & "A" Coy in Reserve. Weather Stormy.	
	8-4-17		Battalion in Front Line "A" & "D" Coys in Front Line, "B" Coy in Support, "C" Coy in Reserve. A Patrol was sent out to F. 29. b. 45. and No 15. Copse. The latter was found to be clear of the Enemy. Weather Fair.	
	9-4-17		Battalion relieved by the 1/6th Bn. Worcesters and moved to Camp at F. 29. b. 72 Weather Stormy	
	10-4-17		Battalion in Camp at F29. b. 72 Company Inspections. Weather fair.	
	11-4-17		Battalion in Camp at F.29. b. 72 Weather Stormy At 8. p.m. they moved to Front Line and relieved the 1/6th Bn. Glosters. "C" Coy. - Right Front Company "B" Coy. Right Support Company "D" Coy. - Left Front Company "A" Coy. Left Support Company A Patrol was sent out from Cross-roads at F.16. a. 96 and found SART FARM occupied Weather Stormy	Roger Wilkinson

A5834 Wt. W4973/M687 750,000 8/16 D. D. & L. Ltd. Forms/C.2118/13.

Instructions regarding War Diaries and Intelligence Summaries are contained in F. S. Regs., Part II. and the Staff Manual respectively. Title pages will be prepared in manuscript.

WAR DIARY
or
INTELLIGENCE SUMMARY.

Army Form C. 2118.

(*Erase heading not required.*) 1/4th Battn. Gloucestershire Regiment

Place	Date	Hour	Summary of Events and Information	Remarks and references to Appendices
	12-4-17		Battalion in Front Line. When dark "D" & "C" Coys were relieved by two Companies of 1/6th Glosters. "A" Coy relieved Left Front Company of 1/7th Worcesters "D" Coy was in Support in preparation for an Attack on Enemy Line running through F17 in the early morning of the 13th	
	13-4-17		"B" & "C" Coys attacked Enemy Line and had captured all objectives by 4 a.m. "B" Coy was immediately Counter-attacked, but drove the Enemy back. During the day our New line was heavily Shelled. Our Casualties were fairly light. At night Battalion was relieved by 1/5th Glosters and moved to Billets at HAMEL.	
	14-4-17		Battalion in Billets at HAMEL. Company Inspections.	
	15-4-17		Battalion in Billets at HAMEL. Training of Specialists "A" & "B" Coys on Working Parties Weather Stormy	
	16-4-17		Battalion in Billets at HAMEL. Training of Specialists "A" "C" & "D" Coys on Working Parties Weather Fair.	
	17-4-17		Battalion in Billets. Working Parties "B" "C" & "D" Coys Training of Specialists	
	18-4-17		do do "A" "B" & "D" Coys do	
	19-4-17		do do "A" & "D" Coys. In the afternoon Battalion moved to ST. EMILIE and relieved the 1/4th Bn Royal Berks	
	20-4-17		Battalion on Railway Cutting. ST EMILIE. Training of Specialists	

Roger Wilkinson
Lt. Col.
Commanding 1/4th Batt. Gloster Regt.

A5834 Wt. W4973/M687 750,000 8/16 D. D. & L. Ltd. Forms/C.2118/13.

Instructions regarding War Diaries and Intelligence Summaries are contained in F. S. Regs., Part II. and the Staff Manual respectively. Title pages will be prepared in manuscript.

WAR DIARY *or* INTELLIGENCE SUMMARY.

(*Erase heading not required.*) 1/4th Battalion Gloucestershire Regiment.

Army Form C. 2118.

Place	Date	Hour	Summary of Events and Information	Remarks and references to Appendices
	21-4-17		Battalion in Railway Cutting. At night they moved to the Front Line and relieved the 6th Bn. Glosters Regt. "A" + "D" Coys in Front Line, "B" Coy in Support "C" Coy in Reserve. Patrol was sent up the Valley as far as A.7.d.69 which they found occupied	
	22-4-17		Battalion in LEMPIERE. dispositions the same as previous day Enemy Artillery quiet. Patrolling carried out at night.	
	23-4-17		Battalion relieved by the 6th Bn. Glosters Regt, and moved back to Railway Cutting, at. ST EMILIE.	
	24-4-17		Battalion at Railway Cutting. In the afternoon Orders received to attack the KNOLL, in conjunction with 1/7th Bn. Worcesters on Right Flank, and 126th Brigade on Left. At dusk Battalion moved up into position "D" Coy on Left "A" Coy in Centre + "C" Coy on Right. "B" Coy were in Support The attack took place at 11-p.m, and by the early morning "C" Coy had gained their objective, but "A" + "D" Coys had pushed too far forward. The 126th Brigade failed to attack.	
	25-4-17		Our dispositions unchanged. Just before dusk "D" + "A" Coys were forced to retire, in order to avoid being surrounded. "C" Coy however were able to extend their line further up the S.E. Slope of the KNOLL At night Battalion was relieved by 1/5th Bn. Glosters Regt and moved to Camp at VILLERS FAUCON	

Roger Wilkinson

Instructions regarding War Diaries and Intelligence Summaries are contained in F. S. Regs., Part II. and the Staff Manual respectively. Title pages will be prepared in manuscript.

WAR DIARY
or
INTELLIGENCE SUMMARY.

Army Form C. 2118.

(Erase heading not required.) 1/4th Battalion Gloucestershire Regiment.

Place	Date	Hour	Summary of Events and Information	Remarks and references to Appendices
	26-4-17		Battalion at Camp in VILLERS FAUCON Company Inspections.	
	27-4-17		do do B+C Coys Working Parties	
			Training of Lewis Gunners.	
	28-4-17		do do A+D Coys Working Parties	
			At 11-a.m. Battalion was relieved by 1/6th Bn. Gloucester Regt and moved to HAMEL.	
	29-4-17		Battalion at HAMEL. In the afternoon moved up to Left Support Line and relieved the Bucks Battalion. ~~HQ~~ + B Coy at LEMPIERE A C + D Coys Hd Qrs ~~in Railway Cutting ST EMELIE~~ in Camp S.E. of Villers Falcon.	
	30.4.17		at dusk A company relieved B coy in LEMPIERE D coy moved to LEMPIERE Hd Qrs B + C Companies moved to railway cutting St EMILIE.	

Roger Wilkinson Lt Col.

Lieut. Col.
Commanding 4th Batt. Gloster Regt.

A5834 Wt. W4973/M687 750,000 8/16 D. D. & L. Ltd. Forms/C.2118/13.

Confidential

Vol 26

144/48

War Diary

of

1/4th Bn The Gloucestershire Regt.

1st May to 31st May 1917

(VOL. XXVI)

25 P.
8 sheets

Army Form C. 2118.

Instructions regarding War Diaries and Intelligence Summaries are contained in F. S. Regs., Part II. and the Staff Manual respectively. Title pages will be prepared in manuscript.

WAR DIARY
or
INTELLIGENCE SUMMARY.

(Erase heading not required.) 1/4th Batt. Gloucestershire Regiment.

Place	Date	Hour	Summary of Events and Information	Remarks and references to Appendices
	1.5.17		Battalion H.Q. & 'C & B' Coys. in Railway Cutting at ST. EMILIE E.24.a.7.8 'A & D' Coys at LEMPIRE; at night 'C & B' Coys out on working party.	
	2.5.17		Battalion H.Q. & 'C & B' Coys in Railway Cutting at ST. EMILIE. 'A & D' Coys at LEMPIRE; at night 'C & B' Coys out on working party at GILLEMONT FARM.	
	3.3.17		Dispositions the same. At 10 a.m. Battalion was relieved by the 8th LANCASHIRE FUSILIERS & moved to TINCOURT	
	4.5.17		Battalion at TINCOURT. Company inspections	
	5.5.17		Battalion at TINCOURT 'A B & C' Coys on working party. 'D' Coy training	
	6.5.17		Battalion at TINCOURT Company inspections	
	7.5.17		Battalion at TINCOURT 'D' Company on working party 'A B & C' Coys training	
	8.5.17		Battalion at TINCOURT 'B & C' Companies on working party, 'A & D' Coys training The following N.C.Os. & men were awarded the Military Medal 200368 Sgt. C.W. KEMP 200521 Cpl. H.A. BAILEY 200753 Pte. H.G. PRICE 201197 Pte. T ASHCROFT	

R Stephens Major
Commanding, 4th Batt. Gloster Regt.

A5834 Wt. W4973/M687 750,000 8/16 D. D. & L. Ltd. Forms/C.2118/13.

Army Form C. 2118.

Instructions regarding War Diaries and Intelligence Summaries are contained in F. S. Regs., Part II. and the Staff Manual respectively. Title pages will be prepared in manuscript.

WAR DIARY
or
INTELLIGENCE SUMMARY.
(Erase heading not required.)

Place	Date	Hour	Summary of Events and Information	Remarks and references to Appendices
	9.5.17		Battalion at TINCOURT. 'B.C' Companies on working party. A & D Companies training	
	~~10.5.17~~		2nd Lt. (Temp Lt. A/Capt) H MERRICK awarded the Military Cross. 200417 Sgt H. WINTERSON awarded the D.C.M.	
	10.5.17		Battalion at TINCOURT. 'A.C.&D' Coys on working party 'B' Coy training	
	11.5.17		Battalion at TINCOURT 'A.B' Coys on working party 'C&D' Coys training	
	12.5.17		Battalion at TINCOURT. Company Training & inspections. At 6.30 p.m. Battalion moved to PERONNE	
	13.5.17		Battalion at PERONNE. At 5 a.m Battalion moved to COMBLES where the Brigade was inspected by Corps Commander	
	14.5.17		Battalion at COMBLES. At 5.30 a.m Battalion moved to LEBUCQUIRE & relieved the 8th WEST RIDING REGT. Battalion H.Q. & 'D' Coys at LEBUCQUIRE 'A.B.C' Coys ~~out~~ in Sunken road at T4a [illegible] 28.C	
	15.5.17		Battalion at LEBUCQUIRE & Sunken road. Work continued on billets, shelters & strong points.	
	16.5.17		Battalion at LEBUCQUIRE & Sunken road. Work continued on billets shelters & strong points	

R.D. Eighman Major
Commanding 4th Batt. Glos'ter Regt

A5834 Wt. W4973/M687 750,000 8/16 D. D. & L. Ltd. Forms/C.2118/13.

Instructions regarding War Diaries and Intelligence Summaries are contained in F. S. Regs., Part II. and the Staff Manual respectively. Title pages will be prepared in manuscript.

WAR DIARY
or
INTELLIGENCE SUMMARY.
(Erase heading not required.)

Army Form C. 2118.

Place	Date	Hour	Summary of Events and Information	Remarks and references to Appendices
	17.5.17		Battalion at LEBUCQUIRE Sunken road work continued on billets, shelters & strong points D Coy relieved A Coy who moved into camp at LEBUCQUIRE.	
	18.5.17		Battalion at LEBUCQUIRE Sunken road work continued on billets shelters & strong points, C & D Coys on RE working party. The following N.C.Os & men awarded the D.C.M.	
	~~19.5.17~~		200477 Cpl R.E. CROSSMAN 200478 Pte G. BENNETT	
	19.5.17		Battalion at LEBUCQUIRE Sunken road. A & B Coys on RE working party. The following officers were awarded the Military Cross 2nd Lt E.W.L. TIDDY. 2nd Lt T.N. BENSON.	
	20.5.17		Battalion at LEBUCQUIRE, Sunken road. work continued on shelters & strong points	
	21.5.17		Battalion at LEBUCQUIRE Sunken road At night the Battalion moved to the front line & relieved the 1/6th ROYAL WARWICKS. Battalion HQ J 4 c 8 3 B Coy. right front C Coy. left front A Coy. right ~~front~~ support D Coy left ~~front~~ support	

R S Stephens
Lt Col
Commanding 4th Batt. Glos'ter Regt.

A5834 Wt. W4973/M687 750,000 8/16 D. D. & L. Ltd. Forms/C.2118/13.

Army Form C. 2118.

Instructions regarding War Diaries and Intelligence Summaries are contained in F. S. Regs., Part II. and the Staff Manual respectively. Title Pages will be prepared in manuscript.

WAR DIARY
or
INTELLIGENCE SUMMARY
(Erase heading not required.)

Place	Date	Hour	Summary of Events and Information	Remarks and references to Appendices
	22.5.17		Battalion in front line. Hostile Artillery quiet. Patrolling was carried out during the night but no signs of the enemy were seen. Work wiring front line.	
	23.5.17		Battalion in front line. Hostile Artillery quiet. Patrolling was carried out during the night. Old enemy trenches reconnoitred but found to be unoccupied. Enemy strong point at K.1.b.8.7 was approached & our patrol was fired on. Work wiring continued.	
	24.5.17		Battalion in front line. Hostile Artillery quiet. Patrolling ~~was carried~~ out & large enemy patrols were also observed. Strong point at K.1.b.8.7 was again approached & patrol fired on. Work wiring continued.	
	25.5.17		Battalion in front line. Hostile Artillery quiet. At 11.30 p.m. D Coy left our front line to attack strong point at K.1.b.8.7. On reaching the Sunken road at ... two platoons remained there in support while the other two platoons pushed forward towards the post. On approaching the post the attacking force observed large enemy forces working round their flanks & to avoid being cut off the Company was forced to retire. Work wiring continued.	
	26.5.17		Battalion in front line. Hostile Artillery quiet. Patrolling was carried out during the night, but no signs of the enemy were seen. D Coy relieved C Coy &	

2449 Wt. W14957/M90 750,000 1/16 J.B.C. & A. Forms/C.2118/12.

R Stephens Lieut. Col.
Commanding 4th Batt. Glos'ter Regt.

Instructions regarding War Diaries and Intelligence Summaries are contained in F. S. Regs., Part II. and the Staff Manual respectively. Title pages will be prepared in manuscript.

WAR DIARY
or
~~INTELLIGENCE SUMMARY.~~
(Erase heading not required.)

Army Form C. 2118.

Place	Date	Hour	Summary of Events and Information	Remarks and references to Appendices
	30.5.17.		Battalion at LEBUCQUIRE. Company inspections	
	31.5.17.		Battalion at LEBUCQUIRE. Companies training & training of specialists. At night 'A, B & C' Coys on working party. Battalion strength 675. Casualties for month ending 31.5.17. Killed nil Died of wounds 2 Wounded 3 Missing nil.	

R Stephens Capt.
Commanding 4th Batt. Gloster Regt.

A5834 Wt. W4973/M687 750,000 8/16 D. D. & L. Ltd. Forms/C.2118/13.

Instructions regarding War Diaries and Intelligence Summaries are contained in F. S. Regs., Part II. and the Staff Manual respectively. Title pages will be prepared in manuscript.

WAR DIARY
or
~~INTELLIGENCE SUMMARY.~~
(Erase heading not required.)

Army Form C. 2118.

Place	Date	Hour	Summary of Events and Information	Remarks and references to Appendices
			A Coy relieved 'B' Coy. Work. Wiring continued	
	27.5.17		Battalion in front line. Hostile Artillery quiet. Patrolling carried out during the night & rifle pits inspected but no signs of the enemy seen. Work wiring front line	
	28.5.17		Battalion in front line. Hostile Artillery quiet. At 10.30 pm two platoons 'C' Coy left our front line to take part in a demonstration in front of enemy strong point at K.1.b.8.7 in conjunction with the ~~reserve~~ Artillery. ~~two~~ One platoon remained in support whilst ~~two~~ the other platoons rushed forward & at 11.30 pm opened fire on the post with the intention of drawing large enemy forces on them. They then retired to the support platoon & the whole Company withdrew to our lines whilst our Artillery opened fire on the strong point. It could not be ascertained whether casualties were inflicted on the enemy. Work. Wiring front line.	
	29.5.17		Battalion relieved by the 1/6 ROYAL WARWICKS & moved to camp at LEBUCQUIRE	

R Stephens Major
Commanding 4th Batt. Glos'ter Regt.

A5834 Wt. W4973/M687 750,000 8/16 D. D. & L. Ltd. Forms/C.2118/13.

Confidential

Vol 27

War Diary

of

1/4th Bn The Gloucestershire Regt. (T.F.)

From 1st June to 30th June 1917

(VOL. XXVII)

26. P.
8 sheet

Instructions regarding War Diaries and Intelligence Summaries are contained in F. S. Regs., Part II. and the Staff Manual respectively. Title pages will be prepared in manuscript.

WAR DIARY
or
INTELLIGENCE SUMMARY.
(*Erase heading not required.*)

Army Form C. 2118.

1/4 Bn. Gloucestershire Regiment

Place	Date	Hour	Summary of Events and Information	Remarks and references to Appendices
LEBUCQUIERE	June 1–5th		Battalion moves billets at LEBUCQUIERE. Training carried out working parties furnished on nights of 1/2 + 4/5	
	6th		Lieut Col. R Stephens, Oxf & Bucks L. I. transferred to 4th Bn Oxf & Bucks L.I. Lieut Col. J St. Crosskey, 1/5 Royal Warwick Regiment takes over command	
			Bn relieves 1/6 R. War. R. in LOUVERVAL Section as before. B Coy Right front Coy; C Left; A Right Support Coy; D Left	
LOUVERVAL	6–9		Situation quite normal on whole front	
	10/11th		Inter-company relief A relieves B D relieves C	
	11		Patrol skirmish as in Appendix A: Casualties 2 O.R. missing (1 since returned)	Ref Appendix A
	12th		Raid attempted as in Appendix B Casualties. 1 O.R wounded; 1 O.R " missing; 2 O.R missing	Ref Appendix B
	13th		Situation normal	
	14/15th		Battalion relieved by 1/6 Bn R War. R & move back into same billets at LEBUCQUIERE	
LEBUCQUIERE	15th–18		Battalion in rest billets Training carried out working party found night of 16th/17th	
	19th		Battalion scheme	
	20–21st		Still in rest billets. Working party on night of 20th/21st	
	22nd		Bn relieves 1/6 R War Regt in LOUVERVAL Section as before. Dispositions as before	

J [signature]

Lieut. Col.

Commanding, 4th Batt. Glos'ter Regt.

30. 6. 17

A5834 Wt. W4973/M687 750,000 8/16 D. D. & L. Ltd. Forms/C.2118/13.

Army Form C. 2118.

Instructions regarding War Diaries and Intelligence Summaries are contained in F. S. Regs., Part II. and the Staff Manual respectively. Title pages will be prepared in manuscript.

WAR DIARY
or
INTELLIGENCE SUMMARY.
(Erase heading not required.)

1/4 Bn. Gloucestershire Regiment

Place	Date	Hour	Summary of Events and Information	Remarks and references to Appendices
LOUVERVAL	[illegible] 23		Situation normal. There appears to be more enemy movement than during previous the towns much outgoing transport.	
	24th		Patrol skirmish with the enemy. See Appendix C. Casualties 5 O.R. wounded	Ref. App. C
	25th		Scheme in conjunction with T.M.B. See Appendices D + D1	Ref. App. D + D1
	26th		Patrol capture prisoner of 7th R.I.R. while lying out in D 30 d - Tbc.	
	27th 28th		Situation normal. T.M.B. scheme continued on night of 27/28th. No enemy appears.	
	29th		T.M.B. scheme again continued, but with no results.	
	30th		Situation normal.	
			Ration strength 30.6.17 Officers 27, O.R. 627, Total 654	

[illegible signature]
Lieut. Col.
Commanding 4th Batt. Glos'ter Regt.
30. 6. 17

A5834 Wt. W4973/M687 750,000 8/16 D. D. & L. Ltd. Forms/C.2118/13.

Appendix A

1/4th.Battalion Gloucestershire Regiment.

Patrol on the night of 11th/12th.June 1917.

A patrol of 1 Officer & 20 O.R. left our lines at J.6.centl at 11 p.m. and proceeded in a N.E.direction to J.6.b.83., crossing an unoccupied trench at J.6.b.44. in which was found a German shovel and bombs, but there were no signs of work in progress.

From J.6.b.44. the patrol moved N.W. to J.6.b.18. where they came in sight of a German patrol. After shots were fired and the German patrol moved off.

Our party then took up the position at J.6.b.97. and shortly after the German patrol was seen moving along the skyline. Further shots were exchanged and the enemy retired.

Our patrol were still at this spot when a further enemy patrol came into close contact with them. Both parties at once engaged with fifles at close range and it is believed that two of the enemy were Killed. The enemy retired and our patrol returned. On their return it was discovered that two O.R. were missing. It is thought that these men were not taken by the enemy, but got cut off from the patrol in the darkness and lost their way, ~~and that they will eventually return.~~

One has since returned

12/6/17.

Lieut. Col

Commanding, 4th Batt. Glos'ter Regt

Appendix B

1/4th Battalion Gloucestershire Regiment.

++

Report on attempted Raid carried out on night 13/14th instant, by 2 Companies on the German Post on the CAMBRAI Road at K.2.a.08.

eeeeeeeeeeeeeeeee

(1). Raiding parties commenced to leave our front line at No.3 Post (J.6.d22) at 11.p.m. with 5 minutes interval between parties.

The left flank party (1platoon "C"Company under 2 Lieut E. Shephard) proceeded along the left of the road to about point E.26. d. 22 05.

The attacking party (2 Platoons "B" Coy with right flanking guard of 1 Lewis Gun and 1 Section riflr men under Lieut Wilkins and 2nd Lieut Organ) proceeded to about point K.1.b.73. When they met an enemy patrol.

The parties on the road:-

1 Platoon "B" Company about 200 yards from cross roads in K.1.a.

1.Platoon "B" Company at cross roads in K. 1. a. under Captain Newth.

2. Platoons "C" Company flanking both sides of the CAMBRAI RD. about 400 yards in front of our wire -

All reached their respective positions without any opposition.

(2). At about 12-30 a.m. the two attacking platoons encountered an enemy patrol , about 20 strong ~~xxxxxxxxxxxx~~ moving along to the right of the enemy Post. The party lay quiet, but as the enemy advanced they discovered them and opened fire, whereupon our patrol replied with rifle and Lewis Gun fire, and judging by the shouts that were heard wounded several of the enemy. During the lull that followed, a party prepared to go forward to bring in any wounded, but before they could start another enemy patrol about 20 strong was seen to be advancing from the right rear. When this last party were quite close, our men opened on them with rifle and Lewis Guns. The enemy then sent up Very lights and opened a brisk rifle and machine gun fire supported by rifle grenade fire from the post, forcing our party to retire to the Sunken Road in K.1.a., where they reorganised.

A small party then went forward again under 2/Lieut Organ to look for wounded enemy and our own wounded, but could not find any, though he searched for 20 minutes. At 1-51 a.m. the prearranged signal was sent up and the various parties retired in order.

It was impossible to try to attack at 1-30 a.m. when the guns opened as the enemy was very much on the alert and kept up a brisk machine gun fire which lasted until about 2 a.m.

TOTAL CASUALTIES:- 1 Other Rank Wounded.
1 do. Wounded & Missing.
2 do. Missing.

14/6/17.

[signature]

Lieut Col.

Commanding 4th Batt. Gloster Regt.

Appendix D1

1/4th. Battalion Gloucestershire Regiment.

P A T R O L.

A patrol of 1.Officer and 20 men left J.6.d.0075. at 10-30.p.m. and proceeded along - at a distance of 100 yards parallel to the CAMBRAI RD. until reaching within 100 yards of the Cross roads, where sounds of the enemy where heard. The patrol halted and sent forward two men to reconnoitre the ground a short distance in front. They reported sounds of the enemy activity near the Sunken Road and another party was sent forward to examine the hedge and ruins at the Cross roads. This party reported an enemy patrol of 30 men near the hedge and word was sent back to the O.C. Trench Mortars who had the guns laid on.

A small party again went forward to reconnoitre, but were now unable to locate an enemy and after further examination of the ground the patrol returned at 2-35a.m.

25-6-17

Lieut Col.
Commanding, 4th Batt. Glos'ter Regt.

Appendix C

1/4th. Battalion Gloucestershire Regiment.

Patrol on the night of 24th/25th. June 1917.

A patrol of 1 Officer and 20 O.R. left J.6.a.2500 at 11-30 p.m. and proceeded in an Easterly direction. At J.6.a.65. an enemy party apparently lying in wait, through bombs into the patrol, causing 5 casualties. Rifle shots were exchanged and the patrol extended along a line about J.6.a.42-44 and more of the enemy being located on road in front, the patrol opened five rounds rapid fire.

Soon after this a party of the enemy was detected crawling along the ditch from about J.6.a.38. and the patrol opened fire upon them with their Lewis Gun. A second similar party was also fired upon and at least another 6 Germans doubled back to the road from this point.

During the firing activity a whistle was heard twice from the East side of the road, and also various other sounds pointing to the presence of a further large party

At this time word was sent to the Brigade machine gun on the right of No.8 Post to open bursts of fire on the road and on the trench on the ridge running through J.6.b., where a Very light was sent up by the enemy, during which time the party was re-organised and the work in hand continued.

Two small patrols were sent to reconnoitre ditch to a point D.30.c.57. and the road at about J.6.a.64. No further enemy were found and the patrol pushed forward and reconnoitred road to D.30.c.70. and ground in front to a line about K.1.a.05. to E.25.c.02.

No further enemy were encountered and the patrol returned at 3-20 a.m.

J.B. Crawley

Lieut. Col.

Commanding, 4th Batt. Gloster Regt.

25/6/17.

Appendix D

1/4th. Battalion Gloucestershire Regiment.
+++

nC O P Y.

S E C R E T.

Ref: Map. 57.c. N.E.

To. O.C. "A" Company.

You will commence the Stunt on the CAMBRAI RD. in conjunction with the T.M.B. tonight.

General Scheme.

(1). 1. Platoon - carrying shovels, and concertina wire and a few stakes will leave No. 3 Post at about 10-30.p.m. move along the right of the CAMBRAI RD. to the cross roads in K.1.a. They will reconnoitre the ruins and cross roads at K.1.a. thoroughly and then will lie out there as a covering party to the T.M.B. They willon no account start to dig or make a noise until notified by the O.C. T.M.B. Section that his guns are in position and ready to fire. When notified, they will Spitlock the trench and put out the wire at the spot reconnoitred and found suitable last night. If an enemy patrol approaches, O.C. Patrol will with draw to a suitable position, will signal through to the T.M.B. (2 longs on the buzzer). The latter will at once fire. When the Stokes has finished, the patrol will again move forward, search the ground covered by the Stokes, bring in any wounded enemy, and get identification off any dead that may be there.

(2). 1. Platoon to act as carrying and close covering party to the Stokes Mortar. They will be under the direct command of the O.C. T.M. Section, and will aid him in digging in his guns at the spot reconnoitred last night. Tools required:- shovels and picks.

(3). O.C. Signals will arrange to have a telephone and signallers with each party and to lay a wire between the two parties. This wire must be brought in with the party.

(4). All parties will return to our lines not before 2-30.a.m. and not later than 2-45.a.m.

(5). If the enemy do not approach the cross roads tonight, this Scheme will be continued tomorrow night, in which case further detailed orders will be issued.

(6). A patrol from "D" Company are lying out from D.30.c.70. to J.6.b.49. in order to scupper any enemy approaching the road, in D.30.c. and the high ground in D.30.d. The Machine Gun at J.6.c.38. have orders, that if this patrol gets engaged, they are to place a barrage from E.19.c.01. to E.19.d.55.

Para (5) will not affect your work or patrol, but the latter will give additional security to your left flank.

[signature] 25.6.17

Lieut. Col

Commanding 4th Batt. Glos'ter Regt

Vol 28

27.P
3 sheets

1/4th Batt Gloucestershire Regt

War Diary

of

1/4th Batt Gloucestershire Regt

from 1 July 1917 to 31 July 1917

Volume 28

Instructions regarding War Diaries and Intelligence Summaries are contained in F. S. Regs., Part II. and the Staff Manual respectively. Title pages will be prepared in manuscript.

WAR DIARY
~~or~~
INTELLIGENCE SUMMARY.
(*Erase heading not required.*)

1/4th Bn Gloucester Regt

Army Form C. 2118.

Place	Date	Hour	Summary of Events and Information	Remarks and references to Appendices
LOUVERVAL	1.7.17		Battn relieved by 2nd Royal Scots Fusiliers who take over the dispositions in the front line, Bn proceeds to billets at FREMICOURT for the night.	
FREMICOURT	2.7.17		Battn leaves FREMICOURT goes to ACHIET-LE-PETIT	
ACHIET LE PETIT	3.7.17		Battn leaves ACHIET-LE-PETIT moves to BLAIREVILLE where they occupy billets.	
BLAIREVILLE	4.7.17 to 20.7.17		Battalion in training at BLAIREVILLE. Training including Platoon, Company, Battalion & Brigade scheme was carried out during this time	
BLAIREVILLE	21.7.17		Battn leaves BLAIREVILLE for BERLES-AU-BOIS	
BERLES-AU-BOIS	22.7.17		Battn leaves BERLES-AU-BOIS, marches to SAULTY LARBRET & entrains for POPERINGHE	
POPERINGHE	23.7.17		Battn takes over billets at POPERINGHE	
POPERINGHE	24.7.17		Battn leave POPERINGHE for St JAN TER BIEZEN where it encamps	
St JAN TER BIEZEN	25.7.17 to 30.7.17		Battn in training by Platoons & Companies	
	31.7.17		Battn moves to Camp in woods at A29a (Sht. Belgium 28 N.W. 1/20000)	
			Total Casualties 1	
			Total Reinforcement Officers 7, Men 280	
			Ration Strength 31.7.17 Officers 35, Men 816.	

[signature]
Major
Commanding 4th [illegible] ~~Lieut. Col.~~
31. 7. 17

A5834 W. W4973/M687 750,000 8/16 D. D. & L. Ltd. Forms/C.2118/13.

L.O. 28 P
4 sheet
144
48

W.O. 28

War Diary

of

1/4th Batt: Gloucestershire Regt.

from 1. 8. 17 to 31. 8. 17

Volume 29.

Instructions regarding War Diaries and Intelligence Summaries are contained in F. S. Regs., Part II. and the Staff Manual respectively. Title Pages will be prepared in manuscript.

WAR DIARY
or
INTELLIGENCE SUMMARY
(Erase heading not required.)

August 1917

1/4 Bn. GLOUCESTER REGT.

Army Form C. 2118.

SHEET: BELGIUM 28 NE 1/20000
PILKEM. Ed 1. 1/10000

Place	Date	Hour	Summary of Events and Information	Remarks and references to Appendices
Camp at A29c	Aug 1–5		Battalion in Camp in wood A29c (Sheet Belgium 28 N.W. 1/20000)	
DAMBRE CAMP	6		Battalion moves to DAMBRE CAMP	
FRONT LINE	8/9		Battalion goes into front line Left Bn. Left Brigade & relieves 4th Bn. Royal Berks Regt.	
			Front Company A Coy H.Q. REGINA CROSS Holding posts across STEENBEEK	
			Rt. Spt. C Coy. H.Q. ALBERTA. (C 11 c)	
			Left Spt. B Coy. H.Q. CANOE TRENCH C 10 d 65.	
			Reserve D Coy H.Q. O.G.1 (CANADIAN FARM – C 15 d)	
			Batt. H.Q. CIVILIZATION FARM. C. 16 c 38.	
			Advanced Batt. H.Q. CANOE TRENCH C 10 d 65	
	9/10		Front Company pushes a post forward to road junction at C 5 d 40 15	
SUPPORT	10/11		Battalion goes into support. A + B Coys. CANAL BANK	
			is relieved by the 1/6th Bn. Gloucester Regt. C + D Coys. O.G. 1+2.	
FRONT LINE	13/14		Battalion moves up into the front line & relieves 1/6th Bn. Gloucester Regt.	
			Left Front Coy A C.H.Q. REGINA CROSS (C 11 a)	
			Right B C.H.Q. ALBERTA.	
			Support Coy. C C.H.Q. CANOE TRENCH C. 10 d. 65	
			Reserve D C.H.Q. O.G.1 (CANADIAN FARM – C 15 d)	
			Batt. & advanced H.Q. as before	
	15/16		B Coy take over whole of Battalion front line & is later relieved by the 145 Brigade	
REIGERSBURG CAMP	16th		Battalion moves back into REIGERSBURG CAMP	
	17th		Battalion still at REIGERSBURG CAMP	
	18th		C + D Coys move to the CANAL BANK	

E. Reeves Major
~~Lieut.-Col.~~
Commanding 4th Batt. Glos'ter Regt.

2449 Wt. W14957/M90 750,000 1/16 J.B.C. & A. Forms/C.2118/12.

Army Form C. 2118.

Instructions regarding War Diaries and Intelligence Summaries are contained in F. S. Regs., Part II. and the Staff Manual respectively. Title Pages will be prepared in manuscript.

2

WAR DIARY (Cont) or ~~INTELLIGENCE SUMMARY~~

(Erase heading not required.)

1/4th Bn. Gloucester Regt

Place	Date	Hour	Summary of Events and Information	Remarks and references to Appendices
	Aug 20th		C & D Coys moved to O.6.1 Advanced B.H.Q. CIVILIZATION FARM	
CANAL BANK	21st		A & B Coys & Batt HQ moved to CANAL BANK.	
FRONT LINE	22nd		Battalion moves into Front Line relieving 1/6th Bn. Gloucester Regt.	
			Batt H.Q. 'ALBERTA' (C 11 c)	
			D Coy Left front Coy H.Q. MON DU HIBOU (C 6 c)	
			C Coy Right H.Q. C 11 b 64	
			B Coy Support Coy H.Q. ALBERTA	
			A Coy Reserve Coy H.Q. C. 22 a 66.	
	22/23rd		One prisoner captured of the 231st R.I.R.	
	23rd/24th		Situation normal.	
	25th		One prisoner captured. 413th R.I.R.	
CANAL BANK	25/26		Battalion relieved by 1/7th Bn. Worcestershire Regiment & proceeds to CANAL BANK.	
REIGERSBURG CAMP	26th		Battalion moves to REIGERSBURG CAMP	
BROWN CAMP	27th		Battalion moves to BROWN CAMP (A 22 d 88)	
SCHOOL CAMP	29th to 31st		Battalion moves to SCHOOL CAMP (WATAU – POPERINGHE R.)	
			Total Casualties killed [illegible]	
			Total Reinforcements 18 [illegible]	
			Ration Strength 31st 718	

E. Brooke [illegible] Major ~~Lieut. Col.~~
Commanding 4th Batt. Glos'ter Regt.

2449 Wt. W14957/M90 750,000 1/16 J.B.C. & A. Forms/C.2118/12.

E.W. 29 P
3 sheets

WO 30

1/4 th. Battalion Gloucestershire Regt.

WAR DIARY.

Period No 30.

Sept 1st 1917 to Sept 30th 1917.

Instructions regarding War Diaries and Intelligence Summaries are contained in F. S. Regs., Part II. and the Staff Manual respectively. Title Pages will be prepared in manuscript.

WAR DIARY

or

~~INTELLIGENCE SUMMARY~~

(Erase heading not required.)

Sept. 1917

Army Form C. 2118.

1/4 Battn GLOUCESTER REGT

Place	Date	Hour	Summary of Events and Information	Remarks and references to Appendices
SCHOOL CAMP	1.9.17 to 17.9.17		Battn in camp (Sheet. Belgium & France 27NE L 3 d 3 6) Platoon, Coy & Battn training carried out.	
NIELLES (les ARDRES) P de C	18.9.17 to 30.9.17		Battn moves to NIELLES (les ARDRES. P de C) Entraining at ABEELE at 7.30 PM 17.9.17 & detraining at AUDRUICQ at 4.30 AM 18.9.17 and marches to billets in NIELLES area.	
			Platoon, Company, Battn, Brigade and Divisional training carried out	
	~~30.9.17~~		~~Battalion moves to~~	
			Total Casualties — Nil	
			Total Reinforcements: Nil	
			Ration Strength 30th 668.	
			J H Comley(?) Lieut Col. Commanding 1/4 Battn Glosters Regt	

2449 Wt. W14957/M90 750,000 1/16 J.B.C. & A. Forms/C.2118/12.

Confidential

144/48

Vol 31

1/4th Gloucestershire Regiment

WAR DIARY

1st October – 31st October 1917

VOLUME XXXI

30 P.
13 sheet

Army Form C. 2118.

Instructions regarding War Diaries and Intelligence Summaries are contained in F. S. Regs., Part II. and the Staff Manual respectively. Title pages will be prepared in manuscript.

No I

WAR DIARY
or
~~INTELLIGENCE SUMMARY.~~

(Erase heading not required.)

OCTOBER 1917

1/4th BATTN GLOUCESTERSHIRE REGT

Place	Date	Hour	Summary of Events and Information	Remarks and references to Appendices
NIELLES LES ARDRES (P. de C)	1.10.17		At 2 AM the Battn left the billets in the NIELLES area and marched to AUDRUICQ for the purpose of entraining for VLAMERTINGHE (BELGIUM Sheet 20 SW). At AUDRUICQ "D" Company was left behind ~~[illegible]~~ to follow on 2nd train.	
			The Battalion detrained at VLAMERTINGHE. HQ. "B" and "C" Coys marched to BRAKE CAMP (A30d 1.9) and "A" Company proceeded to REIGERSBERG CAMP (H 6 b 35) for night working parties in the forward area.	
BRAKE CAMP	2.10.17		During the morning 3 hours company training was carried out and work on the improvement of the camp undertaken.	
			During the afternoon "D" Company arrived in camp.	
BRAKE CAMP	3.10.17		Company training carried out during the morning. "A" Company also arrived in camp.	
BRAKE CAMP	4.10.17		At about mid-day the Battn received orders to proceed to the CANAL BANK (St JULIEN 28 NW2) C 25 d and I 1 b and remain there in Divisional reserve until further orders.	
			The Battn therefore left BRAKE CAMP at 12.45 and proceeded by road to the CANAL BANK where HQ & the four companies were billeted in dugouts along the East bank.	
			During the evening orders were received to leave the CANAL at 9 AM 5.10.17 and proceed to REIGERSBERG CAMP.	
	5.10.17		The Battn left the CANAL at 9.15 AM and proceeded to REIGERSBERG CAMP (H 6 b 35).	

A7092). Wt. W12839/M1295 750,000. 1/17. D. D & L., Ltd. Forms/C2118/14.

Instructions regarding War Diaries and Intelligence Summaries are contained in F. S. Regs., Part II. and the Staff Manual respectively. Title pages will be prepared in manuscript.

WAR DIARY
or
~~INTELLIGENCE SUMMARY.~~
(Erase heading not required.)

Army Form C. 2118.

No II OCTOBER 1917 1/4th GLOUCESTERSHIRE REGT

Place	Date	Hour	Summary of Events and Information	Remarks and references to Appendices
REIGERSBERG CAMP	6.10.17		During the morning, two hours Company inspections & training was carried out. No work was done during the remainder of the day	
	7.10.17		At 8.45 AM the Battn left REIGERSBERG CAMP and marched to IRISH FARM (St JULIEN 28 NW 2) C 26a 26. where bivouacs were erected during the morning.	
			At about 5 PM orders were received to leave IRISH FARM and proceed to DAMBRE CAMP. This was accordingly done.	
DAMBRE CAMP	8.10.17		At 3.30 PM the Battn proceeded by motor lorry to the forward area, to take up position for the attack on the morning of the 9th. The Battn "debussed" at ADMIRALS RD (C 28 b) and proceeded via the ALBERTA TRACK (See APPENDIX "A")	
	9.10.17		ATTACK (See APPENDIX "A")	
	10.10.17		On the night 10/11th the Battn was relieved by the Fifth Camerons, and proceeded to SIEGE CAMP via IRISH Fm	
SIEGE CAMP	11.10.17		The Battn rested during the day the only parades being Sick parade and Foot friction parade.	

A7092). Wt. W12839/M1297 750,000. 1/17. D. D & L., Ltd. Forms/C2118/14.

Instructions regarding War Diaries and Intelligence Summaries are contained in F. S. Regs., Part II. and the Staff Manual respectively. Title pages will be prepared in manuscript.

Army Form C. 2118.

WAR DIARY
or
~~INTELLIGENCE SUMMARY.~~
(Erase heading not required.)

OCTOBER 1917

Nº III

1/4th BATTN GLOUCESTERSHIRE REGT

Place	Date	Hour	Summary of Events and Information	Remarks and references to Appendices
SCHOOLS CAMP	12.10.17		The Batt. left SIEGE CAMP at 2.45 and marched to SCHOOLS CAMP on the POPERINGHE – WATOU Rd. [illegible] 5% men and Draft of ex-A.S.C. men joined the Batt.	
	13.10.17		The Batt. left SCHOOLS CAMP at 6.30 am and marched to HOPOUTRE SIDINGS (POPERINGHE) entraining for SAVY ([illegible]) at 9 am and detraining at LIGNY ST FLOCHEL about 4.20 pm and marched to billets in SAVY. "B" Coy was left behind at HOPOUTRE as loading party & joined the Batt. at SAVY on 14th	
SAVY	14.10.17		Four hours company parades for reorganisation etc carried out during the morning.	
	15.10.17		The Battn marched from billets in SAVY to VILLERS-AU-BOIS ([illegible])	
VILLERS-AU-BOIS.	16.10.17		During the morning 3 hours company and specialist training carried out	
	17.10.17		The Battn relieved the 29th Canadian Battn in the front line during the night 17/18th. The left Battn boundary being ([illegible] 36c SW) N33d 5.5 and the right Battn boundary being T3 d 5.2 "A" Company right front company "B" Company left front company "C" Company right support company "D" Company left support Company Battn H.Q. at T8 a 5.6	

A7092). Wt. W12839/M1297 750,000. 1/17. D. D & L., Ltd. Forms/C2118/14.

WAR DIARY

or

INTELLIGENCE SUMMARY.

(Erase heading not required.)

Army Form C. 2118.

Instructions regarding War Diaries and Intelligence Summaries are contained in F. S. Regs., Part II. and the Staff Manual respectively. Title pages will be prepared in manuscript.

Nov IV — OCTOBER 1917 — 1/4th Batt. GLOUCESTERSHIRE REGT.

Place	Date	Hour	Summary of Events and Information	Remarks and references to Appendices
FRONT LINE	18.10.17		The usual trench routine carried out. Work on the trenches, dugouts, wire etc. The two support companies relieved the two front companies, who went back into support. Lieut Col. A. E. Williams D.S.O. Wiltshire Regt took over command of the Battn from this date.	
	19.10.17		Battn in front line, usual trench routine support companies relieved front companies.	
	20.10.17		Ditto ditto ditto	
	21.10.17		Ditto ditto ditto	
	22.10.17		During the night 22/23rd the Battn was relieved by the 1/6th Batt Glosters Regt and moved back to OTTAWA CAMP (Sheet 36 S.W.) F.8.a by light railway from BON SUMMIT S 29 d 6 2	
	23.10.17		During the morning companies paraded for one hour for inspection of kit equipment etc. And at 12 mid-day the Battn was inspected by the Commanding Officer	
	23.10.17		Three hours training parades for all companies and specialists were carried out during the morning. A new company (X company) was formed, composed of the draft of ex A.S.C. men who required further training	

[illegible] Lieut [illegible] Adjt 1/4th Glouc Regt

A7092). Wt. W128:9/M129? 750,000. 1/17. D. D & L., Ltd. Forms/C2118/14.

Instructions regarding War Diaries and Intelligence Summaries are contained in F. S. Regs., Part II. and the Staff Manual respectively. Title pages will be prepared in manuscript.

No 5

WAR DIARY
or
INTELLIGENCE SUMMARY.
(Erase heading not required.)

OCTOBER 1917

1/4 BATTN GLOUCESTERSHIRE REGT

Army Form C. 2118.

Place	Date	Hour	Summary of Events and Information	Remarks and references to Appendices
OTTAWA CAMP.	24.10.17		Three hours training parades carried out during the morning by A.B.C.D and X Companies and specialists.	
OTTAWA CAMP.	25.10.17		"A" "B" "C" and "D" Companies left OTTAWA CAMP for work in the forward area.	
			"A" and "D" Companies proceeded to HILLS CAMP where they worked upon the CAMP which was unfinished. Putting up Huts etc.	
			"B" and "C" Companies proceeded to (Sheet 28 S.W.) S.23.d.2.6 and carried out work upon the trench system 144 Bgde area.	
OTTAWA CAMP.	26.10.17		Specialists and "X" Company carried out 3 hours training parades during the morning	
"	27.10.17		Three hours parade for X Coy & specialists.	
			"A" Coy & "D" Coy returned to OTTAWA CAMP	
	28.10.17		Sunday Church parade at 11 AM in YMCA hut in the camp	
	29.10.17		The Battn Relieved 1/8th Worcestershire Regt in support. B.H.Q. at S.24.a.2.0. "A" Coy in GERTIE TRENCH T.14.c.2.6. "B" Coy in VIMY T.19.c.2.6.	

A7092). Wt. W12839/M1295 750,000. 1/17. D. D & L., Ltd. Forms/C2118/14.

Instructions regarding War Diaries and Intelligence Summaries are contained in F. S. Regs., Part II. and the Staff Manual respectively. Title pages will be prepared in manuscript.

WAR DIARY
or
~~INTELLIGENCE SUMMARY.~~
(Erase heading not required.)

Army Form C. 2118.

No VI — OCTOBER 1917 — 4th Battn GLOUCESTERSHIRE REGT

Place	Date	Hour	Summary of Events and Information	Remarks and references to Appendices
	29.10.17	(Continued)	"C" Company in the BRICKFIELDS S.18.d.4.6. and "D" Company in CANADA TRENCH with company H.Q. at T.20.a.85.	
			Working parties, for wire in front of line, carrying parties and of party for work on the trench system, during each night.	
	30.10.17		No work done during daylight parties working on the wire, and trenches during the night	
	31.10.17		Working parties during the night	
			Total Casualties. Missing: 15 O.R. Wounded: 4 officers 137 O.R. Killed: 5 officers 43 O.R. Wounded & Missing: 1 officer	
			Total Reinforcements: 149 O.R.	
			Ration strength 31st: 19 officers 639 O.R.	
			List of awards attached	

A. W. Williams
Lieut. Col.
Commanding, 4th Batt. Glos'ter Regt.

A7092). Wt. W128.9/M1295 750,000. 1/17. D. D & L., Ltd. Forms/C2118/14.

1/4th. Battalion Gloucestershire Regiment.

REPORT OF OPERATION ON 9TH. OCTOBER & SUBSEQUENTLY

1/4th. Battalion Gloucestershire Regiment.

REPORT OF OPERATIONS ON 9th. OCTOBER 1917. & SUBSEQUENTLY.

Reference Map POELCAPPELLE Ed.4. 1/10,000.

---

1. The plan for moving the Battalion to the jumping - off position was as follows :-

The Second-in-Command went on an hour in advance of the Battalion with 3 N.C.Os., per Company, this party was to lay out the tape lines 50 yards and 200 yards respectively behind Country Cross Roads and then to return to TWEED HOUSE to guide the Battalion in. The Battalion was to move up by the ALBERTA Track and then along the POELCAPPELLE Road to V 30.d.63 80, where they were to have been met by Bucks Battalion guides, who would guide them to TWEED HOUSE by the taped track via BAVAROISE HOUSE.

On arrival at V.30.d.63 80, Lieut-Coln: Crosskey found that the guides were not there and after waiting for a time decided that he would turn about and move up via the Trench board track and HUBNER FARM a route which he knew himself to some extent. This he did and arrived at TWEED HOUSE about 1-45 a.m. but then discovered that the three rear Companies and about one platoon of the leading one had lost touch, Battalion Headquarters runners were sent out to look for the missing Companies and "C" Company, the leading Company was guided down to the jumping - off point.

At about 4-30 a.m. "A" "B" & 2 platoons of "D" Company were brought to TWEED HOUSE and were taken on down to the jumping - off point. These Companies were just forming up along the tape when our barrage came down, so that the Battalion started the attack less 2 platoons "D" Company and a few men from "A" & "C". "B" Company was complete.

2. The leading Companies "A" on the right and "D" on the left, started off at once and got to within about 50 yards of the barrage before the first lift. "B" & "C" Companies, "B" on the right, moved forward a few minutes after "A" & "D" Companies.

At the first lift the barrage was lost and owing to the sodden condition of the ground was never caught up again.

Immediately the advance commenced our men came under Machine Gun fire from the Cemetry in V.26.d., a Machine Gun in a post about V.26.b.60 25, 2 Machine Guns in a breastwork in front of OXFORD HOUSES at V.26.b.33 45 , and a Machine Gun about V.26.a.97 60. Snipers were also very active from the large rectangular hedge South of the Road in V.26.b., OXFORD HOUSES, BEEK HOUSES, and other points North of LEKKERBOTERBEEK.

3. The bulk of our men were held up approximately on a line 150 yards East of COUNTY CROSS ROADS, but a party of 1 Officer & 6 men , the remains of a platoon, pushed on as far as V.26.b.40.15.. Another small party under a sergeant got into the enclosure about OXFORD HOUSES and fortified a shell hole at V.26.b.25 40. Another party under a sergeant dug in at about V.26.b.05 50. No advance appeared to be made on our left at all and so "C" Company found a defensive flank facing North with three posts and one Lewis Gun post.

4. The Machine Gun in the Cemetery was silenced almost at once by the 6th Battalion Gloucestershire Regiment and a number of Germans retiring North East of the Cemetery came under Lewis Gun and rifle fire and suffered casualties. There was a lot of movement during the

4. the day between the MEBUS at V.26.b.60.35 and the enemy post at V.26.b.60.25, this was always fired at and numerous casualties were caused, as was proved by the large numbers of stretcher parties about that point on the 10th inst. A lot of movement around OXFORD HOUSES was kept under fire.

The two Machine Guns in the breastwork about V.26.b.33 45 were dealt with by rifle grenades and during the morning some of the enemy doubled round to the back of OXFORD HOUSES with the guns and returned later with a light Machine Gun.

The Machine Gun at V.26.b.97 60 was also dealt with by rifle grenades but unfortunately no Number 23 grenades were available on the spot and Number 20 s had rather too long a range to fire accurately at that short distance.

5. What actually happened during the 5 p.m. attack will no doubt be dealt with by O.C. 1/8th.Battalion Worcestershire Regiment, I have seen none of the Officers or men who took part in it but my own men report that the Worcesters went through our line well up to the barrage, which came down just in front of our main line but was right on top of the advanced posts mentioned in para 3 - these fortunately sustained no casualties, though several blind shells landed very near them. The party in OXFORD HOUSES enclosure report that they were 50 yards in front of the barrage. It was this barrage which made the Officer and N.C.Os ~~XXXXXXXXXX~~ Commanding Companies in the line decide to retire and consolidate after dark 100 yards in rear of their present positions. This was carried out and it was that rearline that was handed over to the Camerons.

6. Very few messages were received back from the line after the attack, owing chiefly to the fact that most of the Officers became casualties and also that the heavy and accurate sniping made movement very difficult.

This also greatly hindered the collection of casualties, the Germans sniped a great deal at our stretcher bearers on the 9th.inst. On the 10th., however, they were left alone probably because large enemy stretcher parties were out collecting their wounded under the Red Cross Flag.

7. The chief lessons learnt were with regard to the barrage; 4 minutes before the first lift was not sufficient; with the ground in its present condition, 10 or even 15 minutes would not be too much to allow the infantry to get well up to it.

The 100 yards lift was too much, after it had "jumped" away from the infantry for the first time it was never caught up again. It also failed to deal effectively with enemy snipers and machine gunners who were situated between the first and the second lifts; if it is practicable the 50 yards lift is much better.

In my opinion, the reasons why we failed to take our objectives were:

(a) The exhaustion of the men, most of whom had been tramping over the heavy ground for the greater part of the night.
(b) The sodden condition of the ground.
(c) That the barrage was lost after the first lift and never again caught up.

[signature]

14/10/17.

Major.
Commanding 1/4th.Battalion Gloucestershire Regiment.

1/4th.Battalion Gloucestershire Regiment.

APPENDIX A.

ANSWERS TO QUESTIONS BY DIVISIONAL COMMANDER.

1. Along tape lines running N.N.W. & S.S.E. 50 yards & 200 yards respectively W. of COUNTY CROSS ROADS.

2. By Trench Board Track to HUBNER then across country to TWEED HOUSE (order by BUCKS guide.) and direct to tapes.

3. Just as our barrage came down 5-20 a.m.

4. 2 Platoons of 1 Company and a few men from other Companies who got lost on the POELCAPPLLE ROAD when their Companies came under shell fire.

5. Two day's rations and emergency rations were carried on the men. Rum was got up to the front line on night 9/10th. A certain amount of rest was obtained as the front line was troubled more by sniping than shell fire.

6. TWEED HOUSE.

7. Battalion Headquarters did not move. Lieut-Coln:J.H.Crosskey went forward at about 8-30 a.m. to try and ascertain the situation but got hit.

8. Communication was very difficult owing to the sniping, runners had to be used as there was no suitable point on our front from which shutters could be used.

10. We were in touch with HUBNER by lamp right through and by telephone from about 3 p.m. the wires were hit by shell fire during the night.

11. Not by this Battalion.

12. It was fairly good. Seemed a bit scrappy in places.

13. There was no really weak spot.

14. German Machine Gunners & Snipers were firing during the whole period.

15. The exact situation was not clear until the return of an officer's patrol sent forward at 6-30 p.m. that one was able to get a pretty clear idea of what had happened from the few messages received and from questioning the wounded who came back about midday.

16. V.26.b.25.40.

17. Until dark.

18. Retired 100 yards then because the N.C.O. considered he was beyond our barrage line.

19. No prisoners were actually captured by this Battalion but I think a number were driven over to the 8th.Bn.Gloucesters by our fire during the morning.

21. The only Officer left in "A" Company and the Sergeant Commanding "C" Company.

22. The men consolidated in the shell holes by day, but a more or less

22. straight line of shell holes was consolidated after retiring, after dark. The Battalion Intelligence Officer helped to supervise this work under orders by the Commanding Officer.

23. The only covering parties out were those posts who got forward, mentioned in para 3 of attached report. They became covering parties more by accident than design.

22. Observation was kept from Battalion Headquarters at TWEED HOUSE by Headquarter Officers. No other parties were out.

26. Machine Gun gave covering fire from back positions.

27. Rifles & Lewis Guns kept in action well chiefly owing to the fact that great care had previously been taken to see that all muzzles and breach covers were attached to the rifle or Lewis Gun and that all were supplied with these articles.

28. A good deal as shewn in para 4 of attached report.

29. About 20 but the hostile guns were not silenced by them.

30. No.

31. 2 Vickers Guns were used on evening of 9th. in consolidation, and 2 kept in reserve at TWEED HOUSE. Lewis Guns were used a great deal.

32. No.

33. Yes, as indicated in para 4.

34. 2 Companies attacking 1st.Objective, 2 Companies the 2nd.Objective, the objective consisted of areas. Companies advanced with their skirmishing line in front and remaining sections in file in approximate echelons in rear. Definite platoons were detailed to take each prominent object.

35. Yes.

36. Yes.

37. We were able to bury very few of our dead.

38. Missing 39. 32

39. No men were taken prisoners.

[signature]

14/10/17.

Major.
Commanding 1/4th.Battalion Gloucestershire Regt.

1/4th. Battalion Gloucestershire Regiment.

Appendix B.

CASUALTIES TO 14/10/17.

	Officers.	Other Ranks.
Missing.	–	32.
Killed in Action.	4.	31.
Died of Wounds.	-	3.
Wounded in Action.	6.	104.

[signature]

14/10/17.

Major.
Commanding 1/4th. Battalion Gloucestershire Regiment.

OPERATION ORDERS No.38
by
Lt.Col.H.St.G.Schomberg, Comdg. 1/6th Bn.Gloucestershire Regt.

Ref. Sheet 27 & 28 - 1/40,000

1. MOVE. The Battalion will move by route march tomorrow, to School Camp, ST.JAN TER BIEZEN.
Starting point : Bridge junction B.20.b.36.
Route : Hospital Farm - Dirty Bucket Corner - Chemin Militaire - Elverdinghe Poperinghe Road - Switch Road, thence Poperinghe to Watou Road.

2. PARADE. Head of Headquarters column will pass starting point at 3-18 pm. Order of march :-
"H.Q." "A" "B" "C" "D"
Dress : marching order. Distance between Coys. : 200 yards.

3. TRANSPORT. Cookers, mess cart & water carts will accompany the Battalion and will move 200 yards in rear of the Battalion. Remainder of transport will move under orders of B.T.O.

4. ADVANCE PARTY. 1 N.C.O. per Company, 1 from Headquarters Details, and 1 from the Q.M.Stores, will report to Lieut.W.J.H.POPE at Battalion Hdqrs., tomorrow at 11 am., This party will proceed to ST. JAN TER BIEZEN and meet the Staff Captain at Brigade Hdqrs., School Camp at 1 pm. Every N.C.O. detailed must be able to ride a bicycle. N.C.Os' packs may be handed in to the Q.M.Stores with the surplus packs at 10 am.

5. BLANKETS. Blankets will be handed in to the Q.M.Stores at 10 am. These will be rolled in bundles of ten and clearly labelled.

6. OFFICERS' VALISES & MESS STORES will be handed in at the Q.M.Stores at 10 am. Surplus packs will be handed in at the Q.M.Stores at 10 am.

7. MESS CART. 1 mess box from Headquarters and 1 from each Company may be placed on the mess cart by 2 pm.

8. LEWIS GUNS will be loaded at the transport at 10 am.

9. LORRIES. Officer i/c Headquarters Details will detail 2 runners to be at Brigade Hdqrs. at 11 am tomorrow, to act as guides for lorries which are allotted to the Battalion for carrying blankets, etc.

10. BILLETS. O's C. Companies and Officer i/c Headquarters Details will render to the Orderly Room by 2-45 pm tomorrow, a certificate that billets have been left clean.

11. ADVANCE PARTY TO NEW DIVISIONAL AREA.
O.C. "D" Company will detail 1 Serjeant to proceed to the new Divisional Area to arrange the billeting of the Battalion. This N.C.O. will report to the Orderly Room for instructions immediately on receipt of these orders.

12. DUMP PARTY. All details from HOUTKERQUE will re-join the Battalion at School Camp.

13. Sick parade 9 am. Orderly Room 12 noon.
Letters 7 pm.

F. J. Keen

Lieut. & A/Adjt.,

11/10/17. for O.C. 1/6th Bn. Gloucestershire Rgt.

O P E R A T I O N   O R D E R S   No.39
by
Lt.Col.H.St.G.Schomberg, Comdg. 1/6th Bn. Gloucestershire Regt.

Ref. Sheet HAZEBROUCK 5A - 1/100,000

1. MOVE. The Battalion will proceed by rail to the First Army Area, tomorrow.
Entraining Station : HOPOUTRE.
Detraining Station : LIGNY ST FLUCHEL.
Approximate time of journey : 7 hours.

2. PARADE. The Battalion will parade at 6-45 pm.
Order of march :-

"H.Q." "A" "B" "C" "D"
Dress : marching order. Distance between Coys. : 200 yards.

3. LEWIS GUNS. Lewis Guns will be loaded by 12 noon. One Lewis Gunner per Company will accompany the limbers.

4. MESS STORES. Surplus mess stores will be loaded at the Q.M.Stores by 2-30 pm. Mess stores required during the train journey, will be handed in at the Q.M.Stores at 4 pm.

5. BLANKETS. Blankets, rolled in bundles of ten and clearly labelled, will be handed in at the Q.M.Stores by 2 pm.

6. OFFICERS' VALISES will be handed in at the Q.M.Stores by 4 pm.

7. MEAT. Meat for consumption on the 14th instant should be cooked tomorrow morning.

8. Sick parade 9 am.

[signature]

Lieut. & A/Adjt.,

12/10/17. For O.C. 1/6th Bn. Gloucestershire Regt.

O P E R A T I O N   O R D E R S   No.40
by
Lt.Col.H.St.G.Schomberg, Comdg. 1/6th Bn. Gloucestershire Regt.

Ref. Sheet LENS II.

1. MOVE. The Battalion will move to VILLERS AU BOIS tomorrow, 15th October, 1917.
Starting point : Cross roads N. of AUBIGNY Station.
Route : CAPELLE - FERMONT - ACQ - VILLERS AU BOIS.

2. PARADE. The Battalion will parade at 8-40 am. Formation : column of route. Head of column to be opposite Battalion Headquarters. Order of march :-

"H.Q." "A" "B" "C" "D"

Dress : marching order. Distance between Coys. : 100 yards. Transport will move in rear of the column.

3. ADVANCE PARTY.
One other rank per Company will report to Lieut.W.J.H.POPE outside Battalion Headquarters Mess at 8 am tomorrow. Lieut.POPE will report to Staff Captain at VILLERS AU BOIS at 10 am. at S. entrance to the village. Every other rank detailed must be able to ride a bicycle.

4. LEWIS GUNS.
Lewis Guns will be loaded at 7-30 am. One Lewis Gunner per Company will accompany limbers.

5. MESS STORES will be handed in at the Q.M.Stores by 8 am.

6. BLANKETS.
Blankets, rolled in bundles of ten and clearly labelled, will be handed in at the Q.M.Stores by 7-15 am.

7. OFFICERS' VALISES will be handed in at the Q.M.Stores by 8 am.

8. BILLETS. Attention is drawn to yesterday's order to the effect that billets must be left scrupulously clean.

9. PIONEERS. The Pioneers will report to the Quartermaster at 7-15 am. and will attend to the loading of the stores.

10. OFFICERS' CHARGERS will be at respective Headquarters at 8-15 am.

11. Sick parade 7 am.

J. Pope.

Lieut. & A/Adjt.

14/10/17. for O.C. 1/6th Bn.Gloucestershire Rgt.

O P E R A T I O N   O R D E R S   No.37a
by
Lt.Col.H.St.G.Schomberg, Comdg. 1/6th Bn.Gloucestershire Regt.

Ref. Sheet 28 N.W. and
POELCAPPELLE Sheet.

1. RELIEF. The 26th Brigade will take over the line tonight.

4th SEAFORTHS - Right Front.
5th CAMERONS - Left Front.

The Dividing Line between Battalions in the line, will be BURNS HOUSE inclusive to the Left Battalion.

2. GUIDES. "D" Company will provide 5 guides (1 per Company Hdqrs. and 1 per platoon) to be at Battalion Headquarters at 5-30 pm. When the Companies of CAMERONS arrive at "D" Company Hdqrs., O.C. "D" Company will have post guides awaiting them.

Officer i/c Headquarters Details will detail 5 guides to accompany 2/Lieut.WEBB to the Headquarters of the 1/7th Worcester Regt.. This party in conjunction with 2/Lieut.S.F.SULLIVAN, will guide the Company of SEAFORTHS into position.

3. LEWIS GUN LIMBERS.

Limbers for Lewis Guns will be at TRIANGLE (where ALBERTA Track cuts POELCAPPELLE Road) at 9 pm. A representative from each Company to accompany guns.

4. PETROL TINS.

Petrol tins will be carried out of the line and placed on limbers at the TRIANGLE.

5. DESTINATION.

Destination : IRISH FARM SHELTERS. We shall proceed to SIEGE CAMP tomorrow.

Lieut. & A/Adjt.,

16/10/17. for O.C. 1/6th Bn. Gloucestershire Rgt.

Copies :-
1 & 2 War Diary
3 - 6 Companies
7 Quartermaster
8 Transport Officer.

O P E R A T I O N   O R D E R S   No.41
by
Lt.Col.H.St.G.Schomberg, Comdg. 1/6th Bn.Gloucestershire Regt.

Ref. MAROEUIL Sheet and
36 C. S.W. - 1/20,000

1. RELIEF. The Battalion will relieve the 28th Canadian Battalion in the Support Line tonight.

2. DISPOSITIONS. Companies will take over as under :-

"A"	Company	from	"A"	Coy.	28th	Can.Bn.
"B"	"	"	"B"	"	"	"
"C"	"	"	"C"	"	"	"
"D"	"	"	"D"	"	"	"

3. PARADE. The Battalion will parade at 3 pm.
Formation : Column of route. Head of column facing S.E. to be opposite Battalion Guard. Order of march - "H.Q." "A" "C" "B" "D"
Dress : fighting order - greatcoat rolled around the haversack.
Distance between Companies : 500 yards.

4. GUIDES. 1 guide will report to Battalion Headquarters and 1 to each Company before the Battalion moves. These will guide the Battalion to point where HUMBER Trench crosses road at S.29.b.24.86. At this point an Officer from the 28th Canadian Battalion and 16 Company guides (1 guide per platoon) will meet the Battalion and guide Companies to their respective positions.

5. WATER. Waterbottles will be filled before the Battalion moves. One water cart will move with "A" Coy. "C" Coy. will also use this cart in the support line.
O's C. Companies will arrange that all water drawn from wells and taps in the support line is chlorinated before use.

6. COOKERS. These will be left behind. 2 cooks per Company will move up to the line with their Companies and take with them sufficient dixies for cooking purposes. The dixies will be loaded with the mess stores for the trenches, at 1-45 pm. The 2 cooks will move with limber.

7. TEA. Tea will be made and distributed by Companies on completion of relief.

8. BLANKETS. O's C. Companies and Officer i/c Hdqrs. Details will arrange parties to transfer blankets from Billet No.37 to Billet No.58 immediately on receipt of these orders.

9. LEWIS GUNS, VALISES & MESS STORES as per preliminary Order.

10. OFFICERS' CHARGERS.will be at respective Headquarters at 2-45 pm.

11. TAKING OVER. Receipts are to be given for all trench stores and equipment taken over on relief, and a list sent to Battalion Hdqrs. as soon after completion of relief, as possible.

T J Lewis

Lieut. & A/Adjt.,

17/10/17. for O.C. 1/6th Bn. Gloucestershire Rgt.

OPERATION ORDERS No. 41 w
by
Lt.Col.H.St.G.Schomberg, Comdg. 1/6th Bn. Gloucestershire Regt.

Ref. Sheet 36 C. S.W.

1. RELIEF. The Battalion will relieve the 1/8th Bn. Worcestershire Regiment and the 1/4th Bn. Gloucestershire Regiment in the front line tonight.

2. DISPOSITIONS. "C" & "D" Companies will relieve the 1/8th Worcesters,

"D" Coy. on the Right.
"C" Coy. on the Left.

"A" & "B" Companies will relieve the 1/4th Gloucesters,

"A" Coy. on the Right.
"B" Coy. on the Left.

Each Company will have two platoons in the front line, one platoon in immediate support and one platoon in Battalion Reserve in DORIS - TEDDIE GERRARD Trench.

Sketch maps of dispositions will be rendered by O's C. Companies as soon as possible after taking over the line.

3. GUIDES. Guides from 4th Gloucesters for "A" & "B" Companies will be at BRICKWORKS at 6 pm. One guide per Coy. Hdqrs. and 1 per platoon. A guide for B.H.Q. will also be at BRICKWORKS at 6 pm. Order of move :-

"H.Q." "A" "B"

Guides from 1/8th Worcesters for "C" & "D" Companies will be at junction of PEGGIE - TEDDIE GERRARD T.15.a.7.8. at 7 pm. One guide for Coy. Hdqrs. and 1 per platoon. Order of move :- "D" "C" and will leave their present positions on being relieved by 1/7th Worcesters.

4. LEWIS GUNS will be carried to the front line by the men.

5. MESS STORES. "A" "C" & "D" Coys. will carry their stores to front line. "H.Q." and "B" Coys. mess stores are to be dumped at present dumps at 6 pm. "H.Q." & "B" Coys. mess stores will be unloaded at B.H.Q. (front line) dump TEDDIE, T.8.d.5.7.

6. WATER. Water bottles are to be filled before the Battalion moves. Arrangements are being made for full petrol tins to be placed at a point where Companies can pick them up on way to line. Further information later. "B" & "A" Coys. will carry petrol tins at present in their possession to front line.

7. COMPLETION OF RELIEF.

Completion of Relief will be notified to Battalion Hdqrs. by using code word WINCHESTER.

8. RUNNERS. A runner from B.H.Q. will accompany each Company to the line. On completion of relief this runner will return to B.H.Q. accompanied with company runner.

9. BATTALION HEADQUARTERS - T.8.d.5.7. AID POST at B.H.Q. RELAY POST - PEGGIE (T.15.a.7.7.) where casualties from "C" & "D" Coys. should be brought.

[signature]

Lieut. & A/Adjt.,

21-10-17. for O.C. 1/6th Bn. Gloucestershire Rgt.

Copies :- 1 & 2 War Diary 7, 1/4 Glouc.
3 - 6 Companies 8, 1/8 Worc.

www.ingramcontent.com/pod-product-compliance
Lightning Source LLC
Chambersburg PA
CBHW080914230426
43667CB00015B/2679